Entertaining LIGHT and EASY

LOWER-FAT RECIPES for FESTIVE MEALS

❖

Laurie Burrows Grad

SIMON & SCHUSTER

SIMON & SCHUSTER
Rockefeller Center
1230 Avenue of the Americas
New York, NY 10020

DESIGNED BY DEBORAH KERNER

Illustrations on pages 155, 156, 308, and 366 by Jennifer Harper

Manufactured in the United States of America
1   3   5   7   9   10   8   6   4   2

Library of Congress Cataloging-in-Publication Data
Grad, Laurie Burrows.
Entertaining light and easy : lower-fat recipes for festive meals / Laurie Burrows Grad.
p.   cm.
Includes index.
1. Low-fat diet—Recipes.   2. Entertaining.   I. Title.
RM237.7.G73   1998   97-29872
641.5'638—dc21   CIP

ISBN 0-684-82714-X (hbk.)

*Never eat
more than
you can lift.*
—Miss Piggy

ACKNOWLEDGMENTS

❖ ❖ ❖ ❖ ❖ ❖

The acknowledgments page is reserved for a very select few. Fellow authors immediately flip to this page to check out the name of the agent and editor, searching for subliminal innuendoes into the nature of the book deal. Then there are the relatives who, especially in the case of a cookbook, are included lest the Thanksgiving turkey be laced with "eau de salmonella." And, of course, the friends who "all helped to make this a work of epic proportions" (and I just bought the Brooklyn Bridge for a buck forty). Finally, there are the book afficionados who want to psych out the names of the author's nearest and dearest—most applicable in political exposé books. Let's face it, everyone likes to see their name in print, so the more people listed in the acknowledgments, the more books I sell!

Now that I've analyzed the intricacies of this page of dubious repute, I proffer my own list of exceptional gratitude.

THANKS TO ALL:

Thanks to my supremely humane editor, Sydny Miner, for bearing with my constant sturm und drang and keeping this book on its appointed course.

Thanks to my agent, Pam Bernstein, for drawing me out of cookbook burnout and encouraging me despite plagues and pestilence in my path—OK, so I live in L.A. We give new meaning to catastrophe.

Thanks to my amazingly capable tester, Anne Mayer, for helping to make feasts out of my recipe creations. And . . . to her family for their lip-smacking approval.

Thanks to my friends who volunteered to test. No, not drafted, I said volunteered. According to my thesaurus, a "volunteer" is one who offers one's services, puts oneself at someone's disposal, proffers oneself available, steps forward without being asked, and needs no invitation. So . . . a major thank you to my friends for your thoughts, input, and exercitation (yes, I do use my *Webster's*) on my behalf: Amy Cooper, Diane Gomez. Manuela Lopes, Teresa Pazulla, Bernie Rothman, and Beth Schlanger.

Thanks to a special few who propped

me up both mentally and physically. And, yes, they are listed in alphabetical order—I'm no dope! To my brother, Jim Burrows, for his sense of humor (even though I'm funnier). To Betsy Castenir for her ear and her heart even though they were three thousand miles away. To Debbie Easton for her warmth, friendship, and laughter. To Kathleen Gray, my walking partner, listener, and super-pal, for her comfort and mango-cutting. To Andrew Ogilvie for his support in the wake of my complaining. To Diane Worthington for listening to my constant kvetching and putting it all in proportion—one teaspoon at a time.

Thanks to the others too numerous to mention but I will anyway: Susan Baerwald, Judy Berkowitz, Marilyn Bethany, Lisa Birnbach, Andy and Kathy Blue, Connie Chung, Donna Downing, Midori Firestone, Monica Gomez, Sharon Hardy, John Hertz, Elsie Howard, Catherine Bergstrom-Katz, Ellen Levine, Jan Levine, Susan Maxman, Al and Linda Michaels, Pam Reis, Karin and Gary Richman, Barbara Rothman, Bud Rukeyser, Larry Seigler, Lorraine Sheinberg, Dawn Smith, Julie Alter Solomon, Janet Taylor, Barbara Tenebaum, Trish Vradenburg, Jan Weimer, Carol Weisman.

Thanks to the basic structure of my support system. To my husband, Peter, my best friend, my counsel, my lover, my pal of thirty—count 'em—years, who makes every day worth it even though he hates cilantro. To my favorite and only son, Nicholas, who, even though he ate only McDonald's burgers as a child, has grown into a truly discriminating fresser.

And . . . just to cover all my bases: Madame Bovary, Sidney Chaplin, Totie Fields, Dr. Haldanish, Nostradamus, Nigel Tufnel, Sonny Tufts, and Anonymous.

This book is dedicated to the memory
of my mother, Ruth Burrows,
who instilled in me
a great value system.
She taught me the value
of a great bouillabaisse.

CONTENTS

Entertaining
LIGHT
and EASY

INTRODUCTION

Check this out: you go to dinner at a friend's house and pig out to your heart's content on some seriously delicious food. As you're leaving, you thank the host, while patting your very full and satisfied tummy, "This food was so incredible. I ate every bite and now I'll have to pay for it by starving for the next week." Much to your surprise, your host answers, "No way! I'm glad you loved the food and now you'll love this even more. Nothing you ate was loaded with fat!" Sound like a fantasy? Not at all. This book is all about dining pleasurably—entertaining with a conscience.

We are bombarded and overwhelmed with nutritional information on a daily basis. First margarine is good for us and now it's full of the dreaded transfatty acids. First fish oil is a panacea, and a year later, we find out it's not great. In the seventies, pasta was out and protein was in; in the eighties pasta was in and protein was out; in the nineties everything's up for grabs. Come on, let's stop all this crazy nonsense and get back to basics. But more importantly, let's respect good and fresh food again. Let's venerate a fresh tomato. Let's worship a bunch of basil. Let's savor a delicious spice. Once we get back to real and pure tastes without overprocessing we can re-create those fresh and delicious food memories and translate them into elegant, sumptuous lighter dining.

The facts presented to us seem very simple. We have been told that too much saturated fat will clog our arteries and pad our bellies. Too much fat means too many calories and too much added weight. This is perfectly clear. The way to lose weight is to cut down on fats, specifically the saturated ones. But Americans need to understand the whole culinary picture. We need to rethink our entire way of eating. We need to add more fruits, vegetables, and grains and reduce processed foods laden with saturated fats and empty sugar calories.

This doesn't mean we have to eat olestra or any other manufactured fat. It doesn't mean that we have to make mock lasagne or faux cake. This means that we have to integrate fresh ingredients into dishes that please the eye, the mind, and the palate. Nonfat cottage cheese will always taste like a reject from Miss Muffet's Tuffet. Nonfat cream cheese reminds me of the cold goo the dentist puts in your mouth to make impressions. Forget the proliferation of fat-free and nonfat products and move up the food chain to moderation. This book is full of fresh and exciting recipes that exhilarate the spirit, delight the eye, and inspire the taste buds.

The word *diet* literally means a regimen of limited food or drink. As Erma Bombeck said: "I've been on a constant diet for the last two decades. I've lost a total of 789 pounds. By all accounts, I should be hanging from a charm bracelet." For years whenever my husband announced that he was going on a diet, we all ran for the hills. He griped and kvetched so much that I ended up begging him to get off the diet and eat a hamburger. But then he got smart. He followed my lead and began to lose weight and keep it off without effort.

People have always asked me how I keep my figure with all the cooking I do. True, I do have a good metabolism, but there are other factors. The first is that I exercise every day. We're not talking about running until my knees crumble. We're talking just simple walking. My girlfriend Kathleen picks me up four times a week and we walk and talk and before we know it we're home and eating breakfast. Two times a week I lift weights (I must admit I do complain through most of it), which

helps to tone my body, and even better, works wonders on burning up calories. On the last day of the week, my husband and I walk to breakfast.

The other factor that keeps me fit is that I prefer to eat fresh food that is generally lower in fat. Sure, I eat fries on occasion or once in a while I drown myself in some Häagen Dazs, but on a regular basis, I enjoy eating a fresh salad, light sandwich, or grilled meal more than a heavy fat-laden one.

In October 1990, I was one of fifty participants in a historic ongoing coalition-building conference sponsored by the American Institute of Wine and Food entitled "Resetting the American Table: Creating a New Alliance of Taste and Health." On one side of the arena stood Julia Child and other chefs and food writers espousing our theories of Americans' "fear of food" due to alarming nutrition reports. On the other side of the room were the nutritionists, doctors, and scientists delivering their dictates and diet regimens. By the end of the weekend the two coalesced and the combined theories became one statement: "In matters of taste, consider nutrition and in matters of nutrition, consider taste. And in all cases consider individual needs and preferences." The goal of this book is to follow this credo and encourage Americans to make meals both healthful and pleasurable occasions. This is about eating without fear. There will be no calorie or fat gram numbers to confuse the issue. Just trust that the recipes are low in fat, low in calories, low in sodium, and most importantly, high in flavor and good taste.

*L*IGHT AND EASY DOES IT

Light and easy cooking is a way of life for me. It's healthful, it keeps me slim, and I find the natural tastes of fresh foods to be so much better than anything that comes in a package or out of a can. The reality is, however, that most of us are so busy, we don't think we have time to eat right. We start to rely on convenience foods that may be easier, but in truth, may also be high in fat and not taste all that good.

This book shows you that it is possible to prepare absolutely delicious meals and fabulous desserts that are good for you, are easy to prepare, and take very little time. I have spent the last fifteen years talking about light and easy cooking, writing cookbooks, demonstrating on television shows, and writing magazine articles. And I get lots of letters from people like you, telling me the same thing over and over again. You want to eat right, you want to cut down on fats, you want food to taste great without any hassle in the kitchen. To quote Shirley Conran: "Life is too short to stuff a mushroom."

The techniques that I use are simple to follow and require very little time and energy in the kitchen. Yes, low-fat cooking does require some shopping (no not at Saks) and chopping. We need to find very fresh ingredients to create these dishes. We need to rely on the natural taste of the produce, herbs, poultry, meat, or fish to en-hance the dish without added fats. We need to add flavor and zest without exhausting ourselves in the process. Grilling is my absolute favorite. OK, so I live in California and can grill outside 365 days a year, but I have also found that indoor grills and stovetop pans with grids can add grilled flavor without being outdoors. I like to steam vegetables to enhance their natural flavors but I insist on selecting the freshest vegetables and have given lots of tips in each recipe to help you select the best produce available. Another technique is poaching, which works well for fish and for creating fresh and delicious fruit desserts without added fats. For years I have been creating fruit and vegetable salsas as a sub-stitute for heavy sauces on meats, poultry, and fish. These are just some of my tech-niques to ease kitchen chores while allow-ing me to create the freshest and most healthful dishes with the least effort.

There are some dishes in the book such as osso buco or shepherd's pie that require going the extra mile, but I promise you that the results will justify the added time. Most of the dishes are put together easily, and I have added do-ahead prep tips for those who prefer to organize their time.

*E*NTERTAINING LIGHT

Make It Easy, Make It Light was the cookbook that chronicled my light lifestyle. This book takes that concept and moves it into the entertaining arena. You don't have to use butter and cream to create beautiful parties. The delicious recipes in this book will guarantee you success at any type of celebration you create.

When entertaining, remember that appearances do count, especially when it comes to food. Spa chefs have shown us that light food must be aesthetically appealing. This doesn't mean we have to carve birds out of apples like an experienced sushi chef. It just means we have to garnish and decorate the food to make it as appealing to the eye as to palate. A few sprigs of a fresh herb, a slice of citrus fruit, an edible flower, or even a cherry tomato can make the difference in the presentation of a dish. I pay special attention to color when selecting a garnish. Look for contrasts. If the dish is green spinach then top it off with red tomato. If the dish is orange squash then garnish it with a sprig of thyme. The garnishes specified in the recipes are only suggestions. Be inventive and creative with what is seasonal and available.

Remember to set a beautiful table, either for an elegant dinner party or for a casual family supper. It doesn't have to be complicated to be a knockout. Use some colorful ribbon to tie up napkins. Buy some inexpensive bud vases, fill each with wild flowers and baby's breath, and place one at each setting. Prepare puddings and baked fruit desserts in individual ramekin dishes that can be placed on saucers and garnished with sprigs of mint. Entertaining is about pleasing, gratifying, and indulging all the senses at one time.

ABOUT INGREDIENTS

I adhere to a few tenets when I select ingredients. The first is to buy the freshest produce, meat, poultry, and fish that are available. I take weekly trips to a local farmers' market and buy seasonal fruit and vegetables that not only taste home-grown but cost half the price of those sold at supermarkets.

I strongly suggest that you make friends with your local butcher or fishmonger. Both of these experts will give you tips on the best buys, and will take the extra time to butterfly, bone, or fillet and save you time in the kitchen.

I still adamantly oppose artificial sweeteners. There are too many unanswered questions about them and I detest the aftertaste. If you do not have any physical condition that prevents you from using sugar, I see no problem in using it in moderation. Fat-free products load up on sugar to make up for the lack of fat, but sugar should not be used as a substitute for fat. It should be used as a flavoring.

In most of the recipes in this book, I suggest using salt to taste. Salt is specified only in certain baking recipes where it must be accurately defined. I find that preferences for salt vary so greatly that it is better for each individual to add salt according to his or her own taste requirements. Those on a reduced-salt diet should feel free to increase the amount of garlic, fresh herbs, or lemon juice to enhance flavor. I love Asian flavors, and you will find many recipes inspired by the foods of the Pacific in this book. Asian condiments and flavorings are particularly useful in my style of cooking because they add lots of flavor without a lot of fat; they can be found in Asian groceries, the Asian foods section of the supermarket, or by mail order (see page 387). Following are some of the ingredients I use most often:

❖ Asian-style sesame oil has a nutty taste and aroma; it is prepared from roasted sesame seeds. It is used sparingly and only to add flavor, never as a cooking oil.

❖ Chili paste with garlic is a seasoning paste prepared with crushed chile peppers, vinegar, garlic, and other seasonings. You can use either the Chinese or the Vietnamese brands. An equal amount of crushed red pepper may be substituted if the paste is unavailable.

❖ Chinkiang rice vinegar, also known as Chenkung, Chekiang, or Chen-jung vinegar, is an aged sweet black Chinese vinegar with a distinctive mellow flavor. If you cannot find it, a good balsamic vinegar is an adequate substitute.

❖ Hoisin sauce, also called haisein sauce or Peking sauce, is a thick, sweet sauce prepared from soybeans, flour, chili, red beans, and red coloring. Refrigerate the sauce after opening.

❖ Preserved ginger, also called pickled ginger, is used in Asian cooking as a tangy garnish. Whole, sliced, or shredded peeled gingerroot is preserved in brine, rice wine, or rice vinegar, where it acquires a light pink color. Often red food coloring is added to enhance the color, turning it into "red ginger" that is used as a garnish in Chinese cooking.

❖ Toasted sesame seeds add flavor and texture to recipes. It you can't find them, simply toast regular sesame seeds in a nonstick pan for three to four minutes over medium heat, until they turn golden. You can also bake them in a toaster oven for five to six minutes at 350°F. Do not allow them to burn, or they will taste bitter.

I strongly recommend using fresh herbs whenever possible. The flavor is incomparable and if you find it difficult to obtain them in different parts of the country, try growing a few in boxes on your window sill. Once you get used to the intense and aromatic flavor of fresh herbs, it will be difficult to go back to using the dried. I do use dried herbs when cooking for longer periods of time in soups and stews, but I use less than a recipe suggests since dried herbs can become overpowering and bitter in large quantities.

Always use fresh lemon juice and avoid the bottled version. There is nothing that can replace the taste or flavoring ability of fresh lemon juice. If you can't get fresh lemons all the time, squeeze a bunch when they are plentiful, and freeze the juice in small containers for use year-round.

When using Parmesan cheese, I recommend using the finest quality, Parmigiano Reggiano, and grating it just before use. This finer quality cheese is more expensive but the flavor is so far superior that less can be used in recipes. The result is a more flavorful dish that is lower in fat.

When white wine is called for in a recipe, I recommend using dry white vermouth, a white wine that has been infused with herbs. The screw-topped bottle can be opened and sealed and stored on the shelf easily without any waste. I also find that dry Marsala is a good substitute for red wine because of both the added flavor and the convenience factor of easy storage.

For the most part, I use olive or canola oil as my fat of choice. They add flavor and are monounsaturated fats—the good guys. I find using the wonderful nonstick cooking sprays also a great boon in reducing fats as well. I even fill one of the new spray pumps with olive oil, which saves money and is safer on the environment. As for the controversy over butter and margarine, I prefer just a little bit of butter to the ersatz margarine. We are learning more about the harmful effects of transfatty acids in hydrogenated fats such as margarine, so I stick (forgive the pun) to butter when necessary, but generally use oils in most of my cooking, including my breads.

The differences in olive oils can be confusing. "Light" olive oil, which is filtered to remove some of the olive oil's usual flavor, color, and fragrance, is *not* lower in calories or fat. It is, however, a good choice for sautéing since it has been filtered more than most olive oils. Extra-virgin olive oil, extracted from olives in a cold-press process, is the highest grade, the most expensive, and the least acidic type. Extra-virgin oil is more fruity and aromatic and is best used at the end of the cooking process as a flavor enhancer or as a delicious addition to salad dressings.

Garlic, also called the stinking rose, must be given its proper respect. You can't find a better seasoning agent than this age-old flavor enhancer. Supermarkets are making it easier and easier to use garlic since it is now being sold conveniently peeled and ready to use. But use garlic with caution. Slowly roasted, it is a divine fat-free "butter" that can be used to heighten sauces or mashed potatoes, or as a delicious spread on bread. But when sautéed and allowed to brown, garlic turns bitter. In most of the recipes in this book using sautéed garlic, you will find it is sautéed for just a few seconds or often added with the liquid ingredients of a dish.

Although fresh pasta is delicious and has a wonderful texture, it is often overcooked. Dried pasta is easier to use and does not overcook and become mushy as easily. Many of the American pastas are worthy of competition with the finest of the Italian-made versions. In a taste test in *Cook's Illustrated* magazine, Ronzoni was the number-one recommended pasta, while the hugely popular De Cecco dropped to number three.

No matter what type of pasta you select, you must follow the following basic rules for cooking the pasta: Begin with a large pot that will allow the pasta to move around freely and cook evenly. For each pound of pasta bring at least four to six quarts of cold water to a boil. Add salt if desired and once the water is boiling, add the pasta in batches, keeping the water at a constant boil. Stir the pasta during the first minute of cooking to keep it from sticking to the bottom of the pot. After about six minutes, begin testing the pasta for doneness. Despite the instructions on the box, the best criterion for judging whether the pasta is al dente is taste. *Al dente* comes from the Italian phrase "to the tooth," referring to the slight resistance pasta offers when it is eaten. Pasta should never be overcooked or it will be mushy and gummy. When the pasta is finished, drain it thoroughly in a colander, put the cooked hot pasta in a warm bowl, and immediately toss it with a sauce. If using fresh pasta, remember to cook it only about one to two minutes, testing diligently. If using pasta for a salad, rinse the pasta with cold water immediately after draining and add a few drops or teaspoons of oil to prevent sticking.

I find that risotto makes a wonderful light dish for entertaining. Many cooks shy away from preparing risotto because it requires constant stirring. But for an informal party, it is a perfect dish to get the guests involved and participating in the kitchen. I use Arborio rice, which can be purchased at ethnic groceries, supermarkets, health food stores, or by contacting one of the mail-order sources in the back of the book.

Because potatoes are having a resurgence in popularity comparable to pasta, I have included a large variety of potato recipes in this book. Instead of rice or pasta, potato gratins, herb-roasted potatoes, and even potato pancakes are wonderful light side dishes to accompany any entrée.

Since we are talking about easy cooking, I recommend using canned broths, which are a great time-saver. There are some very good quality canned or frozen fat-free chicken and beef broths on the market. Try a few until you find one you like. Since I personally do not like the canned vegetable broths I have sampled, I have included a recipe for making a very easy vegetable broth that can be prepared in large batches and frozen in small containers for constant use. A good fish stock is also hard to find, but preparing one from scratch can be very time-consuming and create quite an odor in the house. I have an easy "doctored-up" instant fish broth that is simple to prepare and enhances cioppino and other fish-based dishes.

Use large eggs for the recipes in this book, either brown or white, since there is no qualitative difference. The color of the egg shell is determined by the breed of the hen. I buy white eggs one week and then brown the next, so I can tell which is the freshest. I also hard cook only brown eggs since it is easier to see the peel.

ℒIGHT AND EASY TECHNIQUES

There are lots of cooking techniques that facilitate light and easy entertaining without sacrificing quality.

❖ Use heavy pans with good-quality nonstick coating. To maintain their nonstick surface, use plastic or wooden spoons, never metal.

❖ Use nonstick cooking sprays when sautéing or grilling, which cuts down on the use of fat or fill one of the new spray pumps with olive or canola oil.

❖ Learn from spa chefs: garnish food to make it attractive to the eye as well as to the palate.

❖ Buy fresh, seasonal produce. If a recipe calls for asparagus and it is not in season, feel free to substitute broccoli or other noted suggestions in the recipe variations.

❖ Use yogurt cheese as the base for dips and salad dressings in place of mayonnaise or sour cream.

❖ Use buttermilk or egg white instead of whole egg when coating meat, fish, or poultry with crumbs.

❖ Prepare soups and stews a day or two in advance and refrigerate them overnight. The fat will rise to the top, congeal, and can be removed easily. If time is a problem, use a fat or gravy strainer to remove fat from sauces and soups before serving.

❖ Use fat-free canned chicken or beef broth, but if they are not available use regular canned broths; refrigerate them first, and you can easily remove any excess fat.

❖ Use cooked and pureed vegetables as natural thickeners for soups and sauces in place of butter, flour, and cream. Cooked potatoes are very good thickeners for soup.

❖ Grill meats, fish, and poultry to remove excess fat and add flavor. Instead of sautéing meats in stews and braised dishes, grill them to remove fat and save on clean-up.

❖ Roast meat, fish, poultry, and vegetables to intensify flavor without added fat. Make sure to place the roasting foods on a rack to allow the fat to drip off and be discarded.

❖ To intensify flavor, toast nuts and seeds like pine nuts and sesame seeds. A few toasted nuts will add more flavor than a whole bunch of plain ones.

❖ Replace ground beef with ground turkey for meat loaves, pasta sauces, chilis, and casseroles.

❖ Cook *en papillote* (in paper or foil packets). The natural flavors and juices of the ingredients are sealed inside the parchment paper packet without added fats.

❖ Use 1% low-fat milk or nonfat milk. Whole milk contains 3.25 percent fat by weight, 2% milk contains 2 percent fat, 1% milk contains 1 percent fat, and nonfat milk contains almost no fat. Both 1% milk and nonfat milk provide the same nutrients as whole milk or 2% milk, while providing much less saturated fat and cholesterol and fewer calories.

❖ You can substitute nonfat milk for whole milk by adding a spoonful of powdered milk into the nonfat milk to give it more body.

❖ Use lowfat or reduced-fat cheeses but avoid nonfat cheeses, which are rubbery in texture and bitter in taste.

❖ Use mustard, particularly the grainy variety, to add thickness to dressings and sauces without added fat.

❖ Use garlic, ginger, onions, lemon juice, vinegar, chiles, mustard, and fresh herbs as natural flavor enhancers.

❖ Add salt after tasting! Remember to taste cold foods after chilling and adjust with salt and pepper accordingly.

❖ Grind pepper as you need it. Once ground, pepper loses its potency and flavor on standing.

❖ Use salsas and chutneys as condiments to enhance breakfast dishes, grilled foods, and sandwiches. Use fruit salsas as a delicious and fat-free topping for grilled fish, poultry, or meat.

❖ Stir-fry small amounts of meat, fish, and chicken with big bunches of vegetables to reduce the amount of protein and increase the amount of fiber.

❖ You can cook chicken with the skin. It will not add any fat to the dish, but will keep the meat moist. The trick is to discard the fatty skin before eating the chicken!

❖ Trim the fat from beef, lamb, and pork before cooking, which reduces the fat content of the finished dish.

❖ Prepare salad dressings with equal amounts of oil and vinegar. Add a little mustard or citrus juice and reduce the oil even further.

❖ Use flavored vinegars and oils to intensify salad dressings and sauces.

❖ Serve foods that take lots of time to eat, such as artichokes or cracked crab. You will find that you are satisfied with much less food.

❖ Whenever possible, substitute monounsaturated oils like olive, canola, or peanut for butter. No matter what type of oil, limit the amount used.

❖ Chop and freeze fresh herbs when available to have on hand year-round.

❖ An easy way to reduce fat in recipes is to substitute egg whites for whole eggs. The ratio is 1½ to 2 egg whites for each yolk. So if a recipe calls for four eggs, use two eggs plus three to four egg whites.

❖ When you see a recipe with cream or milk, try using chicken or vegetable broth instead and adding a few cooked, pureed potatoes or rice for thickening.

❖ To add a smoky flavor with less fat, use small amounts of prosciutto or Canadian bacon, which are lower in fat than regular bacon.

❖ Use vegetables and reduced-fat cheeses as low-fat pizza toppings instead of high-fat pepperoni and sausage.

❖ Top fruit desserts with nonfat vanilla yogurt or frozen yogurt instead of whipped cream or ice cream.

$\mathscr{S}$TREAMLINING YOUR KITCHEN

As a cook who goes gaga over kitchen equipment and gadgets, I am extremely pleased to report that manufacturers are offering a wide variety of products essential to light cooking.

Cookware: Nonstick pans, in all sizes and shapes, are a must for the light kitchen since they reduce the amount of fat required for cooking. My personal choice is the All-Clad LTD, which is a very expensive pan but performed beautifully under all types of cooking conditions during the recipe testing for this book. As a more economic alternative, I would recommend Farberware Millenium pans, which have a particularly wonderful small omelet pan. I recommend owning a large twelve- to fourteen-inch skillet, a large griddle, a deep saucepan, a small saucepan, and a Dutch oven, which is an invaluable piece for making soups, stews, braised dishes, or sauces. If you are interested in making puffy breakfast pancakes, Calphalon makes a Nonstick Everyday Pan that is perfect for these Dutch Babies (page 65) or great for paella and wonderful one-pot meals.

I suggest cooking in a **well-seasoned wok.** I studied Chinese cooking in the late sixties and purchased a heavyweight stainless steel wok in Chinatown. I have been using that same well-seasoned wok for decades and it always performs well even when cooking with very little fat. Of the nonstick woks, I recommend the Joyce Chen Nonstick Peking Pan lined with Excalibur, which withstands the high heat of stir-frying. I also have a vintage well-seasoned **ten-inch cast-iron skillet** that I use constantly for oven-baked cornbread and frittatas.

Baking Pans: When preparing meat loaves I rely on a **fat-free meat loaf pan** that consists of two pans, one fitting inside the other. The inner pan has holes in it to allow the fat to drip off into the other pan during the cooking. I get a crustier pizza by using the **Perfect Crust Pizza Pan** by Rema. These pans come in a variety of sizes and have a solid rim area to protect the outer edge from overbaking, while the main part is full of tiny holes that allow moisture to escape, resulting in a perfectly crisp crust. For baking angel food cakes and bundt cakes, I have purchased a **nonstick ten-inch removable tube pan.** The bread chapter is full of wonderful muffins, both savory and sweet, so I would advise investing in two nonstick pans: a regular **muffin tin** and the **minimuffin** sizes. I also purchased some **nonstick madeleine forms** from Williams-Sonoma that produce delicious madeleines that pop right out of the pan or can double as pans for baking corn sticks.

Grilling Methods: Since grilling is such an integral part of light cooking, it is important to invest in an **outdoor grill:** a gas one or an old-fashioned Weber kettle will both do the trick. In the winter, I suggest trying one of the **electric indoor grills,** or for a more economical method of grilling, a well-seasoned, **heavyweight, nonstick or cast-iron ridged grill pan** will impart a grilled flavor right on top of the stove. The fat collects in the spaces between the ridges and when heated starts to smoke, permeating the food with an outdoor aroma.

Cooking Sharp: I am a **cleaver** kind of woman. As I have previously mentioned, I learned to cook Chinese-style and ever since have been wielding my very sharp cleaver, the same one I purchased in Chinatown in the late sixties. I also own a set of **Henkels knives** and more importantly my electric **Edgecraft knife sharpener** to keep my knives razor sharp at all times. I have never had a better **peeler** than the one made by Oxo with the black rubber handle.

Steamers: You can invest in a large electric steamer or use an **inexpensive metal steamer,** the kind that fans out and can fit in a variety of pot sizes. It is easier to store than a large appliance and has very similar results.

Cooking in Clay: Cooks are discovering the virtues of cooking in **terra-cotta clay pots.** Instead of basting with fat, steam seals in the flavors. Try the Perfect Roast Chicken with Artichoke-Garlic Flavor (page 122) cooked in one of these clay

pots. In lieu of a clay cooker, a **large cocotte**—a deep heavy pan that is large enough to hold a chicken with a heavy, close-fitting lid—will have a similar result, steaming in the natural juices of the poultry.

Food Processors: I cannot function in the kitchen without my **Cuisinart food processor.** For pureeing soups or sauces, for chopping, grating, slicing, dicing, and innumberable time-saving chores this is my Mr. Wizard in the kitchen. I have also become quite attached to the new **Cuisinart Mini-Prep Processor.** For chopping small amounts of garlic, ginger, and herbs, and for making quick dressings and marinades, this relatively inexpensive kitchen device is a great plus for light entertaining. I also like the **Braun immersion blender,** a hand-held food processor that can puree a sauce directly in the pan, with no messy containers to clean up.

Gadgets: My favorite light gadget, the **gravy strainer or fat strainer,** was first introduced to me by my mother who found it years ago on a trip to France. These devices do a great job of separating fats and oils from soups, sauces, and stews when you don't have the time to chill them overnight. They are simply pitchers with the spout based at the bottom. The soup or gravy is poured into the pitcher, the fat quickly rises to the top, the liquid is poured off from the bottom, and the fat remains in the pitcher. The other gadget that I find quite useful is a **yogurt cheese maker.** Yogurt cheese is a wonderfully creamy, rich mixture of nonfat or low-fat yogurt, drained of its liquid, that can be a great healthful alternative for sour cream in dips, desserts, and appetizers. I recommend purchasing both a ridged large and minisize **biscuit cutter** to prepare some of the delicious savory treats in the bread chapter. In lieu of a biscuit cutter, invest in some cookie cutters, which will also do the trick. A box of **parchment paper** for cooking *en papillote* (in paper packets) is useful and is also good for baking cookies. I recommend the unbleached paper that is available by mail order through Zabar's in New York. I also like a good **kitchen scale** for measuring and weighing your food and if all else fails, use this handy tool to weigh your letters and save a trip to the post office!

Microwave Ovens: Since I wrote my last cookbook, I have not changed my opinion about microwave cooking. I use mine lots: to defrost and reheat. But, when I want a grilled, browned, or braised flavor, I cannot achieve that intensity by cooking food in a microwave oven. I would rather take the hour to bake a potato with a crisp crust and soft and powdery center rather than get a steamed, soggy, mushy microwaved potato. On the plus side, I find that reheating rice and cooked leftovers works beautifully in this superspeed appliance, poaching fish is easy and tasty, and many vegetables are delicious and crunchy when steamed in the microwave.

APPETIZERS

❖ ❖ ❖ ❖ ❖ ❖ ❖

Mushroom Pâté

Sweet Pea Guacamole

Roasted Vegetable Spread

Eggplant Caviar Spread with Southwestern Flavor

Yogurt Cheese Caper Dip

Crunchy Radish and Cucumber Dip

Sun-Dried Tomato and Basil Chicken Pâté

Smoked Salmon Tartare

Spinach-Tomato Terrine

Chilled Artichokes with Spicy Mustard Sauce

Corn Blini with Salsa

Potato Slices with Caviar

Skewered Chicken with Papaya Salsa

Spinach Meatballs

Baked Tortilla Chips

Mushroom Pâté

Serves: 6

This light flavorful spread works well as an appetizer or can be used as a stuffing for chicken. It is a variation of duxelles, a thick pastelike mixture of minced mushrooms and shallots used as a stuffing or as a flavoring for sauces. Remember to taste the pâté before serving since chilling diminishes the flavors and it may need added salt and pepper.

    2 tablespoons olive oil
    ½ cup shallots, peeled and roughly chopped
    1 pound mushrooms, stems removed, wiped clean, and
        roughly chopped
    3 tablespoons port, sweet Marsala, or Madeira wine
    2 tablespoons chopped fresh parsley
    ¾ teaspoon chopped fresh thyme or ⅛ teaspoon dried
        thyme, crumbled
    salt and freshly ground pepper to taste

GARNISH: sprigs of thyme

ACCOMPANIMENTS: crackers

1. In a large nonstick skillet, heat the oil to medium and sauté the shallots until just soft, stirring often, about 2 to 3 minutes. Add the mushrooms and continue to sauté until softened, stirring often, about 5 to 7 minutes. Add the port and stir until the liquid is absorbed. Allow the mixture to cool slightly.

2. In a food processor or blender, puree the mushroom mixture until just smooth. Add the remaining ingredients and continue to process until well blended. Place in a crock, cover, and chill.

3. Serve the mushroom pâté chilled or at room temperature garnished with sprigs of thyme accompanied by crackers.

VARIATION:

❖ Fresh dill can be substituted for the thyme.

COOK NOTE:

❖ Refrigerate mushrooms in a brown paper bag or open container, not in the plastic bags from the supermarket, which will cause them to decay rapidly. Mushrooms should not be washed until just before use and they should never be soaked in water.

❖ An egg slicer does double duty as a nifty mushroom slicer.

𝒟o-ahead prep:

❖ The pâté can be prepared a day in advance, placed in a covered container, and refrigerated until ready to serve.

Sweet Pea Guacamole

Yield: 3 cups

𝒞hef Michael Roberts, originally chef at Trumps in Los Angeles and now of Twin Palms restaurant, popularized the concept of using peas in guacamole. He suggests using the frozen peas because the color is more vibrant and the sugar in the peas has not been allowed to turn to starch.

two 10-ounce packages frozen peas, thawed

¼ medium ripe avocado, peeled, pitted, and roughly chopped

3 tablespoon defatted chicken or vegetable broth

2 tablespoons low-fat mayonnaise

2 tablespoons fresh lime juice

2 tablespoons roughly chopped cilantro

2 teaspoons jalapeño pepper, seeded and roughly chopped

¼ teaspoon ground cumin

¼ teaspoon ground chile powder

salt to taste

𝒢arnish: 2 tablespoons chopped tomatoes and 2 tablespoons chopped scallions (green and white parts included)

𝒜ccompaniments: Baked Tortilla Chips (see page 48) or low-fat tortilla chips

1. In a food processor or blender, combine the ingredients and process until just smooth.

2. Place in a serving bowl, garnish with the tomatoes and scallions and serve accompanied by tortilla chips.

*V*ARIATION:

❖ For a lower-fat version, the avocado can be omitted.

*C*OOK NOTES:

❖ About 89 percent of a chile pepper's fire is contained in the ribs. If these ribs and the attached seeds are cut off and discarded, the heat is diminished.

❖ In handling hot peppers, it is a good idea to wear thin rubber gloves; if you do touch the peppers with your bare hands, be sure not to touch your eyes or mouth until you have washed your hands with soap and water and allowed a few hours to elapse.

*D*O-AHEAD PREP:

❖ Since there is avocado in the dip, which tends to discolor, it is best to serve it immediately, but it can be kept for a few hours in the refrigerator.

Roasted Vegetable Spread

Serves: 8 to 10

*O*ther vegetables can be substituted or added to this spread such as red or yellow bell peppers, shallots, zucchini, and for added spice a jalapeño pepper. The spread can also be tossed with linguine or spaghetti for a delicious pasta dish or spread on pizza crust and baked until hot and bubbly.

1 medium eggplant (about 1 pound), quartered lengthwise

1 large onion, thickly sliced

1½ pounds tomatoes, sliced horizontally and squeezed of seeds

3 cloves of garlic, unpeeled

3 tablespoons chopped fresh basil

1½ tablespoons balsamic vinegar

salt and freshly ground pepper to taste

*G*ARNISH: fresh basil leaves

*A*CCOMPANIMENT: toasted thin sliced bread

1.   Preheat the oven to 425°F. Lightly coat a roasting pan with olive oil nonstick cooking spray.

2.   Place the eggplant skin side down in the pan, add the onions, tomatoes, and garlic. Spray the vegetables lightly with the oil and roast for 45 to 50 minutes, or until the vegetables are softened and browned. Allow to cool slightly.

3.   Place the eggplant, onions, and tomatoes (not the garlic) in the food processor or blender and process until just smooth. Squeeze the garlic puree out of the skin into the food processor, add the basil, vinegar, and salt and pepper and continue to puree until smooth.

4.   Serve the spread hot, at room temperature, or even cold on toasted thin-sliced bread garnished with basil leaves.

*V*ARIATIONS:

❖   One pound of Japanese eggplants can be substituted for one medium eggplant.

❖   It is not necessary to peel the eggplant or tomato since the skins will soften considerably. If you prefer, remove the skins easily after roasting and before pureeing the spread.

*C*OOK NOTE:

❖ The younger the eggplant, the fewer seeds and the less bitter the flesh. To select a young vegetable, choose an eggplant that is rich purple in color with a firm flesh. Medium-sized eggplants are preferred since the larger ones tend to have more seeds. The cap should look fresh and green and avoid any eggplants with dark brown spots, a sure sign of decay.

*D*O-AHEAD PREP:

❖ The spread may be prepared up to three days in advance and chilled until ready to serve.

Eggplant Caviar Spread
with Southwestern Flavor

Serves: 8 to 10

*T*his recipe is a variation on one that my Grandmother Sarah used to make when I was a child. She would hold the eggplant over the flame on the stove until it was charred. In this recipe we roast the eggplant for the same effect, but you might want to try grilling it outdoors for added flavor.

2 medium-sized eggplants (1¼ pounds each)

2 large scallions (green and white parts included), finely chopped

2 tablespoons chopped fresh Italian parsley

1½ tablespoons chopped fresh cilantro

2 tablespoons fresh lime juice

1 tablespoon extra-virgin olive oil

1 teaspoon finely minced garlic

½ teaspoon minced fresh jalapeño or serrano chiles, seeds removed and discarded

¼ teaspoon ground cumin

salt to taste

*G*ARNISH: ⅓ cup minced red or yellow bell peppers (or a combination)

*A*CCOMPANIMENTS: Toasted Tortilla Chips (see page 48)

1. Preheat the oven to 400°F.

2. Wash the eggplants, wipe dry, randomly pierce with a fork or knife, and bake for 35 to 40 minutes, or until soft to the touch. Remove from the oven and allow the eggplants to cool slightly.

3. Cut the eggplants in half, scoop out the flesh, discard the peel, and drain the flesh in a colander for several minutes to remove excess juices. Place in a food processor and mash, pulsating until just soft, but not pureed.

4. Place the eggplant in a bowl, add the remaining ingredients, and stir until the mixture is well blended. Place in a sealed container and allow to chill for 3 to 4 hours, or overnight.

5. Taste for seasonings, adjust with salt if necessary, and serve the eggplant spread at room temperature garnished with the peppers and accompanied by the tortilla chips.

$\mathcal{V}$ARIATIONS:

❖ For a milder flavor substitute Anaheim or pasilla chiles.

$\mathcal{C}$OOK NOTE:

❖ Wear rubber gloves when chopping hot peppers. Do not touch your eyes or mouth until you've removed the gloves.

$\mathcal{D}$O-AHEAD PREP:

❖ The eggplant spread can be prepared a day in advance and chilled in a covered container until ready to serve.

Yogurt Cheese Caper Dip

*Y*ogurt cheese is plain yogurt with the whey (liquid) removed creating a creamy, rich mixture that can be substituted for sour cream in dips, dressings, and desserts. This dip can be used to stuff baked potatoes or as a spread for canapés.

   3 scallions, white parts only, finely chopped

   one 4-ounce jar small capers, drained and chopped

   1 cup nonfat or low-fat Yogurt Cheese (see page 50)

   2 tablespoons low-fat mayonnaise

   salt and freshly ground pepper to taste

*A*CCOMPANIMENT: crudités

1. In a food processor or blender, or by hand, chop the scallions and capers together until just minced.

2. Transfer to a bowl, stir in the Yogurt Cheese, mayonnaise, and salt and pepper, and chill for 1 to 2 hours.

3. Adjust the seasonings, and serve chilled accompanied by crudités.

*C*OOK NOTE:

❖ Capers are the flower buds of the caper bush, a tenacious, thorny plant that thrives wild in the hot, dry Mediterranean climate. Experts claim that the best-tasting capers are the tiniest, called *nonpareilles.* Capers should be rinsed and drained before use.

*D*O-AHEAD PREP:

❖ The dip can be prepared several days in advance but remember to pour off any accumulated water that may have collected on standing and adjust the seasonings after chilling.

Crunchy Radish and Cucumber Dip

Yield: 4 cups

*R*adishes, scallions, parsley, dill, and garlic can be chopped together in the food processor, but cucumbers release too much water and should be chopped by hand.

1 large European hothouse cucumber or 2 regular cucumbers, peeled and seeded

8 radishes, washed, dried, and finely chopped

4 large scallions (green and white parts included), trimmed and finely chopped

¼ cup finely chopped fresh parsley

1½ tablespoons snipped fresh dill

1 teaspoon finely minced garlic

2 cups plain nonfat or low-fat yogurt

salt and freshly ground white pepper to taste

*A*CCOMPANIMENTS: celery sticks, carrot sticks, radishes, cucumber spears, cherry tomatoes, or other seasonal raw vegetables

1. Divide the hothouse cucumber in half. Chop ½ the hothouse cucumber (or 1 regular cucumber). Slice the remaining half of the hothouse cucumber (or regular cucumber) into spears and set aside.

2. Combine the chopped cucumber, radishes, scallions, parsley, dill, and garlic in a medium bowl. Add the yogurt and seasonings and stir until smooth.

3. Place in a covered container and chill for 4 to 6 hours, or overnight.

4. Adjust the seasonings after chilling and serve the dip chilled with a crudité tray consisting of the reserved cucumber spears, celery sticks, carrot sticks, radishes, cherry tomatoes, or other seasonal raw vegetables.

*V*ARIATION:

❖ If fresh mint is available, add 2 to 3 tablespoons chopped mint to the dip.

*C*OOK NOTE:

❖ European cucumbers, also known as English, burpless, greenhouse, hothouse, and seedless cucumbers, are about 12 to 15 inches in length with thin skins and very few seeds.

❖ Yogurt has more than twice as much calcium as cottage cheese—300 to 450 milligrams per cup—more than milk, and about one-quarter to one-half of your daily requirements.

*D*O-AHEAD PREP:

❖ The dip can be prepared 1 to 2 days in advance and kept in a covered container until ready to serve.

Sun-Dried Tomato and Basil Chicken Pâté

Serves: 8 to 10

*P*eople think of pâté as rich, but this lean version of chicken pâté is prepared with skinless white meat and egg whites and is enhanced by adding herbs, garlic, sun-dried tomatoes, and a small amount of Parmesan cheese.

¾ pound boneless, skinless chicken breasts, cut into 1-inch pieces

2 egg whites

1 egg

2 medium cloves garlic, coarsely chopped

2 shallots, peeled and coarsely chopped

2 tablespoons pine nuts

one 2½-ounce package sun-dried tomatoes, soaked in boiling water to cover and squeezed dry

3 tablespoons coarsely chopped fresh basil

3 tablespoons freshly grated Parmesan cheese

2 tablespoons extra-virgin olive oil

salt and freshly ground pepper to taste

*T*OPPING:

one 3-ounce package sun-dried tomatoes, soaked in boiling water to cover and squeezed dry

2 tablespoons coarsely chopped fresh basil

2 tablespoons defatted chicken broth

1 tablespoon pine nuts

1 tablespoon freshly grated Parmesan cheese

1 clove garlic, roughly chopped

salt and freshly ground pepper to taste

GARNISH: fresh basil leaves, pine nuts, lemon wedges

ACCOMPANIMENTS: thinly sliced toast or crackers

1. Preheat the oven to 325°F. Lightly coat the inside of a small loaf pan (about 7½ x 3½ x 2 inches) with olive oil nonstick cooking spray.

2. In a food processor or blender, process the chicken with the remaining pâté ingredients, pulsing on and off until well combined and smooth. Place the mixture in the prepared pan, seal tightly with aluminum foil, and place the loaf pan in a larger pan filled with an inch of hot water. Bake for 70 minutes, or until an inserted knife comes out clean.

3. Remove from the oven and cool on a rack for 15 to 20 minutes. Loosen the sides with a sharp paring knife, turn out on a small platter with bottom side up, and blot dry lightly with paper towels. Cover with plastic wrap, and chill for 4 to 6 hours, or overnight.

4. Place the topping ingredients in a food processor or blender and process until smooth.

5. Frost the pâté with the sun-dried tomato–basil mixture. Serve the pâté chilled or at room temperature, garnished with basil leaves, pine nuts, and lemon wedges and accompanied by thinly sliced toast or crackers.

VARIATION:

❖ Walnuts can be substituted for the pine nuts.

COOK NOTE:

❖ Pine nuts, also known as *Indian nuts,* *piñons,* and *pignolias,* come from inside the pinecones of several varieties of pine trees. Removal of the nuts is a labor-intensive process, which is what makes these nuts so expensive. Pine nuts are high in protein and unsaturated fats, they contain significant amounts of vitamin A, and little starch. Once opened, these nuts will turn rancid easily so it is best to refrigerate or freeze them for future use.

❖ Shallots, a member of the onion family, have a mild, delicate flavor and tender texture. Shallots are formed in the same way as garlic with a head made up of several cloves. Select firm, well-shaped shallots that are not sprouting and store them in a cool dry place for up to 1 month.

DO-AHEAD PREP:

❖ The pâté base and topping can be prepared 2 to 3 days in advance and held separately in the refrigerator until ready to serve.

Smoked Salmon Tartare

Serves: 8

*T*his dish can be assembled several hours or even a day in advance and chilled until ready to use. If using a food processor to mince the salmon, remember to pulse, not process, or the tartare will become a pâté.

½ pound smoked salmon, minced

⅓ cup snipped fresh chives or minced scallion greens

3 tablespoons capers, drained

½ teaspoon grated lemon rind

*D*RESSING:

5 teaspoons lemon juice

4 teaspoons extra-virgin olive oil

1 teaspoon Asian-style sesame oil

freshly ground pepper to taste

*G*ARNISH: sliced cucumbers and lemon wedges

*A*CCOMPANIMENTS: pumpernickel toasts

1. Combine the minced salmon, chives, capers, and lemon rind in a large bowl. Whisk the dressing ingredients until smooth, mix with the salmon to combine well, cover, and chill until ready to use.

2. To serve, line the pumpernickel toasts with sliced cucumbers and top with the salmon tartare. Garnish with lemon wedges and serve.

*V*ARIATIONS:

❖ Fresh ahi tuna can be substituted for the salmon.

*D*O-AHEAD PREP:

❖ It is best to prepare the tartare the morning it is to served, but you can also prepare it a day in advance and keep it in a sealed container until ready to serve.

Spinach-Tomato Terrine

Serves: 6 to 8

*T*he green and red colors of this terrine make this an appealing and attractive dish to serve at the holidays or throughout the year. You can easily substitute frozen chopped broccoli for the spinach.

> one 10-ounce packages frozen chopped spinach, thawed and
>   thoroughly squeezed dry
>
> 2 eggs
>
> ½ cup low-fat ricotta cheese
>
> 3 tablespoons grated Parmesan cheese
>
> 2 tablespoons freshly chopped basil
>
> 1 teaspoon finely minced garlic
>
> ⅛ teaspoon ground nutmeg
>
> salt and freshly ground white pepper to taste
>
> 1 medium tomato, drained of seeds and liquid and finely chopped

*G*ARNISH: cherry tomatoes and fresh basil leaves

*A*CCOMPANIMENTS: thin pumpernickel or black bread

1. Preheat the oven to 350°F. Line an 8-x-3-x-2⅜-inch medium loaf pan (or use a disposable aluminum foil loaf pan) with aluminum foil leaving an overhang of about 3 inches and lightly coat the foil with nonstick cooking spray.

2. Place all the ingredients except the tomato in a food processor and puree until just smooth.

3. Place half the spinach mixture in the bottom of the prepared pan and smooth the top with a spatula. Top evenly with the tomato and then finish with the remaining spinach, smoothing the top.

4. Loosely fold the foil over the terrine to cover, place the pan in a larger baking dish filled with 1 inch of hot water, and bake for 55 to 60 minutes or until set and the terrine is firm.

5. Remove the pan from the water and allow to cool about 15 minutes. Loosen the edges with a sharp paring knife and invert the terrine onto a platter. Cover with plastic wrap and allow to chill for 2 to 3 hours.

6. Cut the terrine into slices and serve garnished with cherry tomatoes and fresh basil leaves, accompanied by thin pumpernickel or black bread.

*V*ARIATION:

❖ If time permits, the tomato can be peeled.

*C*OOK NOTE:

❖ For an easy way to peel and chop a tomato, slice the tomato horizontally, and squeeze out and discard the seeds. Grate the tomato halves on the side of the grater with the largest holes. The result will be perfectly grated tomato and no skin.

*D*O-AHEAD PREP:

❖ The terrine can be prepared a day or two in advance, covered, and kept in the refrigerator until ready to serve.

Chilled Artichokes with Spicy Mustard Sauce

Serves: 6

The artichoke originated in Mediterranean Europe and was first brought to America by the French, who settled in Louisiana in the eighteenth century. However, it was the Spaniards, who settled in the Salinas valley area, that grew them with the most success. This area eventually became the "artichoke capital of the world." Steaming or microwaving are the best methods of cooking artichokes because there is less chance of overcooking and they are easier to drain.

6 large artichokes

½ lemon

Spicy Mustard Sauce:

1 cup nonfat or low-fat yogurt

3 tablespoons Dijon mustard, grainy-style preferred

2 tablespoons low-fat mayonnaise

1 teaspoon lemon juice

½ teaspoon horseradish

½ teaspoon Worcestershire sauce

salt and freshly ground pepper to taste

Garnish: lemon wedges

1.   Wash each artichoke and slice off both ends so that it can sit flatly on a surface. Immediately rub the cut ends with the lemon half to prevent discoloration. Cut away any ragged leaves, and snip off the sharp edges of the leaves with a kitchen scissor. Steam the artichokes in a vegetable steamer, or on a rack in a pot with 1 inch of water and cook for 40 to 45 minutes, over medium heat, or until a leaf can be removed easily. (Be careful not to let the water boil away.) Remove from the pan with tongs, drain thoroughly, and chill in a covered container in the refrigerator.

2.   Whisk the sauce ingredients together and chill until ready to use.

3.   Serve each chilled artichoke with a small container of sauce, garnished with lemon wedges.

Cook Note:

❖   Artichokes can be successfully cooked in a microwave oven. Place the trimmed artichokes in a microwave-safe dish and cover with plastic wrap or a domed lid. Cook for 12 to 15 minutes, or until tender.

Corn Blini with Salsa

Serves: 6 to 8

*T*op these light and easy baby appetizer pancakes with salsa, relish, or chutney, smoked salmon, or even with just a dab of caviar.

¾ cup yellow cornmeal

½ cup all-purpose flour

2 teaspoons sugar

½ teaspoon baking soda

¼ teaspoon salt

freshly ground pepper to taste

1 egg

1 egg white

1 cup low-fat buttermilk

2 teaspoons vegetable oil

½ cup fresh or frozen corn, thawed

*G*ARNISH: low-fat or nonfat sour cream; topped with salsa, or caviar with chopped red onion, or smoked salmon and capers

1. Preheat the oven to 200°F.

2. Combine the cornmeal with the flour, sugar, baking soda, salt, and pepper in a large bowl.

3. In a separate bowl, beat the egg and egg white with the buttermilk and oil. Beat the egg mixture into the cornmeal, combining until the mixture is the consistency of pancake batter. Do not overmix. Fold in the corn.

4. Coat a large nonstick griddle or skillet with nonstick cooking spray, heat to medium-hot, and drop the batter by spoonfuls. Cook the blini for about 1 to 2 minutes per side, or until golden brown on the outside and cooked through on the inside. Blot the blini on paper towels and place on a plate to keep warm in the oven until the rest of the batter is used up. (It may be necessary to coat the pan with the nonstick cooking spray periodically.)

5. Serve the blini warm garnished with a low-fat or nonfat sour cream; topped with salsa, or caviar with chopped red onion, or smoked salmon and capers.

*C*OOK NOTE:

❖   Today buttermilk is made by adding bacterial cultures to skim or low-fat milk. Buttermilk made from 1% low-fat milk has far fewer calories and less fat than whole milk. Besides containing calcium and riboflavin, buttermilk is fortified with vitamin D by some dairies.

*D*O-AHEAD PREP:

❖   The blini can be prepared, cooled, and frozen for future use. Thaw and then reheat in a 200°F oven until warmed through and crisp.

Potato Slices with Caviar

Serves: 8

*T*hese special-occasion appetizers are surprisingly easy to prepare and always guaranteed to get rave reviews.

2 medium white rose potatoes (1 pound) potatoes

½ cup Yogurt Cheese (see page 50) or low-fat sour cream

2 ounce jar black whitefish or golden whitefish caviar, drained

2 tablespoons finely chopped fresh chives

1. Preheat the oven to 450°F. Lightly coat a baking sheet with olive oil nonstick cooking spray.

2. Cut the unpeeled potatoes into ¼-inch slices and place on the prepared pan. Coat the potatoes lightly with the cooking spray and bake for 8 to 10 minutes. Turn, coat again, and continue to bake until golden, about 6 to 7 minutes longer.

3. Remove the potatoes with a spatula and place them on a serving tray. Top each with a spoonful of Yogurt Cheese or low-fat sour cream, a dollop of caviar, and a few chives.

4. Serve immediately.

*C*OOK NOTE:

❖ White rose potatoes are a variety of the long white potatoes that have a similar shape as the russet but have a thin pale skins. Also known as California long whites, acknowledging the state in which they were developed, they are good for baking, boiling, or roasting.

*D*O-AHEAD PREP:

❖ The yogurt cheese can be prepared a week in advance, but the potatoes must be cooked just before serving.

Skewered Chicken with Papaya Salsa

Serves: 10 to 12

*T*hese finger foods are a great light treat at a cocktail party accompanied by the refreshing papaya salsa.

*M*ARINADE:

2 tablespoons Chinese vinegar or balsamic vinegar

1 tablespoon lemon juice

2 tablespoons Asian-style sesame oil

1 tablespoon reduced-sodium soy sauce

1 tablespoon hoisin sauce

1 teaspoon finely minced garlic

1 teaspoon finely minced ginger

2 large whole skinless, boneless chicken breasts (about 1 pound), cut into forty 1-inch cubes

*G*ARNISH: lettuce leaves

*A*CCOMPANIMENTS: Papaya Salsa (see page 57), or other fruit salsa, and toothpicks

1. Mix the marinade ingredients in a medium bowl until well combined. Add the chicken, toss to coat, cover the bowl, and refrigerate for 1 hour.

2. Preheat an outdoor or indoor grill, broiler, or a well-seasoned ridged stove-top grill pan.

3. Thread the chicken cubes onto bamboo skewers without crowding them and grill until they are no longer pink, about 3 to 4 minutes a side.

4. Remove the chicken from the skewers and place on a leaf-lined platter accompanied by the Papaya Salsa, or other fruit salsa, and toothpicks.

*V*ARIATION:

❖ The chicken can be dipped in a prepared sweet Chinese plum sauce or hot mustard.

*D*O-AHEAD PREP:

❖ The chicken can be marinated three hours ahead and grilled just before serving. The salsa can be prepared several days in advance and chilled until ready to serve.

Spinach Meatballs

Yield: 3 dozen

*T*hese meatballs have a Middle-Eastern flavor and make a great hot hors d'oeuvre served at a cocktail party. They are prepared with lean ground turkey instead of beef to lower the fat content.

½ pound lean ground white meat turkey

½ pound lean ground dark meat turkey

one 10-ounce package frozen chopped spinach, thawed and
   squeezed dry

1 cup soft fresh bread crumbs

1 egg

2 tablespoons chopped fresh chives

2 tablespoons chopped fresh mint

2 tablespoons raisins

1 teaspoon finely grated lemon rind

1 teaspoon sugar

¼ teaspoon ground nutmeg

¼ teaspoon ground allspice

salt and freshly ground white pepper to taste

1. Preheat the oven to 450°F. Lightly coat a large roasting pan or cookie sheet with nonstick cooking spray.

2. Combine the meatball ingredients with your hands, form into 1-inch balls, and place on prepared pan.

3. Roast for about 20 minutes, shaking the pan occasionally, until browned on all sides. Serve hot with toothpicks.

*V*ARIATION:

❖ The meatballs can be prepared with lean ground veal.

*C*OOK NOTE:

❖ To prepare soft bread crumbs, break apart a few slices of fresh bread and chop in the food processor until fine. Dry bread crumbs can be made out of stale or lightly toasted bread.

*D*O-AHEAD PREP:

❖ The meatballs can be prepared in advance, frozen, and then reheated when ready to serve.

Baked Tortilla Chips

Yield: 32 chips

*U*se these flavorful baked chips as dippers for salsa, Roasted Vegetable Spread (see page 31), or Eggplant Caviar Spread (see page 33), or as a base for Tortilla Soup with Chicken (see page 98).

> 4 nonfat or low-fat flour or corn tortillas
> 1 tablespoon fresh lime juice
> salt to taste
> chili powder to taste

1. Preheat the oven to 375°F.

2. Brush the top of the tortillas very lightly with the lime juice. Sprinkle to taste with the salt and chili powder and cut each tortilla into 8 wedges. Place the pieces on nonstick baking sheets and bake for about 8 minutes, or until crisp and lightly golden.

3. Allow to cool slightly and serve.

*V*ARIATIONS:

❖ For those watching their sodium intake, a salt-free herb seasoning can be substituted for salt.

❖ Other seasoning blends can be used such as cumin and curry or barbecue flavor.

*C*OOK NOTE:

❖ Store limes away from the light, which causes them to turn yellow. Use limes that are turning yellow as quickly as possible. The juice will still be delicious but the rind will not be usable.

*D*O-AHEAD PREP:

❖ The chips can be prepared several days in advance and kept crisp in an airtight container or resealable plastic bags.

BASICS & SAUCES

❖ ❖ ❖ ❖ ❖ ❖ ❖

Yogurt Cheese

Light English Creamy Topping

Marinara Sauce

Apricot Chutney

Cranberry Chutney with Cassis

Caramelized Red Onion Marmalade

Papaya Salsa

Sun-Dried Tomato Pesto

Pico de Gallo

Yogurt Cheese

Yield: 1 cup

*P*art of a light lifestyle is enjoying foods that are flavorful but low in fat. There is an ingenious way to convert plain nonfat or low-fat yogurt into a rich and creamy substitute for sour cream, cream cheese, or even mayonnaise, by removing the whey or liquid. This thickened yogurt cheese is known as lebneh in Arabic, suzme in Turkish, and yaourti tou ponghiou (pocket yogurt) in Greek. In this part of the world this creamy yogurt is served for breakfast with olives and bread. Americans use yogurt cheese in dips and spreads, in salad dressings to add creaminess the low-fat way, in cold soups to add a rich garnish without added fats, and even in baking for low-fat cheesecakes.

You can prepare yogurt cheese very easily with a yogurt funnel or yogurt strainer designed for just this purpose. Yogurt cheese can also be made by lining the filter holder of a drip coffee pot with a coffee filter, placing it over the coffee pot, and allowing the yogurt to drain. Another method is to place several layers of cheesecloth over a small rack, add the yogurt, and allow the whey to drain off into a small bowl.

Remember, the longer you leave the yogurt, the thicker the consistency. The best yogurt to use is a plain nonfat or low-fat one without gelatin or stabilizers. The gelatin holds the whey in the yogurt and does not allow it to drain off. When selecting a yogurt look for ones with live and active cultures with L Acidophilus for optimum health benefits.

one 16-ounce carton plain nonfat or low-fat yogurt without gelatin

1. Spoon the yogurt into the funnel strainer, filter, or layers of cheesecloth placed over a container and allow it to drain in the refrigerator for 8 to 12 hours or at the most 24, depending on the desired consistency.

2. Discard the whey and keep the yogurt cheese refrigerated in a covered container. Note: the whey may continue to release, so make sure to pour off any accumulated liquid before using.

Light English Creamy Topping

Yield: 2¼ cups

*O*K, so we know that clotted high-fat English Devonshire cream is out! But why not enhance low-fat sour cream and serve it as a topping for fruit desserts, pies, or scones?

> 16 ounces low-fat sour cream
>
> ⅓ cup confectioners' sugar
>
> 1½ teaspoons pure vanilla extract

1. In a medium bowl, whisk the sour cream, sugar, and vanilla together until smooth. Place in a covered container and chill until ready to serve.

*V*ARIATIONS:

❖ Substitute 1½ teaspoons almond extract or 2 tablespoons Amaretto liqueur for the vanilla.

❖ Add 1 to 2 teaspoons grated lemon or orange rind.

❖ Adjust the amount of sugar to taste—if you like it sweeter, add more sugar, if you like it tarter, add less sugar.

*C*OOK NOTES:

❖ When refrigerating sour cream, cottage cheese, or yogurt, turn the container upside-down onto a plate. This creates a tighter seal and keeps the product fresher.

❖ When buying vanilla extract, look for bottles labeled "pure vanilla extract," which indicates that the extract has been made with vanilla beans. Pure vanilla extract actually improves with age, becoming subtler and more complex in flavor.

❖ For enhanced flavor, store a sliced vanilla bean in your box of confectioners' sugar.

*D*O-AHEAD PREP:

❖ The cream can be prepared up to a week in advance and kept in a covered container in the refrigerator until ready to use.

Marinara Sauce

Yield: 4 cups

*M*arinara sauce is a highly seasoned Italian tomato sauce prepared with onions, garlic, and oregano. The sauce can be pureed or served chunky-style. This basic version can be used on pasta, as a base for cioppino, or on top of poultry.

1 tablespoon olive oil

1 medium onion, finely chopped

1 carrot, peeled and finely chopped

2 cloves garlic, finely minced

one 28-ounce can crushed tomatoes, packed in puree

2 tablespoons chopped fresh parsley

1 tablespoon chopped fresh basil, or ½ teaspoon dried basil, crumbled

1 tablespoon chopped fresh oregano, or ½ teaspoon dried
   oregano, crumbled

salt and freshly ground pepper to taste

1. In a heavy medium nonstick saucepan, heat the oil to medium and sauté the onion and carrot for about 5 to 6 minutes, stirring often, until softened.

2. Add the garlic and stir to just combine. Add the remaining ingredients, bring to a boil, cover, reduce heat, and simmer for 45 minutes. Allow to cool slightly.

3. Puree the sauce in a blender or food processor or leave chunky-style and refrigerate or freeze in a covered container until ready to use.

*V*ARIATIONS:

❖ ¼ cup red or white wine can be added before the tomatoes.

❖ ½ teaspoon red pepper flakes can be added for a spicy version.

*C*OOK NOTES:

❖ If tomatoes packed in puree are unavailable, use regular whole juice-packed tomatoes; chop, drain off most of the liquid, return the tomatoes to the can, and fill to the top with canned tomato puree.

❖ Freeze the finished sauce in 1-cup containers to have on hand for quick dinners.

*D*O-AHEAD PREP:

❖ The sauce can be frozen for 3 to 4 months in airtight containers.

Apricot Chutney

Yield: 3 cups

*T*his chutney makes a delicious condiment or side dish to be served with grilled poultry or meats or any type of curry. Seal any extra chutney in glass jars, refrigerate, and give it as a thoughtful house gift for the holidays.

2½ cups (12 ounces) dried apricots, coarsely chopped

1 large onion, finely chopped

¾ cup fresh orange juice

½ cup golden raisins

1 tablespoon grated fresh ginger or 1 teaspoon ground ginger

1 tablespoon freshly grated lemon rind

1 tablespoon grated orange rind

1 teaspoon minced garlic

½ teaspoon ground cinnamon

½ teaspoon crushed dried red pepper

¼ teaspoon ground allspice

1.　Combine all the ingredients in a medium nonstick saucepan. Bring to a boil, cover, reduce the heat, and simmer until smooth and thickened, about 1 hour and 15 minutes, stirring occasionally.

2.　Remove from the heat, cool slightly, pack in clean jars with tight-fitting lids, and refrigerate until ready to use.

3.　Serve at room temperature as a condiment or a side dish.

*V*ARIATION:

❖　Dried peaches can be substituted for the apricots.

*C*OOK NOTE:

❖　Once dried apricots have been opened, they should be stored in the refrigerator or on a cool shelf in an airtight container.

*D*O-AHEAD PREP:

❖　The chutney will keep in the refrigerator for several months.

Cranberry Conserve with Cassis

Yield: 6 cups

*T*his fabulous accompaniment to roast poultry is a variation on a recipe from my friends Andy and Kathy Blue, authors of *Thanksgiving Dinner*.

1 thin-skinned navel orange, cut into chunks (rind included)

1 tart Granny Smith or similar apple, peeled, cored, and coarsely chopped

2 cups brown sugar, firmly packed

½ cup raspberry or cranberry vinegar

½ cup dried currants or raisins

1 teaspoon chopped crystallized ginger

¼ teaspoon ground cinnamon

¼ teaspoon almond extract

4 cups (about 1 pound) cranberries

2 tablespoons crème de cassis

1 tablespoon honey

½ teaspoon lemon juice

1. Place the orange chunks in a food processor and pulse until the orange is coarsely diced. Remove to a bowl and chop the apple chunks until finely chopped. Stir the apple into the orange pieces and set aside.

2. In a saucepan, combine the sugar and vinegar and stir. Bring to a boil over medium heat and allow to bubble for about 5 minutes, or until the mixture becomes syrupy. Add the currants, ginger, cinnamon, and almond extract and continue to simmer for an additional 5 minutes. Add the cranberries and continue to cook for 5 minutes longer, or until the cranberries begin to pop and are softened.

3. Add the orange-apple mixtures to the cranberries along with the crème de cassis, honey, and lemon juice and toss thoroughly to combine the flavors.

4. Store in clean glass containers in the refrigerator until ready to serve.

*V*ARIATION:

❖ Pear can be substituted for the apple.

*C*OOK NOTES:

❖ Crystallized ginger is a confection prepared from bits of gingerroot that have been cooked in a sugar syrup and then coated with coarse sugar.

❖ Purchase extra cranberries at holiday season when they are plentiful and freeze them for use throughout the year.

❖ You can prepare your own raspberry vinegar by thawing and draining a 10-ounce package of frozen raspberries and covering them with 3 quarts of red wine vinegar overnight. Heat the mixture the next day, bring to a boil, remove from the heat, and allow to cool. Strain and store in sealed bottles to keep for future use or give as homemade gifts.

❖ Use a garlic press to simplify the sticky and messy job of chopping candied ginger.

*D*O-AHEAD PREP:

❖ The conserve will keep in the refrigerator for several weeks.

Caramelized Red Onion Marmalade

Yield: 2 cups

*T*his fat-free relish can be cooked up to three weeks in advance, placed in covered containers, and kept refrigerated until ready to use. Remember to bring it to room temperature before serving.

> 2 large red onions (about 1¼ pounds), thinly sliced
>
> 3 tablespoons brown sugar
>
> ¾ cup dry red wine
>
> 3 tablespoons balsamic vinegar
>
> salt and freshly ground white pepper to taste

1. In a heavy large nonstick saucepan, combine the onions and brown sugar, and cook over medium heat, stirring often, until the onions begin to caramelize and turn golden, about 20 to 25 minutes.

2. Increase the heat to high, add the wine and vinegar, bring to a boil, reduce heat, and continue to cook over medium-low heat, stirring often, for about 15 to 20 minutes or until most of the liquid has evaporated.

3. Season to taste with salt and pepper, allow to cool, and serve at room temperature.

*C*OOK NOTE:

❖ Don't judge an onion by its size or color. Size does not determine quality or flavor. The seed used, the soil, and weather during the growing season help determine how mild or pungent an onion will be.

Papaya Salsa

*T*his unique fruit salsa can be used as an accompaniment to grilled seafood, lamb, or vegetables, and can be used as a topping when baking fish or chicken.

2 teaspoons olive oil

2 shallots, finely chopped

2 teaspoons finely minced ginger

½ teaspoon curry powder

1 large ripe papaya, peeled, seeds removed, and finely chopped

2 tablespoons fresh lime juice

1 tablespoon finely chopped fresh cilantro

salt to taste

1. In a small nonstick saucepan, heat the oil and sauté the shallots and ginger over medium heat for about 6 to 7 minutes, or until softened, stirring often.

2. Remove the pan from the heat and stir in the curry powder until well blended. Place the mixture in the food processor, add the remaining ingredients, and pulse until just blended. Do not overprocess!

3. Serve at room temperature.

*V*ARIATIONS:

❖ The white portion of scallions can be substituted for shallots.

❖ Mangoes can be substituted for the papayas.

*C*OOK NOTES:

❖ Select papayas that are more than half yellow and yield to gentle pressure between the palms of the hands denoting ripeness. The fruit should be smooth, unshriveled, and free of bruises.

❖ Papaya seeds can be saved for use in a salad dressing.

*D*O-AHEAD PREP:

❖ The salsa can be prepared several days in advance and chilled until ready to use. Bring to room temperature before serving.

Sun-Dried Tomato Pesto

Yield: 1 cup

*P*esto comes from the Italian word *pestare* (to pound), which is traditionally prepared *alla Genoese*, with basil, garlic, pine nuts, Parmesan cheese, and lots of olive oil. This sun-dried tomato pesto uses dry-packed, sun-dried tomatoes and turns them into a delicious topping for pasta, flavoring for fish, topping for roasted vegetables, or flavoring for meat loaf.

one 3-ounce package sun-dried tomatoes (not packed in oil)

2 tablespoons chopped fresh basil

1 tablespoon pine nuts

1 tablespoon freshly grated Parmesan cheese

1 teaspoon minced garlic

salt and freshly ground pepper to taste

1.   Soak the sun-dried tomatoes in boiling water to cover for about 15 minutes. Drain and reserve the soaking liquid. Place in a food processor with ¼ cup of the reserved liquid, the basil, pine nuts, Parmesan, garlic, and salt and pepper and process until smooth.

2.   Place in a covered container and refrigerate until ready to use.

*V*ARIATION:

❖   Walnuts can be substituted for the pine nuts.

*D*O-AHEAD PREP:

❖   The pesto can be prepared up to 2 weeks in advance and kept in a covered container in the refrigerator.

Pico de Gallo

*P*ico de gallo is a cross between a salsa and a relish. It is traditionally served with fajitas but can be used as a dip with Baked Tortilla Chips (see page 48) or crudités. The name *pico de gallo* means "rooster's beak."

½ pound ripe tomatoes, finely diced

1 small onion, finely chopped

1 jalapeño pepper, seeded, ribs removed, and finely minced

2 tablespoons finely chopped fresh cilantro

1 tablespoon fresh lime juice

salt to taste

1.　In a medium bowl, combine the ingredients, stir and allow to stand at room temperature for at least 30 minutes for the flavors to blend.

2.　Serve at room temperature or slightly chilled

*C*OOK NOTE:

❖　About 89 percent of a chile pepper's fire is contained in the ribs. If these ribs and the attached seeds are cut off and discarded, the heat is diminished.

*D*O-AHEAD PREP:

❖　Pico de Gallo can be prepared several days in advance and refrigerated in a covered container; allow to come to room temperature before serving.

Basics & Sauces　59

BREAKFASTS & BRUNCHES

Piquant Light Frittata

Savory Strata

Dutch Babies

Pumpkin Waffles

Lemon-Yogurt Waffles with Raspberry-Orange Syrup

Gingerbread Pancakes

Silver Dollar Blueberry Pancakes with Cinnamon
Applesauce Topping

Oven-Baked Cinnamon French Toast with Orange Syrup

Piquant Light Frittata

Serves: 4

*T*his light fritatta is a slow-cooked, unfolded Italian omelet you can indulge in without squandering your fat grams or raising your cholesterol.

2 teaspoons olive oil

1 large onion, thinly sliced

1 sweet red bell pepper, seeded and julienned

¼ cup (4 thin strips, about ⅛ pound) minced prosciutto

one 6-ounce bag baby spinach or 2 cups firmly packed washed,
    dried, and trimmed spinach leaves

1 clove garlic, finely minced

6 egg whites

2 whole eggs

2 tablespoons freshly grated Parmesan cheese

2 tablespoons chopped fresh basil

2 tablespoons chopped fresh parsley

salt and freshly ground pepper to taste

*G*ARNISH: fresh basil leaves

*A*CCOMPANIMENT: warmed pita bread

1. Preheat the broiler.

2. In a 10-inch nonstick oven-proof skillet, heat the oil to medium and cook the onion and bell pepper for 5 minutes, stirring often, until softened. Add the prosciutto and continue to cook for an additional 2 to 3 minutes, until the prosciutto just begins to crisp.

3. Add the spinach and cook over medium-high heat, stirring often, until the spinach is wilted, about 1 minute. Add the garlic and stir for 30 seconds.

4. Whisk the egg whites with the remaining ingredients until smooth and well combined. Add the egg mixture to the skillet, smoothing down the top with a spatula. Continue to cook over medium heat for 5 to 6 minutes, until the egg is almost set, lifting the sides of the frittata with a spatula to allow the uncooked portion of the egg to run underneath.

5. Place the skillet under the broiler for 2 to 3 minutes, or until golden and set.

6. Slide the frittata out onto a plate, cut into wedges, and serve hot or at room temperature garnished with basil leaves and accompanied by warm pita bread.

VARIATIONS:

❖ The frittata can be chilled and served cold or at room temperature on an herbed roll or foccacia bread as a delicious sandwich.

❖ Frittatas are versatile and can be varied according to seasonal availability and personal preference. Kale or Swiss chard can be substituted for the spinach; yellow or green bell peppers can be substituted for the red; sautéed mushrooms or potatoes can be added; low-fat grated mozzarella, cheddar, or Swiss cheese can be substituted for the Parmesan; freshly snipped chives, thyme, or an assortment of herbs can be substituted for the basil and parsley; jalapeño pepper can be added to taste.

❖ Pico de Gallo (see page 59) or salsa can be served with the frittata.

❖ For a cholesterol-free frittata, use 8 to 10 egg whites and eliminate the 2 whole eggs.

COOK NOTES:

❖ While putting all of your eggs in one basket was never a good idea, neither is taking them out of the egg carton. Store eggs covered in the supermarket carton to prevent the eggs from absorbing odors of the food in the refrigerator, which can alter their flavor.

❖ The color of the shell has no bearing on the cooking performance, flavor, or nutritive value of eggs. For most purposes, the fresher eggs are, the better they will taste. For hard cooking and beating whites, however, it is important that the eggs be at least 3 days old, which will make them easier to peel. To test eggs for freshness, put them in enough salted cool water for them to float. Fresh eggs will lie flat on the bottom, but older eggs will float because there is more air in the shell.

DO-AHEAD PREP:

❖ The frittata can be prepared a day in advance and reheated in a microwave oven or served at room temperature.

Savory Strata

A strata is a sort of savory bread pudding that is a great way to use up stale bread. The point of a strata (which literally means layers) is that the finished product is much more interesting than the main ingredients. Traditionally, stratas consist of buttered bread, eggs, and cheese. This lightened version reduces the fat but still retains that creamy and comforting flavor and texture that makes it a hit for brunch, lunch, or supper.

1 tablespoon olive oil

1 small onion, finely chopped

6 mushrooms, stems removed, wiped clean, and thinly sliced

1 medium zucchini, ends trimmed, washed, dried, and sliced

1 clove garlic, finely minced

one 14½-ounce can ready-cut diced tomatoes, thoroughly drained

5 egg whites

2 whole eggs

1⅓ cups 1% low-fat milk

2 teaspoons snipped fresh dill

2 tablespoons low-fat feta cheese

dash of Tabasco

salt and freshly ground white pepper to taste

6 cups (about 9 slices) Italian, French, or sourdough bread, cut into ½-inch cubes

4 teaspoons freshly grated Parmesan cheese

*G*ARNISH: chopped fresh parsley

1. Preheat the oven to 350°F. Lightly coat an 8-x-12-inch or similar size oven-proof baking dish with nonstick cooking spray.

2. In a medium skillet, heat the oil over medium heat and sauté the onion, mushrooms, and zucchini, stirring often, until softened, about 6 to 7 minutes. Add the garlic and stir for 30 seconds. Add the tomatoes, stir to combine, and set aside.

3. Whisk the egg whites with the eggs, milk, dill, feta cheese, Tabasco, and salt and pepper until smooth.

4. Layer half the vegetable mixture on the bottom of the prepared baking dish.

Top with half the bread cubes, then the remaining vegetables, and the remaining bread cubes. Pour the egg mixture over all and sprinkle the top evenly with the Parmesan cheese. Press the bread down to make sure it gets soaked with the egg mixture.

5. Bake for 30 minutes, or until golden.

6. Allow to cool slightly, cut into squares, and serve warm or at room temperature, garnished with chopped fresh parsley.

Variation:

❖ Stratas are very versatile and should be varied according to seasonal availability and personal preference. Green bell peppers, mushrooms, and other vegetables can be added if desired; whole grain bread can be substituted for white; low-fat cheddar, Swiss, Monterey Jack, goat cheese, or other low-fat cheeses can be substituted for the feta cheese; basil can be substituted for the dill.

Cook Note:

❖ The easiest way to grate cheese is in a food processor, but if grating by hand, make sure the cheese is well chilled and rub a small amount of oil on the grater to prevent sticking.

Do-ahead prep:

❖ The strata can be assembled the day before through Step 4, covered tightly with plastic wrap, and refrigerated until ready to cook.

Dutch Babies

Serves: 4

*D*utch babies, also known as baked German pancakes, are a puffy breakfast delight. I remember eating this luscious confection filled with tart loganberries at Luchow's restaurant in New York when I was a little girl. Like a popover, Dutch Babies must be served immediately after baking.

> 2 eggs, at room temperature
>
> 2 egg whites, at room temperature
>
> ½ cup all-purpose flour
>
> ½ teaspoon salt
>
> ½ cup 1% low-fat milk
>
> 1 tablespoon unsalted butter, melted
>
> 1 teaspoon pure vanilla extract
>
> **GARNISH:** 1 teaspoon lemon juice, sprinkling of confectioners' sugar and cinnamon
>
> **ACCOMPANIMENTS:** 4 cups raspberries, strawberries, or blueberries; or maple syrup

1. Preheat the oven to 450°F. Lightly coat the bottom and sides of a 10-inch heavy nonstick skillet or Dutch baby pan with nonstick cooking spray.

2. In a large mixing bowl, beat the eggs and egg whites with an electric mixer until thoroughly combined. Sift the flour and salt into the eggs and continue to beat until blended. Add the milk, butter, and vanilla and continue to beat until smooth.

3. Pour the batter into the prepared pan and bake for 15 to 20 minutes, or until puffy and golden. The sides and sometimes the center will puff up unevenly, which is the way it is supposed to bake.

4. Cut into serving pieces, sprinkle with the lemon juice and a dusting of confectioners' sugar and cinnamon, and serve topped with the berries or maple syrup.

*V*ARIATION:

❖ The Dutch babies can be prepared in 4 small pans such as mini-pie pans or 4 small 6-inch skillets.

❖   An easy way to separate an egg is to stand a small funnel in a measuring cup, then break the egg into the funnel. The white will slither through, but the yolk stays on top. To remove the yolk, simply tip the funnel into a bowl.

Pumpkin Waffles

Serves: 3 to 4

*T*hese crisp and flavorful waffles can be prepared with other baked winter squash or baked sweet potatoes. Prepare the waffles in a Belgian waffle iron or regular waffle iron according to the manufacturer's directions.

¾ cup canned pumpkin

2 teaspoons melted unsalted butter

1 whole egg

1 egg white

¾ cup 1% low-fat milk

½ cup all-purpose flour

1 teaspoon baking powder

1 teaspoon pumpkin pie spice

pinch of salt

*A*CCOMPANIMENTS: pure maple syrup, or unsweetened applesauce or apple butter

1.   Preheat a nonstick waffle iron. If the instructions specify, lightly coat the iron with nonstick cooking spray.

2.   In a large bowl, whisk the pumpkin with the butter, egg, and milk. Beat the mixture until just combined.

3.   In a small bowl, combine the flour with the remaining ingredients and stir until smooth. Add the dry ingredients to the pumpkin mixture and stir until just smooth.

4.   Pour the batter into the center of each of the waffle iron squares and bake according to manufacturer's instructions, until golden and crisp.

5.   Remove and serve immediately accompanied by pure maple syrup, or unsweetened applesauce or apple butter.

*V*ARIATIONS:

❖ Other toppings for the waffles can be juice-sweetened fruit preserves, sliced bananas and vanilla-sweetened low-fat yogurt, or fresh cut-up fruits.

❖ If pumpkin pie spice is not available substitute a mixture of ground cinnamon, nutmeg, ginger, cloves, and allspice.

*C*OOK NOTE:

❖ Pumpkins are a great source of beta-carotene and potassium, iron, and riboflavin; they are low in calories and sodium and have no fat or cholesterol.

*D*O-AHEAD PREP:

❖ The batter can be prepared an hour or so in advance. The waffles can also be prepared in advance and kept warm in a 275°F oven for about 15 minutes, which will make them crisper.

Lemon-Yogurt Waffles
with Raspberry-Orange Syrup

Serves: 6 to 8

*T*he word *waffle* comes from an old German term for honeycomb, referring to the pattern that comes out when baked in a waffle iron. Thomas Jefferson brought the first waffle to the United States from Holland and introduced waffles at a White House dinner during his tenure as president.

These light and crispy waffles are easy to prepare and delicious as part of an autumn brunch.

RASPBERRY-ORANGE SYRUP:

12 ounce jar seedless raspberry preserves

½ cup orange juice

3 tablespoons corn syrup

WAFFLES:

2 cups all-purpose flour

3 tablespoons sugar

2 teaspoons baking powder

½ teaspoon baking soda

pinch of salt

2 whole eggs

1 egg white

one 8-ounce nonfat or low-fat lemon-flavored yogurt

¾ cup 1% low-fat milk

2 tablespoons vegetable oil

2 teaspoons grated lemon rind

1. Prepare the syrup: In a small nonstick saucepan, combine the syrup ingredients over medium-low heat. Cook, stirring often, until small bubbles appear at the edges of the pan. Reduce the heat to low and simmer for 2 to 3 minutes, stirring often, until smooth. Transfer to a pitcher and keep warm.

2. Preheat a nonstick waffle iron. If the instructions specify, lightly coat the iron with nonstick cooking spray. Preheat the oven to 200°F.

3. In a medium bowl, sift the flour with the sugar, baking powder, baking soda, and salt.

4. In a separate large bowl, whisk the remaining ingredients until smooth. Stir the dry ingredients into the egg mixture and stir until just smooth.

5. Pour the batter into the center of each of the waffle iron squares and bake according to manufacturer's instructions until golden and crisp.

6. Continue to prepare the waffles until all the batter has been used. Transfer the cooked waffles to a platter and keep warm in the oven until all are ready.

7. Reheat the syrup in a microwave oven or on top of the range, and serve the waffles hot topped with the syrup.

*V*ARIATIONS:

❖ Blueberry, strawberry, orange marmalade, or other preserves can be substituted for the raspberry.

❖ Vanilla-flavored yogurt can be substituted for the lemon yogurt.

*C*OOK NOTES:

❖ Always wash and dry lemons well before grating to eliminate any pesticide residue.

❖ When grating lemon or orange peel, grate extra and store it in a sealed container in the freezer.

*D*O-AHEAD PREP:

❖ The syrup can be prepared a day or two in advance and kept in a sealed glass jar until ready to reheat. The batter can be prepared an hour or two in advance and kept in a covered container in the refrigerator. If the batter thickens on standing, whisk in a few tablespoons of milk. The waffles can be prepared and kept in a warm oven for 15 minutes.

Gingerbread Pancakes

*G*ingerbread is not just for the holidays. These delectable low-fat pancakes are perfect for a brunch or breakfast at any time of the year.

2 cups all-purpose flour

1½ teaspoons baking powder

1 teaspoon ground ginger

1 teaspoon ground cinnamon

½ teaspoon ground nutmeg

½ teaspoon baking soda

pinch of ground cloves

pinch of salt

1¾ cup low-fat buttermilk

1 whole egg

1 egg white

¼ cup molasses

1½ tablespoons vegetable oil

*G*ARNISH: pure maple syrup, fruit preserves, or fresh fruit

1. Preheat the oven to 200°F.

2. In a large bowl, sift the flour with the baking powder, ginger, cinnamon, nutmeg, baking soda, cloves, and salt.

3. In a medium bowl, whisk the buttermilk with the egg, egg white, molasses, and oil until smooth.

4. Add the egg mixture to the dry ingredients and stir until just smooth. (Do not overbeat.)

5. Coat a nonstick griddle or skillet with nonstick cooking spray. Heat the griddle to medium.

6. Drop ¼ cup of the batter onto the hot griddle to make 3- to 4-inch round pancakes. Flatten the tops with the back of a spatula and cook until the bottoms are lightly golden and the pancake is covered with bubbles, about 1½ minutes. Flip and cook until golden, about 1 minute longer. Continue to cook the pancakes in batches, coating the griddle with additional nonstick cooking spray as necessary.

7. Transfer the finished pancakes to a platter and keep warm in the oven while finishing up the rest of the batter.

8. Serve the pancakes hot, garnished with pure maple syrup, fruit preserves, or fresh fruit.

*V*ARIATION:

❖ Bananas, blueberries, or chopped stawberries can be added if desired.

*C*OOK NOTES:

❖ Use an ice-cream scoop or ¼-cup measuring cup to perfectly measure and easily drop the pancake batter onto the griddle.

❖ Dried ground ginger is less peppery than fresh gingerroot, with a slightly delayed, musty bite. The finest ground ginger comes from Jamaica. It is available in the spice section of most grocery stores.

*D*O-AHEAD PREP:

❖ The batter can be prepared a few hours in advance. If the batter thickens as it stands, thin it with a few tablespoons of buttermilk.

Silver Dollar Blueberry Pancakes
with Cinnamon Applesauce Topping

Serves: 6

*S*trawberries, peeled chopped peaches, mangoes, papayas, or other seasonal fruits can be substituted for the blueberries.

> 1 cup all-purpose flour
>
> ¾ cup whole wheat flour
>
> ½ cup cornmeal
>
> 1½ teaspoons baking soda
>
> 1 teaspoon salt
>
> 3 egg whites
>
> 1 egg
>
> 2 cups low-fat buttermilk
>
> 2 tablespoons vegetable oil
>
> 1½ cups blueberries, fresh or frozen, thawed and drained

TOPPING: 1 cup applesauce mixed with ½ teaspoon ground cinnamon

GARNISH: orange slices

1. Preheat the oven to 200°F.

2. In a large bowl, combine the white flour, whole wheat flour, cornmeal, baking soda, and salt.

3. In a separate mixing bowl, whisk the egg whites and whole egg with the buttermilk and oil. Lightly whisk the egg mixture into the flour mixture until barely smooth. Do not overmix. Gently fold in the blueberries.

4. Coat a nonstick griddle with nonstick cooking spray and heat to medium-high. Using an ice-cream scoop or similar-sized utensil, drop the batter onto the hot skillet. When the pancakes puff up and bubbles dot the surface, flip them over and cook for 1 minute longer.

5. Remove the finished pancakes to a warm platter and place in the oven until the rest of the batter has been cooked.

6. Serve the pancakes accompanied by the cinnamon applesauce topping and garnished with fresh orange slices.

ℂOOK NOTE:

❖   If using fresh blueberries, dust them with some of the flour first to keep them separate in the batter.

𝒟O-AHEAD PREP:

❖   The batter should be prepared just before cooking but the warmed pancakes will keep in the oven for about an hour.

Oven-Baked Cinnamon French Toast with Orange Syrup

Serves: 6 to 8

𝒯his is a perfect dish for a brunch because it can be prepared the night before and popped into the oven when the guests arrive.

¾ pound (12 ounces) loaf French, Italian, or sourdough bread, cut into ½-inch slices

ℰGG MIXTURE:

3 egg whites

2 whole eggs

1½ cups 1% low-fat milk

1 tablespoon grated orange rind

1 teaspoon pure vanilla extract

1 teaspoon ground cinnamon

½ teaspoon ground nutmeg

butter-flavored nonstick cooking spray

𝒮YRUP:

1 cup water

1 cup brown sugar

6 ounces frozen orange juice concentrate, thawed

𝒢ARNISH: fresh orange slices

1. Place the bread in a single layer in a 10-x-15-inch jelly-roll pan.

2. In a medium bowl, whisk the egg mixture ingredients together until smooth. Pour evenly over the bread to coat, turning to soak up the liquid on both sides, cover with plastic wrap, and refrigerate for 2 to 3 hours or overnight.

3. Preheat the oven to 400°F. Lightly coat a large nonstick baking sheet with butter-flavored nonstick cooking spray and preheat the pan in the oven for 10 minutes.

4. With a spatula, carefully transfer the bread to the preheated baking sheet and bake for 10 minutes, or until golden on top. Turn, lightly coat with nonstick cooking spray, and continue to bake for 5 to 10 minutes longer or until the toast is golden and browned.

5. While the toast is baking, in a small nonstick saucepan, place the water and brown sugar and bring to a boil over high heat, stirring occasionally. Reduce the heat to medium-low and simmer for 2 minutes, stirring until the sugar is dissolved. Increase the heat to high, whisk in the orange juice concentrate, and cook, stirring for an additional 2 minutes until hot and smooth. Transfer to a pitcher and keep warm.

6. Remove the toast from the oven and serve immediately topped with the orange syrup.

VARIATION:

❖ Frozen apple juice concentrate can be substituted for the orange and the orange rind can be omitted from the recipe.

DO-AHEAD PREP:

❖ Prepare the egg mixture through Step 1, cover it, and refrigerate it until you are ready to pop it into the oven. The syrup can be prepared a day or two in advance and kept in a sealed glass jar until ready to reheat.

Soups

❖ ■ ❖ ■ ❖ ■ ❖

Classic Chicken Broth

Instant Fish Broth

Vegetable Broth

Sandy's Chicken Soup with Fine Noodles

Chinese Vegetable Egg Drop Soup

Ribollita

Acorn Squash and Apple Soup

Celery Root and Carrot Soup

Mushroom Barley Soup with Dill

Pea Soup with Roasted Garlic Flavor

Pappa al Pomodoro

Zucchini Soup with Red Pepper Puree

Tortilla Soup with Chicken

Seafood Minestrone

Borscht with Dill Flavor

Broccoli-Leek Vichysoisse

Cucumber Yogurt Soup with Fresh Mint

Mulligatawny Soup

Tomato Corn Soup

Etiquette is the noise you don't make while having soup.
— Anonymous

Classic Chicken Broth

Serves: 6 to 8

A classic chicken broth is prepared from a whole chicken, but can be prepared from less-expensive ingredients such as chicken backs and necks. My mother taught me a few tricks to make a clear, flavorful broth. First, the ingredients must be cooked at a slow simmer—if the soup boils too fast, it may become cloudy. The other trick is to use a little frozen or canned broth to give a boost to the flavors. Freeze the soup in small containers so that you have delicious broth whenever you need it.

1 large chicken, about 5 pounds, rinsed well and cut up into 8
    pieces (liver and giblets removed and saved for another use)
    or 5 pounds chicken backs and necks

2½ quarts water

3 cups defatted chicken broth

3 large carrots, peeled and cut into 2-inch lengths

2 large onions, quartered

2 ribs celery, cut into 2-inch lengths, including the tops

1 parsnip, peeled and cut into 2-inch lengths

1 large leek, thoroughly washed and cut into 1-inch lengths (white
    part only)

3 sprigs fresh dill

3 sprigs fresh parsley

8 peppercorns

2 whole cloves

1 bay leaf

salt to taste

1. Place the chicken parts in the bottom of a large heavy, narrow stockpot. Add the water and broth (the liquid should cover the chicken completely) and bring to a boil; reduce the heat to medium-low heat and allow the soup to simmer for 10 minutes, removing and discarding any scum that comes to the surface with a large spoon.

2. Add the carrots, onions, celery, parsnip, and leek. Place the dill, parsley, peppercorns, cloves, and bay leaf in a piece of cheesecloth, tie up with kitchen twine, and submerge in the soup along with the salt. Reduce the heat, cover, and simmer very slowly for 2 to 2½ hours.

3. Allow the soup to cool slightly. Remove and discard the cheesecloth bag of herbs and spices, squeezing out any excess liquid into the soup. Remove the chicken and vegetables from the pot and save them for another use. Strain the clear soup into a container. Cool and then refrigerate the liquid in a covered container so that the fat can be easily removed.

4. When ready to serve, remove the accumulated fat, and reheat the soup.

*V*ARIATIONS:

❖ The broth can be served with cut-up pieces of the chicken, without the skin, and the vegetables.

❖ The vegetables can be pureed with some of the liquid, seasoned with salt and pepper, and served as a thick and delicious pureed soup.

❖ The clear soup can also be served with starches such as cooked noodles, rice, barley, kreplach, wontons, dumplings, tortellini, meatballs, piroshki (Russian meat-filled pasta), pirogen (Jewish meat-filled ravioli), or matzo balls. Additional vegetables such as snow peas, scallions, turnips, or tomatoes can be added if desired.

*C*OOK NOTES:

❖ For a darker colored broth, leave the brown onion skin intact, which will give a rich brown tone to the broth.

❖ Save chicken backs and necks and freeze them along with other good soup flavorings. When you have collected enough ingredients, thaw and prepare the soup.

❖ Use a heavy, tall, and narrow stockpot so all the chicken parts and vegetables are covered with the liquid and evaporation is slow.

❖ Leeks are the sweetest and mildest member of the onion family. Select leeks with uniform, medium-sized necks. The tops should be fresh and green and the leeks should "give" a bit to the touch to assure their not being woody on the inside.

*D*O-AHEAD PREP:

❖ The soup should be cooked a day or two in advance so that the fat can rise to the top and be removed easily. The broth can be refrigerated in covered containers for up to 5 days or frozen for up to 6 months.

Instant Fish Broth

Yield: 1 quart

*L*ight and easy cooking calls for using shortcuts like canned broth or canned tomatoes. Bottled clam broth can be used in many fish recipes, but if time permits, I like to cook it quickly with a few key ingredients to enhance the flavor.

> two 8-ounce bottles clam juice
>
> 2 cups water
>
> ⅔ cup dry white wine or dry vermouth
>
> 1 medium onion, roughly chopped
>
> 1 rib celery with leaves, roughly chopped
>
> 8 peppercorns
>
> 4 sprigs parsley
>
> 2 tablespoons lemon juice
>
> 1 strip of lemon peel
>
> 1 bay leaf

1. In a large nonreactive saucepan, combine all the ingredients. Bring to a boil over high heat, reduce the heat, and simmer uncovered for 20 minutes. Allow to cool slightly.

2. Pour the broth through a strainer, pressing as much liquid as possible from the solids before discarding them. Allow to cool, pour into small containers allowing an inch for expansion at the top, cover, and freeze.

*V*ARIATION:

❖ 1 teaspoon chopped fresh thyme or ½ teaspoon dried thyme, crumbled, can be added.

*C*OOK NOTE:

❖ Store celery in a perforated plastic bag in the refrigerator for about a week. If the celery is wilting, revive it by submerging the ribs in a bowl of ice water with 1 tablespoon of lemon juice for about half an hour.

*D*O-AHEAD PREP:

❖ The stock can be refrigerated in covered containers for up to a day or frozen for up to 4 months.

Vegetable Broth

*L*ight and easy cooking calls for using shortcuts like canned broth. Unfortunately there is not a good vegetable broth on the market, so I have come up with a master vegetable broth recipe that can be prepared in large quantities and frozen in small covered containers for use any time.

No salt is added to the broth so that it can enhance any dish without adding an extra-salty flavor.

*V*EGETABLE BROTH:

2 onions, thinly sliced

2 whole leeks, thoroughly washed and thinly sliced (white and
    green parts; this is the one time you get to use the whole leek)

4 medium carrots, peeled and roughly chopped

4 ribs celery with leaves attached, roughly chopped

4 garlic cloves, peeled and split

1 bunch watercress, washed and dried

8 sprigs parsley

8 whole peppercorns

4 sprigs thyme or ½ teaspoon dried thyme, crumbled

2 bay leaves

10 cups water

1. In a large nonreactive stockpot, combine all the broth ingredients and cover with the water. Bring to a boil over high heat, reduce the heat, and simmer uncovered for 1½ hours. Allow to cool slightly.

2. Pour the broth through a strainer, pressing as much liquid as possible from the vegetables before discarding them. Allow to cool, pour into small containers allowing an inch for expansion at the top, cover, and freeze.

*V*ARIATIONS:

❖ For an earthier flavor, add turnips, parsnip, celery root, and other root vegetables.

❖ For a richer and darker broth roast the vegetables in a 450°F oven for 25 to 30 minutes. Add a few cups of hot water to the pan to loosen the browned particles, transfer to a stock pot, cover with water, and cook for 1 to 2 hours. Strain.

Cook Notes:

❖   Vegetable broth is a great way to recycle your vegetable castoffs. Save the asparagus, carrot, parsnip, and other vegetable trimmings and add them to the broth.

❖   Select leeks with tight green tops and store them, unwashed, in a perforated plastic bag in the vegetable crisper of the refrigerator for about 1 week. Leeks are fresh vegetables that do not have the staying power of onions or garlic, which are dried.

Do-ahead Prep:

❖   The stock can be refrigerated in covered containers for up to 5 days or frozen for up to 6 months.

Sandy's Chicken Soup
with Fine Noodles

Serves: 8

*M*y friend Sandi Batton from Vail, Colorado, prepares this soul-satisfying soup year-round. The soup needs to be prepared at least a day in advance.

1 whole 3- to 4-pound chicken, cut up

1 large onion, quartered

1 carrot, peeled and cut into 2-inch lengths

1 rib celery, including leaves, cut into 2-inch lengths

8 peppercorns

½ teaspoon dried thyme, crumbled

1 bay leaf

9 cups defatted chicken broth

½ cup julienned carrot strips

½ teaspoon dried sage, crumbled

salt and freshly ground pepper to taste

one 12-ounce package fine noodles such as Kluski, cooked until
    just al dente and drained

1. In a deep large Dutch oven or soup pot, place the chicken parts. Add the onion, carrot, celery, peppercorns, thyme, and bay leaf. Add the broth and additional water until all the ingredients are covered by liquid. Bring to a boil, cover, reduce heat, and simmer slowly for 45 minutes.

2. Remove the chicken from the broth and allow it to cool slightly. Remove the skin and bones from the chicken and return them to the pot; wrap the meat tightly in aluminum foil, allow it to cool, and then chill the meat. Bring the soup to a boil again, reduce the heat, and continue to simmer for an additional 2 hours.

3. Strain and remove excess fat from the broth. Cool and chill the soup in a covered container for 6 to 8 hours or overnight if possible.

4. Remove any excess fat from the congealed broth and return it to the soup pot. Bring the broth to a boil, add the carrot strips, sage, and salt and pepper; cover, reduce heat, and simmer slowly for 15 minutes. Cut the chicken into 1½-inch cubes or in thin strips, add to the hot broth, and cook until just warmed. Add the cooked noodles, stir to heat for a few seconds, and serve piping hot.

*V*ARIATION:

❖ The gizzard, neck, and heart can be cooked with the other chicken parts, but the liver should be reserved for another use.

*C*OOK NOTE:

❖ You know carrots are fresh if they still have their fresh-looking tops on. But remove the greens at the market to prevent drainage from the roots.

*D*O-AHEAD PREP:

❖ The soup is best if prepared a day or two in advance so that the fat is allowed to congeal and be easily removed. The finished soup can also be frozen in covered containers for up to 6 months.

Chinese Vegetable Egg Drop Soup

Serves: 8

*T*his is a sort of hot and sour soup that I whip up for lunch or supper at the spur of the moment. The only basic ingredients are broth, noodles, eggs (or egg whites only), and tofu, which I usually have on hand. The rest is up to you. Add mushrooms, pea pods, spinach, Chinese dumplings, asparagus, broccoli, or whatever is in season.

3 ounces dried shiitake mushrooms, soaked in hot water to soften

6 cups defatted chicken or vegetable broth

one 10-ounce package spinach, stems removed, washed and
    drained (or substitute frozen leaf spinach, thawed and drained)

one 7.25-ounce package cooked udon noodles or ½ pound
    spaghetti, cooked and drained

1 to 2 teaspoons reduced-sodium soy sauce, or to taste

1 teaspoon Chinese Chinkiang vinegar (or balsamic vinegar), or
    to taste

Tabasco to taste

½ pound firm Chinese-style tofu, cut into small cubes

freshly ground white pepper to taste

2 egg whites

1 egg

1. Drain the mushrooms, remove and discard the stems, cut them into small pieces, and set aside.

2. In a large nonreactive saucepan, bring the broth to a boil; add the spinach and cook until just wilted, stirring often. Add the mushrooms and noodles and cook just to heat through.

3. Season the soup with soy, vinegar, and Tabasco. Add the tofu and pepper and stir just to heat through.

4. Scramble the egg whites and egg together and while the soup is simmering, stir it with a fork in one hand and gradually pour the egg mixture into the soup in a stream, scrambling constantly.

5. Serve the soup immediately.

*V*ARIATIONS:

❖   Vegetable or chicken gyoza potstickers can be substituted for the noodles or added along with them.

❖   Other vegetables such as straw mushrooms, baby sweet corn, baby bok choy, or peas can be added if desired.

❖   You can use 3 egg whites instead of 2 egg whites and 1 whole egg.

*C*OOK NOTE:

❖   Shiitake mushrooms are also known as Oriental black mushrooms, Chinese black mushrooms, black forest mushrooms, and golden oak mushrooms. Dried shiitake have a strong, woody taste and aroma and add a distinctive and intense flavor to Asian soups and stir-fries. Dried shiitake mushrooms will keep indefinitely in a tightly sealed jar in a dark area.

*D*O-AHEAD PREP:

❖   The soup can be prepared a day in advance and reheated but the tofu tends to toughen. If preparing a day or two in advance, add the tofu and any crunchy vegetables just before serving.

Ribollita

Ribollita, which means "boiled again" in Italian, is a hearty Tuscan-style bean and cabbage soup that is thickened with bread. Tuscan cooks say that you should start cooking the soup one day and finish it the next. This is a great winter lunch or supper dish that is meant to be cooked to a thick and flavorful consistency.

The soup requires a lot of chopping, but can be prepared several days in advance.

2 teaspoons extra-virgin olive oil

1 medium onion, finely chopped

2 ribs celery, finely chopped

2 medium carrots, peeled and finely chopped

2 cloves garlic, finely minced

4 cups defatted chicken broth

one 14½-ounce can ready-cut diced tomatoes, including liquid

3 cups shredded savoy cabbage

one 6-ounce package baby spinach

2 tablespoons chopped fresh Italian parsley

2 teaspoons minced fresh sage or ½ teaspoon dried
    sage, crumbled

2 teaspoons minced fresh thyme leaves or ½ teaspoon dried
    thyme, crumbled

salt and freshly ground pepper to taste

one 15-ounce can cannellini or Great Northern beans, drained

four to six 1-inch-thick slices day-old Italian bread, cut into
    1-inch chunks

GARNISH: 2 to 3 tablespoons chopped Italian parsley and 2 to
    3 tablespoons freshly grated Parmesan cheese

1. In a nonstick Dutch oven or large saucepan, heat the oil to medium and sauté the onion, celery, and carrots, stirring often, until softened, about 5 to 6 minutes. Add the garlic and stir to combine.

2. Add the broth, tomatoes, cabbage, spinach, parsley, sage, thyme, and salt and pepper; bring to a boil, cover, reduce heat, and simmer for 2 hours, or until the vegetables are very tender.

3. Stir in the beans and bread and continue to cook for about 30 minutes, or until the bread dissolves into the soup.

4. Serve hot in deep soup bowls garnished with the parsley and Parmesan cheese.

VARIATIONS:

❖ Green beans, Swiss chard, kale, potatoes, zucchini, and other seasonal vegetables can be added to the soup. When adding extra vegetables, add enough broth to keep the ribollita thick but soupy.

❖ You can puree the beans for an extra-rich texture.

COOK NOTES:

❖ Savoy cabbage, milder and less crisp than green cabbage, is round with crinkled, ruffly, yellow-green leaves. Savoy cabbage is rich in beta carotene—enough to supply 20 percent of the RDA for vitamin A—while green and red cabbage have very little.

❖ If you substitute red cabbage: to prevent the color change, add a tablespoon of vinegar or lemon juice to the cooking liquid.

DO-AHEAD PREP:

❖ Cook the soup through Step 2 several days in advance and refrigerate in a covered container until ready to add the beans and bread.

Acorn Squash and Apple Soup

Serves: 6

*T*his soup is delicious hot in the winter and makes a great presentation served in hollowed-out acorn squash shells.

- 2 medium acorn squash (about 2½ pounds)
- 2 teaspoons vegetable oil
- 1 medium onion, coarsely chopped
- 1 tart Fuji, pippin, or Granny Smith apple, peeled and coarsely chopped
- 2¾ cups defatted chicken or vegetable broth
- 1 tablespoon lemon juice
- 1 teaspoon grated lemon rind
- ½ teaspoon chopped fresh thyme or a pinch of dried thyme, crumbled
- salt and freshly ground white pepper to taste

*G*ARNISH: 2 teaspoons grated lemon rind mixed with 1 tablespoon chopped parsley

1. Preheat the oven to 350°F.

2. Cut the squash in half horizontally, remove the seeds, and place cut side down in a roasting pan. Add 1 cup hot water to the bottom of the pan and bake for about 30 minutes, or until the squash pulp is softened.

3. In a large nonstick saucepan, heat the oil to medium. Add the onion and apple and sauté for about 5 to 7 minutes, stirring occasionally, until softened.

4. Remove the squash from the oven, scoop out the pulp, and add to the saucepan. Add the broth, lemon juice, lemon rind, and thyme, bring to a boil, cover, reduce heat, and simmer for 25 minutes, until softened. Allow the soup to cool slightly.

5. Puree the soup in a food processor or blender until smooth, adjust seasonings with salt and pepper to taste, and serve hot garnished with lemon-parsley garnish.

*V*ARIATION:

❖ The soup can also be served chilled with a large dollop of plain yogurt, but make sure to add additional salt and pepper as needed.

*C*OOK NOTE:

❖ When selecting acorn squash, choose ones that are heavy for their size with clean, hard, unbruised skins. Avoid squash that show signs of softening or mold, especially on the stem end. Store acorn squash in a moderately cool and dry area and it will keep for several weeks. Do not store in the refrigerator or the starch will convert to sugar and give the squash an overly sweet taste.

*D*O-AHEAD PREP:

❖ The soup can be made a day or two in advance and refrigerated in a covered container or it can be frozen for several months. If the soup thickens on standing or freezing, gradually add about ¼ cup of chicken broth until the right consistency is achieved.

Celery Root and Carrot Soup

Serves: 6 to 8

*C*elery root, also known as celeriac, is a big bulbous vegetable with fibrous brown skin that is actually the root of a special celery cultivated for its root. The flavor is both mellow and earthy—a cross between celery and parsley. Europeans are familiar with this knobby vegetable and use it raw in rémoulade, but it can also be cooked into a thick and flavorful low-fat soup.

    1 tablespoon olive oil
    1 large onion, coarsely chopped
    2 medium carrots, peeled and roughly chopped
    2 medium celery roots (about 2¼ pounds), peeled and cut into
        small cubes
    1 clove garlic, finely minced
    6½ cups defatted chicken or vegetable broth
    salt and freshly ground pepper

*G*ARNISH: chopped fresh parsley

1. In a large nonstick Dutch oven or deep saucepan, heat the oil to medium and sauté the onion and carrots, stirring often, until slightly softened, about 4 to 5 minutes.

2. Add the celery roots and continue to sauté, stirring often, until softened, about 5 minutes. Add the garlic and stir for 30 seconds. Add the remaining ingredients, bring to a boil, cover, reduce heat, and cook for 45 to 50 minutes, or until the vegetables are very soft. Allow to cool slightly.

3. Puree the soup in batches in a food processor or blender until smooth.

4. Reheat and serve the soup piping hot, garnished with chopped parsley.

*V*ARIATION:

❖ The soup can be served cold as well but remember to adjust the salt and pepper after chilling.

*C*OOK NOTES:

❖ Select firm celery roots without soft spots and refrigerate them in plastic bags for about a week.

❖ Peeled celery root darkens on contact with the air, so it should be mixed with other ingredients and cooked immediately. If using celery root raw, soak it briefly in water with added lemon juice to prevent discoloration.

❖   The soup can be prepared several days in advance, refrigerated in a covered container, and reheated before serving. If the soup has thickened on standing, stir in additional broth until a smooth consistency is achieved.

Mushroom Barley Soup with Dill

Serves: 8

*B*arley is the world's most ancient cultivated grain, dating from at least 5000 B.C. Today there are new reasons to embrace barley. This healthful grain is an excellent source of soluble fiber, which can be effective in lowering cholesterol levels.

½ cup pearl barley

1 tablespoon olive oil

1½ pounds mushrooms, stems removed, wiped clean, and
     thinly sliced

2 large onions, finely chopped

2 large carrots, peeled and finely chopped

1 teaspoon finely minced garlic

8 cups defatted chicken broth

2 tablespoons finely snipped fresh dill

freshly ground white pepper to taste

*G*ARNISH: sprigs of dill

1.   In a small bowl, place the barley; cover with hot water, and allow it to soak for 30 minutes. Drain and set aside.

2.   In a large nonstick Dutch oven or deep heavy saucepan, heat the oil over medium-high heat, and sauté the mushrooms, onions, and carrots until softened, stirring often, for 6 to 7 minutes. Add the garlic and stir to coat. Add the barley, broth, dill, and salt and pepper; bring to a boil, reduce heat, cover, and simmer slowly for 1 hour.

3.   Serve the soup hot garnished with dill sprigs.

$\mathcal{V}$ARIATION:

❖   Dried soaked porcini (cèpes) mushrooms can be added to intensify the flavor of the soup.

$\mathcal{C}$OOK NOTE:

❖   Select mushrooms that are plump and clean without bruises or pitting. Look for ones with closed *veils*, the area where the cap and stem meet. An open veil indicates aging, while a closed one means the mushroom is fresher. Store mushrooms loosely in a brown paper bag. If left open, they will dry out, and if left in a sealed plastic bag, they will become soggy and decay.

$\mathcal{D}$O-AHEAD PREP:

❖   The soup can be cooked several days in advance and refrigerated in a covered container. Remember to adjust the seasonings with salt and pepper before serving since cold diminishes the intensity of the flavors. The soup can also be frozen success-fully for several months.

Pea Soup with Roasted Garlic Flavor

Serves: 4

*A*s long as you've got the oven on, why not roast a couple of heads of garlic to use as a nonfat spread, in a sauce for fish, or to add as a flavor enhancer for soups.

2 cloves garlic, unpeeled

2 teaspoons olive oil

1 medium onion, roughly chopped

3 cups fresh or frozen green peas

4 cups defatted chicken or vegetable broth

salt and freshly ground white pepper to taste

1 teaspoon lemon juice

*G*ARNISH: chopped fresh mint leaves

1. Preheat the oven to 275°F. Lightly coat small roasting pan with olive oil non-stick cooking spray.

2. Place the garlic cloves in the pan and roast slowly until soft, about 40 to 45 minutes. When cooked, allow to cool slightly, squeeze the garlic from the peel, chop finely, and set aside.

3. In a large nonstick saucepan, heat the oil to medium and sauté the onion, stirring often, until softened, about 5 minutes. Add the peas, broth, salt and pepper, and the roasted garlic. Bring to a boil, cover, reduce heat, and simmer until the peas are very soft, about 10 to 15 minutes. Allow to cool slightly.

4. Puree the soup in batches with the lemon juice in a food processor or blender until smooth.

5. Reheat the soup and serve piping hot, garnished with the mint leaves.

*V*ARIATIONS:

❖ You can roast the garlic at 400°F for 20 minutes, but watch carefully to prevent burning.

❖ Two medium carrots can be sautéed with the onion for added color and flavor.

❖ The soup can be served cold with ½ cup plain low-fat or nonfat yogurt blended into the chilled soup. Remember to adjust the seasonings after chilling.

$\mathcal{C}$OOK NOTES:

❖   Green peas are a good source of carbohydrates; they contain plenty of vitamins A and C, and thiamin, riboflavin, and niacin; and they are rich in phosphorus, iron, and potassium.

❖   The lemon juice is added after cooking since it may diminish the bright green color.

❖   Frozen green peas do not need to be thawed before being used in soups.

$\mathcal{D}$O-AHEAD PREP:

❖   The soup can be prepared several days in advance, refrigerated in a covered container, and reheated before serving. If the soup has thickened on standing, stir in additional broth until a smooth consistency is achieved.

Pappa al Pomodoro

Serves 8

*T*his wonderfully comforting dish of cooked fresh tomatoes and grilled bread is a regional specialty of Tuscany. It can be served as a hearty first course, a light main dish, or a creative luncheon entrée. It is best to prepare this Italian favorite during the summer months when ripe tomatoes and basil are in plentiful supply.

8 slices Italian, sourdough, or French bread

1 tablespoon extra-virgin olive oil

3 large leeks, thoroughly washed and finely sliced (white parts only)

3 cloves garlic, finely minced

3 pounds ripe tomatoes, peeled, cored, seeded, and coarsely chopped

4 cups defatted chicken or vegetable broth

salt and freshly ground white pepper to taste

½ cup fresh basil, coarsely chopped

*G*ARNISH: small clusters of basil leaves

1.   Preheat the oven to 300°F.

2.   Place the bread on cookie sheets and bake for 10 to 15 minutes or until golden on both sides. Remove and set aside.

3.   In a large nonstick saucepan, heat the olive oil to medium. Add the leeks and sauté for 5 to 7 minutes, stirring often, until softened. Add the garlic and cook for 30 seconds longer.

4.   Add the tomatoes and chicken or vegetable broth, bring to a boil, cover, reduce heat, and simmer very slowly for 45 minutes, until the vegetables are softened. Allow to cool slightly.

5.   Puree the soup in a food processor or blender until smooth. Return to the saucepan, season with salt and pepper, add basil, and cook until piping hot, about 2 to 3 minutes.

6.   Place a slice of toasted bread in the bottom of each soup bowl, pour the soup over, and serve piping hot garnished with small clusters of basil leaves.

*V*ARIATIONS:

❖   One large onion can be substituted for the leeks.

❖   For added flavor, the bread can be lightly coated with nonstick olive oil vegetable spray and then grilled for a few minutes until golden.

*C*OOK NOTE:

❖   The easiest way to peel tomatoes is to submerge them in boiling water for about a minute, place in icy cold water, and then peel off the skin. If desired this dish can be prepared with the skins on and then the cooked vegetables can be strained through a food mill.

*D*O-AHEAD PREP:

❖   The soup can be prepared in double batches through Step 3, cooled, and frozen in a covered container for future use. When ready to serve, defrost, reheat, add seasonings and basil, and proceed with the recipe.

❖   The bread can be prepared a day in advance and kept in a sealed tin until ready to use.

❖   The soup can be prepared a day or two ahead through Step 4 and refrigerated in a covered container.

Zucchini Soup with Red Pepper Puree

Serves: 8

*T*his recipe is a variation of one served at The General's Daughter in Sonoma, California. The contrast of red pepper puree and green soup makes it a great dish to serve for the Christmas holidays.

2 large sweet red bell peppers

1 teaspoon balsamic vinegar

salt and freshly ground pepper to taste

1 tablespoon olive oil

1 large onion, roughly chopped

6 medium zucchini or yellow summer squash (about 2¼ pounds), washed, dried, and roughly chopped

4½ cups defatted chicken or vegetable broth

2 cloves garlic, roughly chopped

salt and freshly ground pepper

*G*ARNISH: snipped fresh chives

1. Preheat broiler or outdoor grill.

2. Char the red bell peppers under a broiler or over an outdoor grill until blackened on all sides, turning as each side blisters. Immediately wrap the peppers in heavy foil or place them in a paper bag and allow to stand for about 10 to 15 minutes or until cool enough to handle. Peel the peppers and remove and discard stems, seeds, and ribs.

3. Place the peppers in a blender or food processor with the vinegar and salt and pepper and process until smooth. Set aside.

4. In a heavy large nonstick saucepan, heat the oil over medium heat. Add the onion and continue to sauté until softened, about 3 to 4 minutes, stirring occasionally. Add the zucchini and continue to cook for an additional 2 to 3 minutes. Add the broth, garlic, and salt and pepper; bring to a boil, reduce heat, cover, and simmer for 30 minutes, until all the vegetables are very soft.

5. Puree the zucchini soup in batches in a blender or food processor until smooth and ladle into bowls. Place a dollop of the red pepper puree on each of the portions, top with the chives, and serve hot.

$\mathcal{V}$ARIATIONS:

❖　The soup is delicious served both hot and cold. If serving cold, remember to add salt after chilling to augment the flavor.

❖　Yellow bell peppers can be substituted for the red bell peppers.

$\mathcal{C}$OOK NOTES:

❖　Bell peppers are an excellent source of vitamin C—green bell peppers have twice as much as citrus fruit and red bell peppers have three times as much! In addition, red bell peppers are a good source of beta-carotene.

❖　Select well-shaped peppers that are firm and glossy. The stems should be very fresh and green and the skins should be unwrinkled, smooth, and taut. Bell peppers should be heavy for their size without soft spots. Store bell peppers in a perforated plastic bag in the refrigerator for up to a week.

$\mathcal{D}$O-AHEAD PREP:

❖　The pepper puree and zucchini soup can be prepared a day or two in advance and kept in a covered container in the refrigerator.

Tortilla Soup with Chicken

Serves: 6

*T*ortilla soup originated in Mexico and is a favorite in the Southwest. Traditionally the tortilla chips are fried, but here we bake them as a bed for this hearty, comforting, yet very light one-dish meal.

This soup is a great way to use up leftover chicken, shrimp, pork, or vegetables.

    4 corn tortillas
    2 teaspoons olive oil
    1 large onion, finely chopped
    2 cloves garlic, finely chopped
    2 teaspoons chili powder
    2 teaspoons ground cumin
    7 cups defatted chicken or vegetable broth
    2 cups crushed tomatoes packed in puree
    one 4-ounce can chopped mild green chiles, drained
    2 jalapeño peppers, seeded and finely minced
    salt and freshly ground pepper to taste
    2 cups cooked shredded chicken
    1 cup fresh or frozen corn, thawed

*G*ARNISH: 2 to 3 tablespoons chopped fresh cilantro, 2 to 3 tablespoons freshly grated low-fat Monterey Jack, Swiss, Cheddar, or Muenster cheese

1.　Preheat the oven to 375°F.

2.　Cut the tortillas into strips, lightly coat them with nonstick coating spray and bake for about 8 minutes, or until crisp and golden. Set aside.

3.　In a large nonstick Dutch oven or deep saucepan, heat the oil to medium and sauté the onion, stirring often, for 5 to 6 minutes, or until glazed and softened.

4.　Increase the heat to medium-high, add the garlic, chili powder, and cumin and stir for 30 seconds. Add the broth, tomatoes, chiles, jalapeños, and salt and pepper; bring to a boil, cover, reduce heat, and simmer for 30 minutes.

5.　When ready to serve, bring the soup to a boil, add the chicken and corn and cook for 2 to 3 minutes or until just warmed through. Ladle the soup into bowls, top each with the tortilla strips, cilantro, and cheese, and serve hot.

$\mathcal{V}$ARIATIONS:

❖ If tomatoes packed in puree are unavailable, use regular whole juice-packed tomatoes; chop, drain off most of the liquid, return the tomatoes to the can, and fill to the top with canned tomato puree.

❖ If pressed for time use the meat of a cooked barbecued chicken with the skin removed and packaged low-fat tortilla chips, lightly crushed.

$\mathcal{C}$OOK NOTES:

❖ Cilantro does not hold up well under long periods of high heat, so always add it toward the end of the cooking time or as a garnish for optimum flavor.

❖ There are some new low-fat salad crisps on the market made with ground corn flavored with chili and lime that are a quick and easy substitute for the baked tortilla strips.

$\mathcal{D}$O-AHEAD PREP:

❖ The soup base can be prepared a day or two in advance through Step 2, cooled, and chilled in a covered container until ready to serve.

Seafood Minestrone

Serves: 4 to 6

*I*n America, *minestrone* is often used as a fancy name for vegetable soup—mainly served as the soup du jour at coffee shops or served right out of the can. In Italy, minestrone is a revered thick soup derived from the Latin verb *ministro*, "to serve." It was originally a specialty of the port at Genoa served to satisfy the vegetable-deficient sailors.

Monkfish, cod, or other firm-fleshed white fish may be substituted for the shrimp and/or scallops.

> 1 tablespoon olive oil
>
> 1 small onion, finely chopped
>
> 2 leeks, thoroughly washed and chopped (white parts only)
>
> 1 rib celery, finely chopped
>
> 2 cloves garlic, finely minced
>
> 3 cups Instant Fish Broth (see page 78), defatted chicken broth, or vegetable broth
>
> one 14½-ounce can ready-cut diced tomatoes, undrained
>
> 2 tablespoons tomato paste
>
> 2 teaspoons finely chopped fresh basil or ½ teaspoon dried basil, crumbled
>
> 1 teaspoon finely chopped fresh oregano or ¼ teaspoon dried oregano, crumbled
>
> 1 bay leaf
>
> salt and freshly ground pepper to taste
>
> 2 ounces tiny pasta shells, farfalle, or orzo
>
> 1 cup cooked canellini beans or other white beans
>
> 12 medium shrimp, peeled and deveined
>
> ½ pound bay scallops or sea scallops, cut in half
>
> *G*ARNISH: chopped fresh Italian parsley, toasted bread rounds

1.   In a nonreactive Dutch oven or a deep saucepan, heat the oil to medium, and sauté the onion, leeks, and celery until just softened, about 5 to 7 minutes, stirring occasionally.

2. Add the garlic and cook for 30 seconds. Add the broth, tomatoes, tomato paste, basil, oregano, bay leaf, and salt and pepper; bring to a boil, cover, reduce heat, and simmer for 25 minutes. Add the pasta and cook, covered, for 10 minutes longer.

3. Add the beans, shrimp, and scallops and cook, covered, for 4 minutes, or until just cooked.

4. Serve hot, garnished with parsley and toasted bread rounds.

𝒱ARIATIONS:

❖ ¼ teaspoon anise seed can be added with the tomatoes.

❖ If using other types of seafood, add so that each piece of seafood is finished cooking at the same time.

❖ Drained and rinsed canned white beans can be used but added just to heat through for the last 1 to 2 minutes or they will become too mushy.

𝒞OOK NOTES:

❖ To make toasted bread rounds, or "croutes," spray ½-inch-thick slices of French bread lightly with nonstick olive oil cooking spray, then toast in a 400°F oven until brown, watching carefully to prevent burning. Immediately rub with the cut side of half a garlic clove.

❖ Buy scallops that are free of excess cloudy liquid and are sweet-smelling with no hint of sulfur odor.

𝒟O-AHEAD PREP:

❖ The liquid soup base without the pasta, beans, or seafood can prepared a day or two in advance and refrigerated in a covered container or frozen for future use. When ready to cook, reheat and add the remaining fresh ingredients.

Borscht with Dill Flavor

Serves: 6

*T*his light soup is enriched with the addition of pureed vegetables that give it a thick and rich consistency without the addition of cream.

1 teaspoon olive oil

3 large leeks, thoroughly washed and thinly sliced (white parts only)

2 large beets, peeled and coarsely chopped

1 medium potato (about ½ pound), coarsely chopped

3¾ cups defatted chicken or vegetable broth

2 teaspoons snipped fresh dill

½ teaspoon freshly ground white pepper

salt to taste

1 cup nonfat plain yogurt

GARNISH: plain nonfat yogurt and sprigs of fresh dill

1. In a large nonstick saucepan, heat the oil, add the leeks, and sauté over medium heat, stirring often, until just glazed, about 3 to 4 minutes.

2. Add the remaining ingredients except the yogurt, bring to a boil, cover, reduce heat, and simmer for 35 to 40 minutes or until the vegetables are very tender.

3. Allow the soup to cool slightly and then puree in a food processor or blender until smooth. Chill in a covered container for 4 to 6 hours or overnight.

4. Place the chilled borscht in a food processor or blender, add the yogurt and salt and pepper to taste and puree until pink and smooth. Serve the soup chilled garnished with a dollop of yogurt and a sprig of fresh dill.

VARIATION:

❖ The soup can also be served hot, without the pureed yogurt, but topped with a generous dollop of low-fat sour cream.

COOK NOTES:

❖ Designer beets—orange, white, and even striped—are gaining popularity today. Unlike red beets, they do not bleed when boiled.

❖ Beets are rich in potassium, but are otherwise not especially good sources of essential nutrients.

❖   The soup can be cooked several days in advance and refrigerated in a covered container. Remember to adjust the seasonings with salt and pepper before serving since cold diminishes the intensity of the flavors.

Broccoli-Leek Vichyssoise

Serves: 6

*T*raditionally vichyssoise is a rich and creamy French potato and leek soup that is served chilled. The texture of this flavorful low-fat version is achieved by adding a potato instead of cream to enrich the consistency.

    1¼ pound broccoli

    3 leeks, thoroughly washed and thinly sliced (white parts only)

    1 medium potato, peeled and cut into large dice

    4 cups defatted chicken or vegetable broth

    salt and freshly ground white pepper to taste

*G*ARNISH: Plain nonfat yogurt and finely snipped chives

1.   In a medium saucepan, place the broccoli florets. Peel the stems with a paring knife, cut into 2-inch lengths, and add to the pan. Add the leeks to the pan along with the potato.

2.   Cover the vegetables with the broth, add the salt and pepper, bring to a boil, cover, reduce heat, and simmer slowly for about 40 minutes, or until the potatoes are very tender. Allow the soup to cool slightly.

3.   Puree the soup in a food processor or blender in batches until very smooth. Adjust the seasonings if necessary with salt and pepper, and chill in a covered container in the refrigerator for 4 to 6 hours or overnight.

4.   Adjust the seasonings with salt and pepper and serve chilled with a dollop of yogurt and snipped chives.

*V*ARIATIONS:

❖   Broccoflower or cauliflower can be substituted for broccoli.

❖   The soup can be served hot.

❖ Broccoli is highly perishable and should be stored unwashed in a perforated plastic bag in the refrigerator.

DO-AHEAD PREP:

❖ The soup can be cooked several days in advance and refrigerated in a covered container. Remember to adjust the seasonings with salt and pepper before serving since cold diminishes the intensity of the flavors.

Cucumber Yogurt Soup with Fresh Mint

Serves: 4

*T*his soup uses nonfat or low-fat yogurt as the base in place of the more traditional sour cream. Not much salt is needed since the flavor of the soup is enhanced naturally with the fresh herbs.

Cucumbers, a relative of melons, are very high in water, giving them refreshing properties that no doubt prompted the description "cool as a cucumber."

> 1 large European hothouse cucumber, split and coarsely chopped, or 2 medium cucumbers, peeled, seeded, and coarsely chopped
>
> 3 tablespoons chopped fresh mint
>
> 2 large scallions (green and white parts included), roughly chopped
>
> 1½ tablespoons snipped fresh dill
>
> 1 clove garlic, crushed
>
> 2 cups nonfat or low-fat plain yogurt
>
> salt and freshly ground white pepper to taste
>
> **G**ARNISH: sliced cucumbers, sliced radishes, chopped scallions, and grated hard-cooked egg (optional)

1. In a food processor or blender, process the cucumber, mint, scallions, dill, and garlic until well combined but not smooth. Add the yogurt and continue to puree until smooth.

2. Chill in a covered container for 4 to 6 hours or overnight.

3. Adjust the seasonings with salt and pepper and serve the soup, chilled, with the accompanying garnishes of cucumbers, radishes, scallions, and egg.

*V*ARIATION:

❖ If you are fortunate enough to pick up the little pickling cucumbers, which are crisper, have less water, and, like the European hothouse cucumber, don't need to be peeled, they can be substituted; use 5 small ones in place of 1 large European cucumber.

*C*OOK NOTES:

❖ Fresh mint is not always available year-round. In the summer months when mint is plentiful, wrap washed and dried bunches of fresh mint in foil and freeze them. When you need fresh mint, just cut off what you need and chop. Mint can also be chopped and frozen in small containers.

❖ Cucumbers should be stored separately from fruits and vegetables such as tomatoes, apples, and pears, which produce a natural ethylene gas that hastens the ripening process.

*D*O-AHEAD PREP:

❖ The soup can be prepared a day in advance and kept in a covered container in the refrigerator. Remember to adjust the seasonings with salt and pepper before serving since cold diminishes the intensity of the flavors.

Mulligatawny Soup

Serves: 4 to 6

*M*ulligatawny is a thick, chicken- or lamb-based soup flavored with curry from India. The name comes from the Tamil word *milakutanni*, which means "pepper water." Here I have replaced the traditional cream with yogurt.

2 teaspoons olive oil

1 medium onion, finely minced

1 large tart apple, peeled, cored, and diced

1 clove garlic, finely minced

1 to 2 teaspoons curry powder, or to taste

2½ cups defatted chicken or vegetable broth

1 large baking potato, peeled and diced

1 teaspoon grated orange rind

¼ teaspoon ground ginger

salt to taste

1 cup plain nonfat or low-fat yogurt

*G*ARNISH: chopped fresh cilantro leaves

1. In a deep large nonstick saucepan, heat the oil over medium heat and sauté the onion and apple, stirring often, for 5 to 6 minutes, until softened. Add the garlic and stir for 30 seconds. Add the curry powder and stir until smooth.

2. Add the broth, potato, orange rind, ginger, and salt; bring to a boil, cover, reduce heat, and simmer slowly for 25 minutes until the potato is very tender. Allow to cool slightly.

3. Puree the soup in a food processor or blender in batches until smooth. Refrigerate the soup in a covered container for 4 to 6 hours or overnight until thoroughly chilled.

4. Whisk in the yogurt, adjust the seasonings with salt and pepper, garnish with the cilantro, and serve chilled.

*V*ARIATION:

❖ Buttermilk can be substituted for the yogurt.

𝒞OOK NOTE:

❖   Commercial curry powder varies greatly since it generally contains an assortment of the following spices: coriander, cumin, fenugreek, turmeric, black pepper, hot red pepper, powdered mustard, kari leaves, cinnamon, clove, mace, nutmeg, caraway, bay leaf, dill, cardamom, fennel, anise, saffron, ginger, onion, and garlic. Most of the distinctive flavor comes from coriander, cumin, and fenugreek; the color comes from turmeric; and the fire from the hot peppers. Taste a few curry powders before selecting one that best appeals to you.

𝒟O-AHEAD PREP:

❖   The soup can be prepared up to 2 days in advance and refrigerated in a covered container until ready to serve. Remember to adjust the seasonings to taste just before serving because cold diminishes the flavors.

Tomato Corn Soup

Serves: 4

*T*his delicious chilled soup combines those wonderful ripe abundant tomatoes and corn of August and September. If you like it spicy, by all means use a heavy hand with the Tabasco.

2 scallions (green and white parts included), roughly chopped

1 clove garlic, finely minced

1½ tablespoons chopped fresh basil

3 very ripe large tomatoes, seeded and cut into large chunks

2 cups tomato juice

1 tablespoon lemon juice

Tabasco to taste

salt and freshly ground pepper to taste

1 cup cooked fresh or frozen corn (about 2 ears), or canned corn drained

*G*ARNISH: low-fat or nonfat yogurt and freshly chopped basil

1. In a food processor or blender, chop the scallions, garlic, and basil.

2. Combine the remaining ingredients except the corn and pulse until just smooth. Add the corn and refrigerate the soup in a covered container.

3. Taste for seasonings, adjust with salt and pepper, and serve chilled with a dollop of yogurt and chopped basil.

*V*ARIATION:

❖ Chopped green bell pepper can be added with the corn.

*D*O-AHEAD PREP:

❖ The soup can be prepared 1 to 2 days in advance and refrigerated in a covered container until ready to serve. The chopped basil garnish should be cut just before serving because it will discolor on standing.

POULTRY

❖ ❖ ❖ ❖ ❖ ❖

Chicken Breasts Stuffed
with Basil Spinach Puree

Marinated Grilled Chicken Breast

Balsamic Vinegar Glazed Chicken with Braised Apples
and Chestnuts

Stir-Fry of Chicken and Mushrooms with Spinach Fettuccine

Chicken Fajitas

Cold Poached Lemon Chicken with Mustard-Chive Sauce

Perfect Roast Chicken with Artichoke Garlic Flavoring

Light Coq au Vin

Chicken Cacciatore

Roasted Rock Cornish Game Hens with Raspberry Flavor

Turkey Roasted on a Covered Charcoal Grill

Roast Butterflied Turkey Breast with Orange Mustard Glaze
and Raisin Bread Stuffing

Grilled Turkey Burger

Outstanding Turkey Chili

Savory Shepherd's Pie

> *A chicken in
> every pot is a
> fine idea for
> everyone but
> the chicken.*
> —Anonymous

Chicken Breasts Stuffed with Basil Spinach Puree

Serves: 4

*T*his simple-to-assemble dish is delicious and quite rich in flavor but not in fat. The stuffing is very versatile and can be used on roasted tomato halves, on baked potatoes, on pizzas, or even tossed with hot pasta.

*S*TUFFING:

one 6-ounce package baby spinach leaves

2 tablespoons snipped fresh chives or minced scallion greens

2 tablespoons chopped fresh basil or ½ teaspoon dried
    basil, crumbled

1 teaspoon freshly minced garlic

1 cup low-fat ricotta cheese

2 tablespoons freshly grated Parmesan cheese

¼ teaspoon ground nutmeg

salt and freshly ground white pepper to taste

4 whole skinless, boneless chicken breasts, halved

3 tablespoons all-purpose flour seasoned to taste with salt and
    freshly ground white pepper

2 tablespoons olive oil

*G*ARNISH: basil leaves

1. Place the spinach leaves in a nonstick pan with a few tablespoons of water and wilt over medium heat until the leaves soften. Drain and squeeze dry of any moisture.

2. Preheat the oven to 375°F. Lightly coat a roasting pan with nonstick cooking spray.

3. Place the chives, basil, and garlic in a food processor and chop until fine. Add the spinach and remaining stuffing ingredients and process until well combined.

4. Make a pocket in each of the chicken breasts by slicing horizontally about ¾ of the way through the meat, fill the pocket with the stuffing, and make sure the pocket is closed over the stuffing. Dust each piece in the seasoned flour and shake off any excess.

5. In a heavy-bottomed nonstick skillet, heat the oil and sauté the chicken breasts on both sides over high heat until lightly golden, about 2 minutes a side. Place the chicken in the prepared pan and bake for about 20 minutes, or until cooked through.

6. Serve hot garnished with basil leaves.

*V*ARIATIONS:

❖ If baby spinach is not available, substitute 7 to 8 ounces of fresh spinach leaves, coarse stems removed, washed and dried. To make it even easier, substitute half of a 10-ounce package of frozen chopped spinach, thawed and squeezed dry.

❖ The Mushroom Pâté (see page 28) can be substituted for the spinach stuffing.

*C*OOK NOTE:

❖ Don't buy pre-grated Parmesan cheese; it has no flavor. A chunk of imported Parmesan will keep for a long time wrapped airtight in plastic and placed in the warmest section of the refrigerator. Grate the cheese as you need it.

*D*O-AHEAD PREP:

❖ The stuffing can be prepared a day in advance and refrigerated in a covered container, but stuff the chicken just before cooking.

Marinated Grilled Chicken Breast

Serves: 6

*P*ounding the chicken will produce uniform thickness that will ensure even cooking. This dish is wonderful accompanied by Caramelized Red Onion Marmalade (see page 56), or Apricot Chutney (see page 53).

3 whole skinless, boneless chicken breasts, halved (about
   1¼ pounds)

*M*ARINADE:

3 tablespoons Dijon mustard

3 tablespoons balsamic vinegar

3 tablespoons orange marmalade

3 tablespoons reduced-sodium soy sauce

2 tablespoons molasses

1 tablespoon Asian-style sesame oil

1 teaspoon finely minced garlic

1 teaspoon finely minced ginger

salt and freshly ground pepper to taste

*G*ARNISH: whole grilled scallions

1.   Pound the chicken to uniform thickness between sheets of waxed paper, and set aside.

2.   In a large or small food processor, combine the marinade ingredients and process until smooth; pour into a resealable plastic bag, add the chicken, seal tightly, and press and turn the bag until all sides of the chicken are coated. Marinate at room temperature for about 15 minutes or 2 to 3 hours in the refrigerator.

3.   Lightly coat an outdoor or indoor grill, broiler, or a well-seasoned ridged stove-top grill pan with nonstick cooking spray and preheat.

4.   Remove the chicken from the marinade, reserve the marinade in a small saucepan, and grill for about 3 to 4 minutes per side, or until just cooked (do not overcook).

5.   While the chicken is cooking, bring the marinade to a boil, and cook for 1 to 2 minutes until slightly thickened.

6.   Arrange the cooked chicken breasts on a platter, top each with the heated marinade, garnish with the grilled scallions, and serve immediately.

Cook notes:

❖ When grilling skinless, boneless chicken breasts make sure the fire is not too hot or you will scorch the outside and dry out the chicken. Check when you think it is done by cutting into the thickest part to see if the meat has turned from pink to white. Remember that meat continues to cook on standing.

❖ To grill scallions, cut away the root end and any damaged outside layers and trim the tops so that about 3 inches of green remains. Lightly coat the scallions with olive oil nonstick cooking spray and grill them over hot coals for 2 to 3 minutes a side, or until they are lightly browned. Sprinkle with salt and pepper to taste and serve.

Do-ahead prep:

❖ The marinade can be prepared several days in advance and refrigerated in a covered container. The chicken should not be marinated longer than 2 to 3 hours and should not be grilled until just before serving.

Balsamic Vinegar Glazed Chicken with Braised Apples and Chestnuts

Serves: 4

*T*his elegant and unusual dish will impress your most jaded guests. Chestnuts are delicious all year round, not just for Thanksgiving and holiday dinners, are low in calories, and have absolutely no fat!

2 whole skinless, boneless chicken breasts, halved

3 tablespoons all-purpose flour

salt and freshly ground white pepper to taste

1 tablespoon plus 2 teaspoons olive oil

3 leeks, thoroughly washed and thinly sliced (white parts only)

2 Fuji, pippin, Granny Smith, or other tart and crisp apples, peeled and thinly sliced

3 tablespoons balsamic vinegar

1½ cups defatted chicken broth

1 tablespoon Dijon mustard

1 tablespoon currant jelly

salt and freshly ground white pepper

1 cup peeled, roasted or steamed chestnuts

*G*ARNISH: sprigs of watercress

1. Pound the chicken breasts between layers of waxed paper until evenly flattened. Combine the flour with the salt and pepper; dip the chicken in the mixture, coating on both sides and shaking off the excess.

2. In a heavy, large nonstick skillet, heat 1 tablespoon of the oil to high and sauté the chicken until golden on both sides, about 2 minutes per side. Remove with a slotted spatula or spoon and keep warm on a plate covered with aluminum foil.

3. Add the additional 2 teaspoons of the oil if necessary, add the leeks to the pan, and sauté over medium heat, stirring often, for 3 minutes. Add the apples and continue to sauté, stirring often, until the onions and apples are lightly golden.

4. Increase the heat to high, add the vinegar, and allow the liquid to evaporate. Add the broth, mustard, currant jelly, salt and pepper, and stir together; reduce the heat and simmer for 5 minutes to reduce and thicken slightly. Add the chicken and chestnuts, bring to a boil, cover, reduce heat, and simmer for about 5 to 6 minutes, or until the chicken is just tender.

5. Serve immediately, garnished with sprigs of watercress.

𝒱 ARIATIONS:

❖ This dish can be prepared with turkey scaloppine instead of chicken.

❖ Raspberry vinegar can be substituted for balsamic vinegar.

𝒞 OOK NOTE:

❖ Since chestnuts are such a seasonal item, make sure to stock up on the jars of roasted or steamed chestnuts at holiday times.

𝒟 O-AHEAD PREP:

❖ It is best to cook the chicken just before serving. It can be cooked earlier in the day and reheated, but the white meat of the chicken tends to dry out.

Stir-Fry of Chicken and Mushrooms
with Spinach Fettuccine

Serves: 6

*S*tir-fry cooking is usually associated with Chinese food, but here I combine chicken with mushrooms and peppers and serve it over pasta for a delicious one-dish meal. Although there is some chopping involved, the preparation can be done very early in the day and then stir-fried at the last minute.

½ ounce dried porcini mushrooms

½ cup hot water

8 ounces spinach fettuccine

2 whole skinless, boneless chicken breasts, cut into 1-inch cubes

2 tablespoons all-purpose flour seasoned with salt and freshly ground pepper to taste

2 tablespoons olive oil

1 medium onion, thinly sliced

½ pound mushrooms, stems removed, wiped clean and thinly sliced

1 sweet red bell pepper, seeded and julienned

1 teaspoon finely minced garlic

¼ cup dry white wine or vermouth

1 tablespoon lemon juice

¾ cup defatted chicken broth

½ teaspoon chopped fresh thyme or pinch of dried thyme, crumbled

salt and freshly ground pepper to taste

*G*ARNISH: sprigs of thyme

1. Soak the mushrooms in the hot water for 20 seconds, until softened. Strain out the mushrooms, chop, and set aside; reserve the strained liquid.

2. Drop the pasta into a large pot of boiling water and cook until just al dente.

3. Toss the chicken pieces with the seasoned flour and set aside.

4. In a large nonstick wok or deep skillet, heat 1 tablespoon of the oil to high and when hot, stir-fry the chicken until it loses its pink color, about 3 minutes. Remove with a slotted spoon and set aside.

5. Add the remaining tablespoon of oil to the pan, and when hot stir-fry the onion, mushroom, and red bell pepper over high heat for about 3 to 4 minutes, until lightly golden. Add the garlic and stir to just combine. Add the wine and lemon juice and allow the liquid to boil away. Add the broth, thyme, salt and pepper, reserved chicken, porcini mushrooms, and liquid. Bring to a boil and stir over high heat until slightly thickened, about 1 to 2 minutes, or until the chicken is cooked through.

6. Drain the hot pasta, toss with the chicken and sauce, and serve immediately garnished with sprigs of thyme.

𝒱ARIATION:

❖ Turkey scaloppine cut into strips can be substituted for the chicken.

𝒞OOK NOTE:

❖ When selecting dried porcini mushrooms, look for mostly cap pieces, which are dark—the darker the color the more intense the flavor. Avoid porcini with lots of tiny holes and ones that are mainly stems.

𝒟O-AHEAD PREP:

❖ Although it is best to eat this stir-fried dish immediately after cooking, the chicken mixture can be cooked in advance, reheated, and then tossed with the pasta just before serving.

Chicken Fajitas

*F*ajitas are a Mexican dish, traditionally prepared with marinated skirt steak or flank steak and served with tortillas and assorted accompaniments. This lighter chicken version has many accompaniments. Use all of them or select the ones that you and your guests might prefer.

two 6- to 7-ounce whole skinless, boneless chicken breasts, pounded slightly

*M*ARINADE:

3 tablespoons lime juice

2 tablespoons olive oil

1 clove garlic, finely minced

1 teaspoon Worcestershire sauce

salt and freshly ground pepper to taste

1 tablespoon extra-virgin olive oil

2 large green bell peppers, seeded and cut into julienne strips

1 large red onion, thinly sliced

*A*CCOMPANIMENTS: warmed nonfat or low-fat flour or corn tortillas, shredded lettuce, slices of avocado, fresh Pico de Gallo (see page 59) or fresh tomato salsa, nonfat or low-fat sour cream, nonfat or low-fat refried beans, grilled scallions (see page 113), and slices of lime

1. Place the chicken breasts in a resealable plastic bag. Combine the marinade ingredients, stir well, and toss with the chicken in the bag. Seal the bag tightly and marinate for several hours in the refrigerator, turning occasionally.

2. Lightly coat an outdoor or indoor grill, broiler, or a well-seasoned ridged stove-top grill pan with nonstick cooking spray and preheat to medium-high.

3. In a large nonstick skillet or wok, heat the oil to medium and sauté the bell peppers and onions until golden for about 6 to 7 minutes, stirring often.

4. Remove the chicken from the marinade and pat dry. Grill the chicken breasts over medium-high heat, occasionally basting with the marinade and turning, until no longer pink but still moist and juicy, about 7 to 9 minutes (do not overcook).

5. Quickly slice the chicken into strips, toss with the sautéed vegetables, and serve immediately accompanied by warmed nonfat or low-fat flour or corn tortillas, shredded lettuce, slices of avocado, fresh Pico de Gallo or fresh tomato salsa, nonfat or low-fat sour cream, nonfat or low-fat refried beans, grilled scallions, and slices of lime.

*V*ARIATION:

❖   For beef fajitas, substitute lean flank steak for the chicken.

*C*OOK NOTE:

❖   Tortillas can be warmed wrapped in foil in a 350°F oven for 10 to 15 minutes, or in the microwave for 30 seconds.

*D*O-AHEAD PREP:

❖   The onions and bell peppers can be cooked an hour in advance or even re-heated if necessary. The chicken can be marinated earlier in the day and grilled just before serving.

Cold Poached Lemon Chicken
with Mustard-Chive Sauce

Serves: 4 to 6

*T*his is the perfect cold dish to serve at a spring or summer luncheon or as a light supper.

3 whole skinless, boneless chicken breasts, halved

1 large onion, thinly sliced

1 large lemon, thinly sliced

3 tablespoons lemon juice

2 sprigs of parsley

6 peppercorns

1 bay leaf

salt to taste

¼ cup dry vermouth or white wine

2 to 3 cups defatted chicken broth, or enough to cover

*S*AUCE:

1½ cups low-fat or nonfat plain yogurt

3 tablespoons low-fat mayonnaise

2 tablespoons lemon juice

2 tablespoons grainy-style Dijon mustard

2 tablespoons freshly snipped chives

2 teaspoons brown sugar

1 teaspoon grated lemon rind

salt and freshly ground pepper to taste

*G*ARNISH: mixed greens, lemon slices, and sprigs of parsley

1. In a large nonreactive deep skillet, place the chicken breasts in a single layer. Top with the onion, lemon, lemon juice, parsley, peppercorns, bay leaf, and salt. Pour over the wine and enough chicken broth to cover.

2. Bring to a boil, cover, reduce heat to medium-low, and simmer slowly for 10 to 15 minutes, or until the chicken is just tender and is no longer pink in the center. Remove from the heat and allow the chicken to cool in the liquid. With a slotted spoon, remove the chicken from the broth, place on a platter, cover, and chill until ready to use. (Note: strain and refrigerate or freeze the stock in a covered container for another use.)

3. In a small bowl, combine the sauce ingredients and whisk until smooth. Chill in a covered container until ready to use.

4. At serving time, place the chicken on a bed of greens, generously coat with the sauce, and serve over a bed of mixed greens garnished with lemon slices and sprigs of parsley.

*V*ARIATIONS:

❖ For a thicker sauce, substitute Yogurt Cheese (see page 50) or low-fat sour cream for the yogurt.

❖ The sauce can be used as a topping on fish, as a dip for vegetables, as a dressing for mixed greens, or even as a sandwich spread.

*C*OOK NOTES:

❖ When cooking with lemon juice and other citrus flavors, it is important to use nonreactive pans and utensils and avoid cast iron and aluminum. The acid in the citrus juice can adversely react with these metals, causing the flavor and color of a dish to change.

❖ Most of the lemons sold today are the Eureka, which some say were developed in California, but others debate that they were imported from Sicily in the late 1870s when Italian immigrants were building up vineyards in northern California. The Meyer lemon, available chiefly in California, is a thin-skinned lemon that seems sweeter than the Eureka but does not contain less sugar, just less acid. Legend has it that Meyer lemons were grown in Louis XIV's orangerie where ladies of the court sucked on them to keep their lips lusciously red.

*D*O-AHEAD PREP:

❖ The chicken can be prepared up to 2 days in advance and the sauce can be prepared 3 to 4 days ahead. Both should be stored in a covered containers in the refrigerator until ready to use.

Perfect Roast Chicken
with Artichoke-Garlic Flavoring

Serves: 4 to 5

*O*ne of my favorite food experiences as a child was eating roast chicken for dinner. It was always served with plain white rice, which was topped with the natural juices. I have simplified this comforting meal into a one-pot supper. I use a clay cooker (remember to start it in a cold oven) or covered roaster and it always seems to turn out juicy, moist, and flavorful. If you really want rice or noodles, just omit the potatoes. I followed the idea of *New York Times* food writer Molly O'Neill, who puts a delicious artichoke-garlic puree under the skin of the chicken, adding even more flavor to the finished dish.

> one 14-ounce can artichoke hearts (packed in water), drained and
>   squeezed dry
> 2 cloves garlic
> 1 tablespoon olive oil
> salt and freshly ground pepper to taste
> one 5- to 6-pound roasting chicken
> 12 baby red potatoes or small Yukon gold potatoes, sliced in half
> 12 small onions, peeled
> one 12-ounce package peeled baby carrots or 3 medium carrots,
>   peeled, and sliced into 2-inch pieces
> paprika
> 1 teaspoon herbes de Provence, crumbled
> salt and freshly ground pepper to taste
> 1½ cups defatted chicken broth
> ¼ cup dry white wine or vermouth

*G*ARNISH: sprigs of thyme, oregano, or parsley

1.　Preheat the oven to 450°F.

2.　Place the artichokes, garlic, olive oil, and salt and pepper in a food processor or blender and process until the mixture is a smooth spread. Gently pull the skin away from the breast meat and slide the spread into the space between the skin and meat, smoothing and flattening it down. Season the cavity with salt and pepper and truss the chicken with skewers or string. (Note: if you do not have time to truss, you can eliminate this step.)

3. Place the chicken in a clay cooker (which has been soaked in cold water according to the manufacturer's directions) or on a rack in a covered roaster. Surround the bird with the potatoes (cut-side up), onions, and carrots, distributing them evenly. Coat the chicken and vegetables with olive oil nonstick cooking spray and sprinkle with the paprika, herbes de Provence, and salt and pepper. Pour the chicken broth and wine into the bottom of the pan, cover, place in the oven, and roast for 1¾ hours without basting.

4. Remove the cover, coat the chicken very lightly with olive oil nonstick cooking spray, and return the pan to the oven; continue to cook for 15 to 20 minutes, or until the bird and vegetables are golden brown.

5. Remove the chicken from the oven, carve, and place on a platter with the vegetables. Remove the fat from the pan juices, strain, and serve the natural gravy alongside the chicken garnished with the sprigs of fresh herbs.

*V*ARIATION:

❖ For added flavor and aroma, the cavity of the chicken can be filled with a whole head of garlic or cut-up lemons, which make delicious and attractive garnishes.

*C*OOK NOTES:

❖ Herbes de Provence is an assortment of dried herbs found in the region of southern France. If you cannot locate this blend, combine dried basil, fennel seed, lavender, marjoram, rosemary, sage, summer savory, and thyme or a combination of several of these herbs.

❖ Any leftover broth should be frozen in a covered container for another use. As you keep using the broth it gets stronger and more flavorful.

*D*O-AHEAD PREP:

❖ The chicken can be trussed and seasoned earlier in the day and left in the refrigerator, but the dish should be cooked just before serving.

Light Coq au Vin

Serves: 6

*T*he secret to lightening this dish is to grill or broil the chicken instead of sautéing it. This technique allows the grease to drip away, reducing excess fat. Coq au vin is a fabulous dish for busy people to prepare since it can be cooked well in advance.

1 chicken (about 3 to 3½ pounds), cut into pieces

salt and freshly ground pepper to taste

1 tablespoon olive oil

4 large shallots, finely minced

2 medium carrots, peeled and finely chopped

½ pound mushrooms, stems removed, wiped clean and
thinly sliced

1 large clove garlic, finely minced

1 tablespoon all-purpose flour

¾ cup dry red wine

1 tablespoon brandy

¾ cup defatted chicken broth

2 tablespoons finely chopped fresh parsley

1 teaspoon finely chopped fresh thyme or ¼ teaspoon dried
thyme, crumbled

1 teaspoon finely chopped fresh oregano or ¼ teaspoon dried
oregano, crumbled

1 bay leaf

salt and freshly ground pepper to taste

*G*ARNISH: chopped fresh parsley

1. Lightly coat an outdoor or indoor grill or broiler with nonstick cooking spray and preheat to medium-high. (Note: if using an indoor broiler, place a pan beneath the grill to catch the drippings.)

2. Coat both sides of the chicken pieces with olive oil cooking spray. Place the chicken skin-side up on the grill or prepared rack, season with salt and pepper, and grill or broil for 10 minutes. Turn the chicken, spray again with olive oil cooking spray, season, and continue to cook for an additional 10 minutes or until the chicken is well browned on both sides.

3. In a large nonstick Dutch oven or deep saucepan, heat the oil to medium, and sauté the shallots, carrots, and mushrooms for about 7 to 9 minutes, stirring often, until golden. Add the garlic and cook for an additional 30 seconds. Add the flour and cook, stirring for 2 to 3 minutes, until well blended and slightly browned.

4. Increase the heat to high and add the wine and brandy. Cook over high heat until reduced and slightly thickened. Add the remaining ingredients and stir until smooth. Add the par-cooked chicken, making sure it is covered with the sauce; bring to a boil, cover, reduce heat, and simmer slowly for about 40 minutes, or until the chicken is tender.

5. Remove the bay leaf and discard, adjust the seasonings to taste, and serve the chicken hot, garnished with the chopped parsley.

*V*ARIATION:

❖ 5 to 6 scallions (white parts only) can be substituted for the shallots.

*C*OOK NOTES:

❖ Shallots are a sibling of the onion but are formed in the same way as garlic, with a head made up of individual cloves. A thin, papery skin of reddish brown covers the inside, which is tinged with green and purple. Store them in a cool, dry, well-ventilated place. If stored in the refrigerator, they become moldy.

❖ Store loose mushrooms in the refrigerator in a paper bag or open container loosely covered. Mushrooms stored in plastic bags deteriorate quickly.

*D*O-AHEAD PREP:

❖ This dish can be prepared several days in advance and chilled in a covered container or can be frozen successfully for several months.

Chicken Cacciatore

*C*hicken Cacciatore is a homey Italian peasant dish with earthy flavors. *Cacciatore* means "hunter's style." By using skinless and boneless chicken thighs, you can reduce the amount of fat and time from the original recipe considerably. If the boneless thighs are not available the dish can be cooked with skinless thighs with bones, but add five more minutes to the cooking time.

⅓ cup all-purpose flour

salt and freshly ground pepper to taste

12 skinless, boneless chicken thighs, all visible fat removed

4 teaspoons olive oil

3 leeks, thoroughly washed and thinly sliced (white parts only)

½ pound mushrooms, stems removed, wiped clean and
thinly sliced

1 green bell pepper, trimmed, and thinly sliced

1 sweet red bell pepper, trimmed, and thinly sliced

¾ cup dry red wine

one 28-ounce can tomatoes including liquid or 26-ounce package
aseptic-packed chopped tomatoes

2 garlic cloves, finely minced

2 tablespoons finely chopped fresh basil or 1 teaspoon dried basil,
crumbled

2 tablespoons finely chopped fresh oregano or 1 teaspoon dried
oregano, crumbled

¼ teaspoon red pepper flakes, or to taste

salt and freshly ground pepper

*G*ARNISH: fresh basil leaves

*A*CCOMPANIMENT: hot spaghetti, linguine, vermicelli, or
white rice

1. Combine the flour with the salt and pepper and dip the chicken in the flour mixture, coating lightly.

2. In a nonstick Dutch oven or deep large saucepan, heat 2 teaspoons of the oil to medium-high and sauté half the chicken on all sides, until browned. Add the remaining 2 teaspoons of the oil, and continue to sauté the rest of the chicken in batches, until browned. Remove the chicken with a slotted spoon and set aside.

3.   Add the leeks, mushrooms, and green bell pepper to the skillet and cook over medium-high heat, stirring often, for about 5 minutes, or until softened.

4.   Add all the remaining ingredients including the reserved chicken and increase the heat to high. Bring to a boil, cover, reduce to a simmer, and cook for 20 to 25 minutes, or until the chicken is tender.

5.   Serve the cacciatore over hot spaghetti, linguine, vermicelli, or white rice garnished with fresh basil leaves.

*V*ARIATION:

❖   Veal stew meat can be substituted for the chicken. Increase the cooking time to an hour or cook until the meat is tender.

*C*OOK NOTE:

❖   Select green or red bell peppers that are well shaped, firm, and have a glossy color. They are highly perishable so purchase just before using.

*D*O-AHEAD PREP:

❖   This dish can be prepared several days in advance and chilled in a covered container or can be frozen successfully for several months.

Roast Rock Cornish Game Hens
with Raspberry Flavor

Serves: 4

*T*his recipe can be prepared using small chickens, called *poussins*, although the individual hens make a beautiful and unique presentation.

*M*ARINADE:

⅓ cup red wine or raspberry or balsamic vinegar

¼ cup seedless, juice-sweetened raspberry preserves

¼ cup freshly squeezed orange or tangerine juice

2 tablespoons olive oil

2 tablespoons grainy-style Dijon mustard

1 tablespoon minced orange rind

2 teaspoons minced garlic

2 teaspoons minced fresh thyme or ½ teaspoon dried
    thyme, crumbled

freshly ground pepper to taste

four 1- to 1½-pound Rock Cornish game hens, split

salt and freshly ground pepper to taste

*G*ARNISH: sprigs of fresh thyme, raspberries, and
    orange slices

1. Bring the marinade ingredients to a boil in a small saucepan and cook over medium heat until the raspberry preserves have dissolved. Allow the marinade to cool slightly.

2. Wash and dry the hens, turn them backbone up, and cut through the backbones only. Flatten out the birds with the palm of your hand and sprinkle each with salt and pepper.

3. Place the hens in a shallow nonreactive dish and pour the marinade over, coating on all sides. Allow the hens to marinate at room temperature for about 30 minutes or in the refrigerator for about 3 to 4 hours.

4. Preheat the oven to 475°F. Lightly coat the bottom of a roasting pan with nonstick cooking spray.

5. Remove the hens from the marinade and place them in the prepared pan skinside down. Spread the hens liberally with the marinade and roast them for 15 minutes.

Turn, baste the hens with the remaining marinade, and continue to roast for an additional 15 to 20 minutes or until well browned and cooked through.

6. Remove the cooked hens to a warm platter, strain the sauce into a pitcher, and remove any accumulated fat. Serve the hens hot with the sauce on the side, garnished with sprigs of thyme, raspberries, and orange slices.

VARIATION:

❖ Strawberry, blackberry, blueberry, apricot, or peach preserves can be substituted for the raspberry.

COOK NOTE:

❖ Rock Cornish game hens were developed in America in the nineteenth century by crossing a Cornish game cock with a White Plymouth Rock chicken. These hens usually weigh between 1 and 2 pounds and are low in fat. Rock Cornish game hens are generally sold frozen although they are beginning to appear fresh in many markets.

DO-AHEAD PREP:

❖ The marinade can be prepared 1 to 2 days in advance and refrigerated in a covered container until ready to use.

Turkey Roasted on a
Covered Charcoal Grill

Serves: 8 to 10

*I*f the weather outside is conducive, cooking the turkey on the outdoor grill is a great idea, giving the turkey a delightful smoky flavor. It frees up the kitchen oven for other dinner preparations, especially on Thanksgiving, and it cuts down considerably on the cleanup. Allow about 30 minutes for the fire to be ready, then 11 minutes per pound for an unstuffed bird and 13 to 15 minutes per pound for a stuffed bird. Remember that wind direction, temperature, and humidity may affect cooking time. Be sure to select a bird that isn't too big for your grill. You need to allow at least 1 inch between the turkey and the lid and sides of the grill. A good rule of thumb is that a turkey cooked on an average-sized grill should not exceed 12 pounds.

> mesquite or other scented wood chips (optional)
>
> charcoal briquettes
>
> one 12-pound turkey (fresh or completely thawed frozen turkey), rinsed and dried inside and out
>
> stuffing (optional) (see Sourdough Stuffing with Apricots and Almonds, page 253)
>
> 2 to 3 tablespoons olive oil
>
> salt and freshly ground pepper to taste
>
> **G**ARNISH: parsley sprigs, orange slices, and grapes

1. To prepare the fire: for a rich, smokey flavor, soak about 2 cups mesquite chips in water for about 1 hour. Put a 12-x-9-inch disposable foil drip pan in the bottom of the grill. Build a fire of about 30 briquettes (not self-starting) on each long side of the drip pan. With the vents open and the grill uncovered, light the coals and let them burn about 30 minutes. The fire is ready when the coals are covered with gray ash. Drain the chips well and scatter them over the coals.

2. If using stuffing, place it inside the turkey neck and body cavities. Fold the neck skin under the back and secure with skewers. Close the body cavity with turkey lacers to seal. Twist the wing tips under the back and tie the legs together. Rub the skin all over with olive oil and sprinkle with salt and pepper.

3. Place the turkey breast-side up on a rack that will fit in the pan. Place the rack on the grill, centered over the drip pan. Cover the grill and cook, adding 9 briquettes to each long side of the pan every hour, for about 2 hours and 15 minutes for unstuffed or 2 hours and 40 minutes for stuffed or until an inserted meat thermometer registers 175°F to 180°F and stuffing should read at least 160°F.

4. Transfer the turkey to a cutting board and allow it to stand for 20 to 30 minutes before carving.

5. Remove the fat from any pan juices, strain, and place them in a pitcher. Serve the turkey, accompanied by the pan juices, and garnished with parsley sprigs, orange slices, and grapes.

$\mathcal{C}$OOK NOTES:

❖ Cheesecloth stuffing bags are available in many markets at holiday time and provide a simple way to remove all the stuffing with ease.

❖ Avoid purchasing a self-basting bird, which adds chemicals, additives, and extra fats, many of which are saturated. Look for a butcher who carries fresh turkeys, which will be the most flavorful.

❖ If you are using a frozen bird, begin defrosting it in the refrigerator at least 2 days before cooking.

$\mathcal{D}$O-AHEAD PREP:

❖ You can prepare the stuffing a day in advance and refrigerate it in a covered container. Do *not* stuff the bird until you are ready to put it in the oven!

Roast Butterflied Turkey Breast with Orange Mustard Glaze and Raisin Bread Stuffing

Serves: 8

*T*o quote Benjamin Franklin: "I wish the Bald Eagle had not been chosen as the Representative of our country! The turkey is a much more respectable Bird, and withal a true original native of America." In the past, turkey was restricted to a once- or twice-a-year Thanksgiving or Christmas treat. Today turkey has become a staple of a low-fat diet. The raisin stuffing can be used as a filling here or can be stuffed in other poultry.

one 4½-pound or two 2½-pound turkey breasts, butterflied

1 recipe Raisin Bread Stuffing (recipe follows)

*G*LAZE:

½ cup frozen orange juice concentrate, thawed

¼ cup juice-sweetened cranberry jelly

¼ cup grainy-style Dijon mustard

*G*ARNISH: watercress; sprigs of fresh sage, thyme, or parsley

1. Preheat the oven to 350°F. Lightly coat a roasting rack with nonstick cooking spray.

2. Place the turkey breast between layers of waxed paper and pound until a uniform thickness. Dry the meat with paper towels and season the inside with salt and pepper. Spread the prepared stuffing evenly over the turkey. Roll from the long side as you would a jelly roll, keeping the filling inside and the roll as tight as possible. Secure the roll with kitchen twine, tying every 2 to 3 inches. Transfer the roll to the rack, lightly coat the roll with nonstick cooking spray, and season with salt and pepper to taste. (Any leftover stuffing can be baked in a small casserole alongside the turkey.)

3. In a small saucepan, heat the glaze ingredients until smooth, slather generously over all parts of the rolled breast, and roast for 40 to 50 minutes, or until no longer pink (about 170°F), basting with the remainder of the sauce every 15 minutes. Remove from the oven and allow to rest for 5 minutes before carving.

4. Slice the turkey and place slices in an overlapping circle on a platter, garnish with watercress, and serve hot garnished with sprigs of fresh sage, thyme, or parsley.

$\mathscr{V}$ARIATIONS:

❖ Raspberry, apricot, or other fruit-sweetened jams can be substituted for cranberry.

❖ Leftover turkey is delicious cold on sandwiches with spicy mustard.

$\mathscr{C}$OOK NOTES:

❖ Turkey is an excellent source of protein, niacin, vitamin B_6, vitamin B_{12}, and phosphorus. It also has good amounts of iron, zinc, riboflavin, and magnesium. Almost all of the fat in turkey is found in the skin. However, turkey meat is so low in fat that 3½ ounces of roasted breast meat with skin has only 153 calories, 18 percent of them coming from fat.

❖ Poultry is graded by the USDA and the graded turkey sold in supermarkets is Grade A, which means that it is well shaped, free of feathers, and has a layer of fat. Select turkey that is moist and pink with creamy white, not bluish skin. The skin should be free of any cuts, tears, blemishes, or bruises.

❖ Poultry, meat, or shrimp that is butterflied is split down the center, almost but not quite all the way through, so that the halves can be opened flat like butterfly wings.

$\mathscr{D}$O-AHEAD PREP:

❖ Do not stuff the turkey until just before roasting to prevent food contamination.

Raisin Bread Stuffing

Yield: 6 cups

12 slices raisin bread, crusts trimmed, cut in ½-inch cubes (about
   6 cups)

1 tablespoon vegetable oil

8 shallots, finely chopped

2 medium tart apples, peeled and finely chopped

¼ cup fresh orange juice

¼ cup defatted chicken broth

1½ tablespoons grainy-style Dijon mustard

½ teaspoon dried sage, crumbled

½ teaspoon dried thyme, crumbled

¼ teaspoon grated nutmeg

salt and freshly ground pepper to taste

1. Preheat the oven to 375°F.

2. Spread the bread cubes on a baking sheet and bake for 7 minutes, stirring occasionally, or until lightly golden and crisp. Transfer to a large bowl.

3. In a large nonstick skillet, heat the oil to medium, and sauté the shallots, stirring often, for 3 minutes. Add the apple and continue to cook, stirring often, until softened, about 5 minutes longer.

4. In a large bowl, combine the remaining stuffing ingredients, top with the cooked mixture, and stir to combine. Place the stuffing in a covered container and store in the refrigerator until ready to use.

VARIATION:

❖ Whole grain raisin bread can be substituted for the raisin bread.

COOK NOTES:

❖ Select firm, crisp apples with color that is bright and appropriate for the variety. The apple surface should be smooth and firm with no bruises or blemishes. Brownish colored spots or streaks are likely due to "russeting." Generally, russeting is caused by weather conditions during the growing season. The russeting does not affect the flavor of the apple.

❖ Decay can spread rapidly from one apple to the next, so any decayed or badly bruised fruit should be discarded immediately. Store apples at home, wrapped in a perforated plastic bag, in the coldest part of the refrigerator or crisper drawer. Do not wash apples until just before using.

❖ Dried sage tends to lose its flavor quickly so store it away from direct light or heat in a cool, dry, dark area and replace it every 6 months.

DO-AHEAD PREP:

❖ The bread cubes can be toasted several days in advance and kept fresh in a sealed container. The stuffing can be prepared a day or two in advance and kept in a covered container in the refrigerator until just before stuffing the turkey.

Grilled Turkey Burger

Serves: 6

*L*ean ground turkey or chicken makes a delicious low-fat patty when seasoned and grilled or broiled until golden. Use an outdoor hamburger grill basket to keep the meat intact and for ease in turning during the grilling.

For an extra-special burger, try topping the finished patty with Roasted Garlic Sauce (see page 142).

> 2 teaspoons olive oil
> ¼ cup finely chopped onion
> 1 clove garlic, finely minced
> 1¼ pounds lean ground turkey or chicken
> ½ cup dry bread crumbs
> 1 egg, lightly beaten
> 2 teaspoons Worcestershire sauce
> 2 teaspoons Dijon mustard
> salt and freshly ground white pepper to taste

*A*CCOMPANIMENTS: toasted hamburger buns, lettuce leaves, tomato slices, and Caramelized Red Onion Marmalade (see page 56)

1.　In a medium nonstick skillet, heat the oil to medium high and sauté the onion, stirring often, about 4 to 5 minutes, until lightly golden. Add the garlic, stir to combine, remove from the heat, and allow to cool slightly.

2.　In a medium bowl, combine the turkey or chicken with the remaining ingredients including the cooked onions, mixing with your hands, until well blended. Form into 6 flat burgers, place on waxed paper, cover, and refrigerate until ready to cook.

3.　Lightly coat an outdoor or indoor grill, broiler, or a well-seasoned ridged stove-top grill pan with nonstick cooking spray and preheat to medium-high.

4.　Grill the burgers for 3 to 4 minutes per side, or until no longer pink in the center.

5.　Serve the turkey burgers hot accompanied by toasted buns, lettuce leaves, tomato slices, and the Caramelized Red Onion Marmalade.

*V*ARIATIONS:

❖　Serve the burgers on toasted whole wheat buns.

❖ If you do not have an outdoor burger grill spray 6 squares of aluminum foil with nonstick cooking spray. Place each of the patties on a square and cook the turkey burgers on the foil on one side for 4 minutes. Remove and discard the foil, flip the burgers, and continue to cook until done.

*C*OOK NOTES:

❖ After mixing the turkey with your hands, it is imperative that you wash thoroughly before touching anything else to remove any lurking bacteria often found in raw poultry.

❖ Bread crumbs can be prepared simply by placing slices of any type of whole grain bread in a 300°F oven for 10 minutes or until dry. Place in a food processor or blender and store the crumbs for several days in a sealed container.

*D*O-AHEAD PREP:

❖ The turkey burgers can be assembled early in the day and refrigerated covered, but must be cooked at the last minute.

Outstanding Turkey Chili

Serves: 8 to 10

Chili con Carne, known as "bowl of red," is considered to be the national dish of Texas. Traditionally, chili was prepared with chopped beef, pork, or venison and served with beans on the side. This version is adapted to our lighter eating habits by using ground turkey instead of meat and oil instead of butter or lard. Like many stews, chili is easy to prepare and reheat and actually improves on standing. The most common way of serving chili is in a bowl, accompanied by tortillas, bread, or crackers, and a variety of toppings including salsa, chopped onions, cilantro, diced avocado, and grated cheddar cheese.

If you prefer chili with beans, add two 15-ounce cans rinsed and drained pinto or kidney beans and bake the cooked chili in a covered pot in a 325°F oven for about 30 to 40 minutes until heated through.

- 2 tablespoons olive or canola oil
- 2 large onions, chopped
- 4 large garlic cloves, minced
- 2 pounds lean ground turkey or chicken
- ¼ cup chili powder
- 1 tablespoon ground cumin
- 2 teaspoons dried oregano, crumbled
- 2 teaspoons unsweetened cocoa powder
- ½ teaspoon cayenne powder or to taste
- salt and freshly ground pepper to taste
- one 28-ounce can crushed tomatoes packed in puree
- one 12-ounce bottle dark beer, preferably Mexican
- ½ cup defatted chicken broth
- 1 bay leaf

*A*CCOMPANIMENTS: hot cooked pinto, kidney, red, or white beans, hot low-fat tortillas, diced avocado, salsa, grated sharp low-fat cheddar cheese, chopped onions, chopped cilantro, chopped tomatoes, and low-fat or nonfat sour cream

1. In a large nonstick Dutch oven or deep saucepan, heat 1 tablespoon of the oil to medium and sauté the onions, stirring often, for about 5 to 6 minutes, until softened. Add the garlic, stir just to combine, transfer to a bowl, and set aside.

2. Increase the heat to high, add the remaining 1 tablespoon of the oil, and when hot, cook the turkey, chopping and separating with a wooden spoon, until it loses its pink color, about 5 to 6 minutes. Drain the meat into a colander to remove the excess fat and liquid, wipe the pan with a paper towel, and return the turkey to the pan.

3. Add all the seasonings except the bay leaf, reduce the heat, and continue to cook for an additional minute over moderately high heat to incorporate the spices. Add the reserved onions and garlic, tomatoes, beer, broth, and bay leaf, bring to a boil, reduce the heat, and simmer, uncovered for 45 to 50 minutes, stirring occasionally, until slightly thickened. Remove and discard bay leaf.

4. Serve the chili hot with any or all of the following toppings: hot cooked pinto, kidney, red, or white beans, hot low-fat tortillas, diced avocado, salsa, grated sharp low-fat sharp cheddar cheese, chopped onions, chopped cilantro, chopped tomatoes, and low-fat or nonfat sour cream.

𝒱ARIATIONS:

❖ If the chili is too thick when reheating, add an additional ½ cup of defatted chicken broth.

❖ If tomatoes packed in puree are unavailable, use regular whole juice-packed tomatoes; chop, drain off most of the liquid, return the tomatoes to the can, and fill to the top with canned tomato puree.

𝒞OOK NOTES:

❖ Recipes containing chili powder may not need much salt since salt is one of the ingredients in most commercial chili powders.

❖ If you want to remove just a few cloves of garlic from a head, scrape away the outside papery layers until you can see individual cloves. Work the tip of a knife into the head, and pry out as many cloves as you need.

𝒟O-AHEAD PREP:

❖ Prepare the chili several days in advance and refrigerate in a covered container or freeze this easy-to-prepare buffet dish for several months.

Savory Shepherd's Pie

Serves: 8

*T*his proper British dish is traditionally prepared with ground beef, herbs and seasonings, and topped with a browned mashed potato crust. In this lightened version, lean ground turkey is substituted for the beef and the mashed potatoes are whipped with 1% milk and just a hint of butter.

MASHED POTATO CRUST:

2 pounds all-purpose potatoes

¾ cup potato cooking liquid or warmed 1% low-fat milk

1 tablespoon unsalted butter

salt and freshly ground white pepper to taste

2 tablespoons freshly grated Parmesan cheese

1½ pounds lean ground turkey

2 teaspoons olive oil

1 medium onion, finely chopped

1 yellow or red bell pepper, seeded and finely chopped

2 cloves garlic, finely minced

one 14½-ounce can ready-cut diced peeled tomatoes

¾ cup defatted chicken broth

1 tablespoon Worcestershire sauce

¼ teaspoon dried rosemary, crumbled

Tabasco to taste

salt and freshly ground pepper to taste

2 tablespoons all-purpose flour

GARNISH: cherry tomatoes and sprigs of fresh rosemary

1. In a large saucepan, add enough water to cover the potatoes by 1 inch. Bring to a boil, reduce heat to medium, cover, and simmer for 15 to 20 minutes, or until tender.

2. Drain the potatoes well, reserving ¾ cup of the cooking liquid, if using; return the potatoes to the saucepan along with the reserved cooking liquid or warmed milk, butter, and salt and pepper. Using an electric mixer at medium speed or potato masher, mash the potatoes until just smooth. Stir in the Parmesan cheese and set aside.

3. Preheat the oven to 350°F. Coat a 9-inch square baking dish or 3-quart oval or rectangular casserole with nonstick cooking spray.

4. In a large deep nonstick skillet over medium-high heat, cook the ground turkey for 4 to 5 minutes, until the meat loses its pink color, stirring often to break up the clumps. Drain the meat in a colander.

5. Wipe the skillet clean with a paper towel, add the oil, and when hot sauté the onion and bell pepper over medium heat, stirring often, until just glazed, about 4 to 5 minutes. Add the garlic and stir for 30 seconds. Add the tomatoes, ½ cup of the broth, the Worcestershire, rosemary, Tabasco, and salt and pepper. Bring to a boil, cover, reduce heat, and simmer slowly for 10 minutes.

6. In a small bowl, mix the flour with the remaining ¼ cup of the broth until smooth. Add to the skillet, stir, and cook for 1 to 2 minutes, until slightly thickened. Remove from the heat. Combine with the reserved turkey and set aside.

7. Place the meat mixture in the bottom of the prepared casserole and gently spread the mashed potatoes evenly on top. Bake for 25 to 30 minutes, or until the potatoes are lightly golden at the peaks and the dish is hot and bubbling. (Note: if the potatoes do not color by the end of the baking time, it may be necessary to place the casserole under a broiler for 1 to 2 minutes to brown the tops of the potatoes.)

8. Serve hot, garnished with cherry tomatoes and sprigs of fresh rosemary.

Variations:

❖ Chopped carrots, celery, leeks, and other vegetables can be added with the onions and bell peppers.

❖ Fresh or dried oregano, sage, or thyme can be added in place of the rosemary.

Cook Notes:

❖ Select potatoes that are fairly clean, firm, and smooth with regular shapes so there will not be much waste in peeling.

❖ Dried rosemary's needlelike leaves are too sharp to crush between your fingers, so use a mortar and pestle to crush them.

Do-Ahead Prep:

❖ The shepherd's pie can be assembled in the casserole, covered, and refrigerated overnight. It can also be frozen before or after baking.

FISH & SEAFOOD

Grilled Tuna with Roasted Garlic Sauce

Grilled Salmon with Fresh Tomato
and Feta Relish

Grilled Halibut with Mango Salsa

Grilled Swordfish with Chinese Salsa

Stir-Fried Swordfish with Jicama and Broccoli Florets

Crispy Oven-Baked Catfish Fillets with Mustard-Chive Flavor

Fish Fillets in Parchment with Minced Vegetables

Fish Fillets Veracruz Style

Plaki (*Psari Plaki*)

Chilled Trout Fillets with Creamy Dill Dressing

Fish Cioppino on a Bed of Linguine

Santa Barbara Shrimp with Spicy Lemon Garlic Sauce

Stir-Fried Szechuan Shrimp and Asparagus

Shrimp Curry with Braised Cucumbers

Stir-Fried Scallops with Black Bean Sauce

Spicy Clams in Tomato Sauce with Cumin Flavor

Grilled Tuna with Roasted Garlic Sauce

Serves: 4

*G*rilled fresh tuna bears no resemblance to the canned variety we eat as tuna salad. It has the juicy texture of beef, especially when not overcooked. Tuna is a fatty fish, a good source of those highly unsaturated Omega-3 fatty acids that have been shown to do such a wonderful job of lowering the levels of unhealthful cholesterol. This recipe is especially easy to prepare since the sauce can be assembled four to five days in advance and chilled in a covered container until ready to use.

If fresh tuna is unavailable, or too costly, substitute swordfish, salmon, halibut, or even shark steaks and the recipe will be just as delicious.

ROASTED GARLIC SAUCE:

8 large cloves garlic (about 1 head)

¾ cup plain nonfat or low-fat yogurt

2 tablespoons reduced-fat mayonnaise

1 tablespoon grainy-style Dijon mustard

1 teaspoon lemon juice

salt and freshly ground white pepper to taste

four 1-inch-thick slices fresh tuna (about 1½ to 2 pounds)

3 tablespoons olive oil

½ teaspoon dried rosemary leaves, crumbled

GARNISH: rosemary or parsley sprigs, curled lemon zest

1. Preheat the oven to 275°F. Lightly coat a glass or ceramic baking dish (or a terra-cotta garlic baker) with olive oil nonstick cooking spray. Place the unpeeled garlic cloves on the baking sheet in a single layer and bake for about 35 to 40 minutes, or until very soft. Remove from the oven and allow to cool slightly.

2. Squeeze the garlic cloves from their skins into a small bowl and mash with a fork until smooth. Add the yogurt, mayonnaise, mustard, lemon juice, and salt and pepper, stir until thoroughly combined, and refrigerate in a covered container until ready to use.

3. Lightly coat an outdoor or indoor grill, broiler, or a well-seasoned ridged stove-top grill pan with nonstick cooking spray and preheat to medium-high.

4. Place the tuna in a flat dish in a single layer. In a small bowl, combine the olive oil and rosemary and brush liberally on both sides of the fish. Grill the fish for about 2 to 3 minutes per side, until just cooked through. It is best not to overcook the fish or it will dry out.

5. Serve immediately accompanied by the sauce and garnished with rosemary or parsley sprigs and lemon zest.

*V*ARIATION:

❖ This sauce makes a wonderful dip for raw vegetables, or it can also be used as an accompaniment for other hot or cold fish or poultry dishes.

*C*OOK NOTES:

❖ Whenever possible, have the fish steaks cut to order from fish that has taut, moist skin. If the exposed cut portion of a large fish looks dry, some markets will remove a thin outer slice and cut the steak from the interior, which will be in better condition.

❖ Wipe freshly purchased fish all over with a wet paper towel; wrap and store the fish in the refrigerator until ready to use. Cook and eat fish the same day it is purchased.

❖ To quickly peel a clove of garlic without breaking it, put the clove in the microwave oven on high for about 10 seconds. The heat will create a burst of steam that easily loosens the skin. Remove the garlic from the oven, hold one end, gently press the clove against a hard surface, and the garlic will easily pop out of its papery skin.

*D*O-AHEAD PREP:

❖ The sauce can be prepared a day or two in advance and refrigerated in a covered container until ready to use. Allow the sauce to come to room temperature before serving. The fish should be grilled just before serving.

Grilled Salmon with Fresh Tomato and Feta Relish

Serves: 4

*T*his recipe is cooked by a unique method developed by the well-known Los Angeles chef Michel Richard. The fish is lightly grilled on both sides and then cooked in a 200°F oven for 15 minutes. The result is a juicier more flavorful fish.

GLAZE:

2 tablespoons olive oil

2 tablespoons lemon juice

2 tablespoons Dijon mustard

1 clove garlic, finely minced

salt and freshly ground pepper to taste

four 1-inch thick salmon steaks

RELISH:

2 medium ripe tomatoes

2 shallots, finely minced

1 tablespoon extra-virgin olive oil

1½ tablespoons lemon juice

2 teaspoons snipped fresh snipped dill

salt and freshly ground pepper to taste

1½ ounces (about ⅓ cup) crumbled low-fat feta cheese

GARNISH: bed of mixed greens, sprigs of fresh dill, and lemon wedges

1.   Lightly coat an outdoor or indoor grill rack or a well-seasoned ridged stovetop grill pan with nonstick cooking spray. Preheat the grill or pan to high.

2.   Preheat the oven to 200°F.

3.   In a small bowl, whisk the glaze ingredients together, brush half the mixture on one side of the salmon, and grill for 1 to 2 minutes. Turn the salmon, brush with the remaining glaze, and cook for an additional 2 minutes.

4.   Place the salmon in a 200°F oven and continue to cook for an additional 15 minutes, or until just flaky.

5.   To prepare the relish, core the tomatoes, slice them in half, and squeeze out the seeds and discard. Chop the tomatoes finely. Combine with the shallots, oil, lemon juice, dill, and salt and pepper, stirring to mix well. Fold in the feta cheese until well combined.

6. Place the fish atop a bed of greens, top with the relish, and serve hot, garnished with sprigs of fresh dill and lemon wedges.

*V*ARIATIONS:

❖ If low-fat feta is not available, use only 1 ounce of regular feta cheese.

❖ Goat cheese can be substituted for the feta cheese.

❖ Serve any leftover fish chilled the next day, topped with extra relish.

*C*OOK NOTES:

❖ To reduce the sodium content in feta cheese, drain and rinse it with fresh cold water. Drain again and dry on paper towels before crumbling.

❖ Place not-quite-ripe tomatoes, stem-side up, in a paper bag or fruit ripener with an apple. The natural ethylene gas given off by the apple hastens the ripening process of the tomato. Once ripened, tomatoes will keep for a few days at room temperature. If they are too ripe, place them in the butter compartment, which is the warmest part of the refrigerator, until ready to use.

*D*O-AHEAD PREP:

❖ The relish can be prepared several days in advance and kept in a covered container in the refrigerator. Allow the relish to come to room temperature before serving. The fish should be grilled just before serving.

Grilled Halibut with Mango Salsa

Serves: 4

*T*his recipe can be prepared with any type of fish steak: salmon, tuna, or even shark.

Mango Salsa makes a flavorful low-fat topping for grilled, baked, or poached fish, chicken, or vegetables. The salsa can be prepared in advance, but bring it to room temperature before serving with the fish.

*S*ALSA:

1 ripe mango, peeled, seeded and finely chopped

¼ cup finely chopped red onion

¼ cup chopped fresh cilantro

¼ cup fresh lime juice

1 tablespoon chopped fresh mint

1 tablespoon olive oil

1 small red chili pepper, seeded and minced

salt and freshly ground white pepper to taste

1 tablespoon olive oil

1 tablespoon lemon juice

salt and freshly ground pepper to taste

4 halibut steaks, about 1 inch thick

*G*ARNISH: cilantro sprigs, mango slices

1.   Combine all the ingredients for the salsa in a bowl, mix well, cover, and refrigerate several hours to allow the flavors to blend.

2.   Lightly coat an outdoor or indoor grill, broiler, or a well-seasoned ridged stove-top grill pan with nonstick cooking spray and preheat to medium-high.

3.   In a small bowl, stir together the oil, lemon juice, salt and pepper. Put the fish on a large plate, pour the oil mixture over it, and allow the fish to marinate, turning once, for 10 minutes only. (The acid in the lemon juice will start to "cure" the fish if you let it sit any longer.)

4.   Grill the halibut on the grill over moderately high heat for 4 to 5 minutes per side, or until just cooked through.

5.   Serve the fish on a platter topped with the salsa and garnished with cilantro and sliced mango.

$\mathcal{V}$ARIATIONS:

❖ Salmon, tuna, or swordfish steaks may be substituted for the salmon.

❖ The fish may be served cold the next day.

❖ Papaya, pineapple, or other tropical fruits can be substituted for the mango.

❖ Chile peppers may be mild or hot depending on preference.

$\mathcal{C}$OOK NOTES:

❖ The rule for cooking fish is that it should be cooked for no more than 10 minutes per inch (measured at the thickest part of the steak).

❖ Slightly green mangoes should be ripened in the dark, like tomatoes. Put them in a brown paper bag. They are ripe when they develop a sweet fruity smell and become orange or red in color. Some mangoes are ripe when they are yellow or if they develop small brown spots. You can test their ripeness by pressure.

❖ Take care in peeling mangoes. The skin contains a sap similar to poison ivy and sensitive individuals will get a blistering rash. After peeling mangoes wash your hands and utensils well with soap and water. Never try to eat the fruit off the peel.

$\mathcal{D}$O-AHEAD PREP:

❖ The salsa can be prepared in advance and chilled in a covered container until ready to use. Allow the salsa to come to room temperature before serving. The fish should be grilled just before serving.

Grilled Swordfish with Chinese Salsa

Serves: 4

*T*his fusion-style salsa works well atop any top of firm, fleshy fish such as ahi tuna, halibut, or salmon. If fresh shiitake mushrooms are available and reasonably priced, substitute them for the regular mushrooms.

4 swordfish steaks, cut 1 inch thick

1 tablespoon peanut oil

salt and freshly ground pepper to taste

*C*HINESE SALSA:

2 teaspoons peanut oil

2 cloves garlic, finely minced

1 teaspoon freshly ground ginger

6 mushrooms, wiped clean and thinly sliced

2 tablespoons Chinese Chinkiang rice vinegar or balsamic vinegar

2 tablespoons reduced-sodium soy sauce

1 teaspoon sugar

1 teaspoon Asian-style sesame oil

½ teaspoon chili paste with garlic or pinch of crushed red pepper to taste

3 tablespoons chopped fresh cilantro

3 tablespoons chopped scallion greens

2 teaspoons toasted sesame seeds

*G*ARNISH: sprigs of cilantro

1. Lightly coat an outdoor or indoor grill, broiler, or a well-seasoned ridged stove-top grill pan with nonstick cooking spray and preheat to medium-high.

2. Brush the swordfish steaks with the tablespoon of oil, season with salt and pepper, and set aside.

3. In a nonstick wok or large nonstick skillet, heat 2 teaspoons of the oil and stir-fry the garlic and ginger over high for 30 seconds. Add the mushrooms and continue to cook, stirring constantly, for 3 minutes, or until the mushrooms are tender.

4. Combine the remaining salsa ingredients, stir, add to the mushrooms, and continue to stir-fry for an additional 2 minutes. Remove from the heat, and set aside.

5.   Grill the fish for 3 to 4 minutes per side, or until just cooked through.

6.   Place the fish on a platter and distribute the Chinese Salsa evenly among the pieces of fish. Sprinkle the tops with chopped cilantro, scallion greens, and sesame seeds, and serve immediately garnished with sprigs of cilantro.

*V*ARIATION:

❖   Chinese salsa can be used over grilled poultry or meat.

*D*O-AHEAD PREP:

❖   The sauce can be refrigerated in a covered container for several days but should be reheated before serving. The fish should be grilled just before serving.

Stir-Fried Swordfish with Jicama and Broccoli Florets

Serves: 6

*T*he best type of fish to use for stir-frying is a firm-fleshed fish like swordfish, salmon, tuna, halibut, or even shark. Monkfish, also called lotte, angler, or goosefish, is a chewy fish with the texture of a scallop that is also excellent for use in this Chinese-inspired dish.

2 cups broccoli florets (1 small bunch)

1 cup (about 6 ounces) peeled and julienned jicama

2 teaspoons finely minced ginger

1 teaspoon finely minced garlic

1½ pounds swordfish, or other firm fish, cut into 1½-inch pieces

*S*AUCE:

⅔ cup defatted chicken broth

2 tablespoons reduced-sodium soy sauce

2 tablespoons dry sherry

1 tablespoon cornstarch or arrowroot

1 teaspoon Chinese chili paste with garlic (or use a shot of Tabasco)

2 tablespoons peanut oil

*G*ARNISH: cilantro sprigs

1.　Place the broccoli and jicama on a plate near the cooking area. Combine the ginger and garlic and place alongside the fish. Place the fish cubes within easy reach.

2.　In a small bowl, combine the sauce ingredients and set aside.

3.　Heat a seasoned wok or heavy large nonstick skillet on high heat, add the oil, and when hot, stir-fry the ginger and garlic over high heat for 30 seconds. Add the broccoli and jicama, and continue to stir-fry for 2 minutes, Add the fish and stir-fry for 2 to 3 minutes, or until the fish is no longer opaque.

4.　Stir the sauce ingredients to make sure the cornstarch is thoroughly mixed, add to the wok, stir to combine, reduce the heat to medium, cover, and cook for about 2 minutes longer, or until the fish is cooked but the broccoli is still crunchy.

5.　Serve immediately garnished with cilantro.

$\mathcal{V}$ARIATION:

❖ Cauliflower, broccoflower, zucchini, snow or snap peas, or other vegetables can be substituted for the broccoli

$\mathcal{C}$OOK NOTES:

❖ When selecting swordfish, note that the veins of dark myoglobin, which are easily visible on the steaks, should be in a compact, well-defined V and not spreading out.

❖ Jicama is a tropical root vegetable from Mexico that resembles an overgrown turnip and tastes like a fresh water chestnut. The name means "edible storage root," and this wonderfully versatile vegetable has many uses in addition to stir-frying. Try it as a crudité with light dips, use it as an addition to salads, or by itself with diced fresh oranges and a dusting of powdered chili. If unavailable in your area, substitute rinsed, canned water chestnuts.

❖ Peel the broccoli stems with a sharp paring knife, cut into 2- to 3-inch lengths, and use as a crudité or toss into a salad.

$\mathcal{D}$O-AHEAD PREP:

❖ Remember that stir-frying requires complete organization beforehand since the cooking is done at the last minute. All ingredients should be assembled near the cooking area, ready to be added.

Crispy Oven-Baked Catfish Fillets
with Mustard-Chive Flavor

Serves: 4

*W*hy fry the fish when you can bake it with similar results?

1¼ cups whole grain bread crumbs

1 tablespoon freshly snipped fresh chives or finely minced scallion greens

2 teaspoons finely chopped fresh parsley (Italian is preferable)

1 teaspoon finely minced garlic

½ teaspoon paprika

salt and freshly ground pepper to taste

2 tablespoons olive oil

1 tablespoon grainy-style Dijon mustard

2 teaspoons fresh lemon juice

4 catfish fillets (about 2 pounds)

salt and freshly ground pepper to taste

*G*ARNISH: parsley sprigs and lemon wedges

1. Preheat the oven to 475°F. Spray a small rack that can accommodate the fish in a single layer with nonstick cooking spray. Place the rack in a roasting pan.

2. In a medium bowl, combine the bread crumbs with the chives, parsley, garlic, paprika, salt and pepper and stir until well mixed.

3. In a separate bowl, combine the oil with the mustard and lemon juice; whisk with a fork until smooth.

4. Dip the fish in the mustard mixture and then press into the bread crumbs, coating both sides thoroughly. Place each piece on the prepared rack and bake for 6 to 8 minutes or until cooked through and crisp. (Do not overcook or the fish will be too dry.)

5. Season to taste with salt and pepper and serve hot, garnished with parsley sprigs and lemon wedges.

*V*ARIATIONS:

❖ Turkey breast fillets or pounded chicken breast fillets can be substituted for the fish.

❖ White or sourdough bread crumbs can be substituted for whole grain crumbs.

$\mathcal{C}$OOK NOTES:

❖   Whole grain bread crumbs can easily be prepared by baking any whole grain bread in a 300°F oven for about 10 to 15 minutes. Allow to cool slightly, place in a blender or food processor, and store for several weeks in a tightly sealed container.

❖   Italian flat-leaf parsley, also known as plain-leaf parsley, has a stronger and more intense flavor than the curly leaf variety. Since it is more difficult to find Italian parsley, chop a bunch when you locate it and freeze it in small containers for use in cooking only, not for garnishing.

$\mathcal{D}$O-AHEAD PREP:

❖   The fish can be coated with the crumb mixture earlier in the day and kept in a covered container until ready to bake that evening.

Fish Fillets in Parchment
with Minced Vegetables

*T*he fish fillets in this recipe are sealed in a parchment paper packet with vegetables, seasonings, and liquid and then steamed in the oven to bring out the natural juices and flavors in the ingredients. Parchment paper is the best material to use for the packets. Aluminum foil can be used, but aluminum may react with acids in the wine and affect the taste of the finished dish. Waxed paper should be avoided since it often crumples and the wax can melt off into the food.

1 tablespoon olive oil

2 shallots, peeled and finely chopped

2 stalks celery, finely chopped

2 medium carrots, peeled and finely chopped

1 small tart apple, peeled and finely chopped

1 clove garlic, finely minced

⅓ cup dry vermouth or white wine

3 tablespoons chopped fresh parsley

1½ teaspoons snipped fresh dill or ⅓ teaspoon dried
    dill, crumbled

four 6- to 8-ounce fish fillets such as sole, flounder,
    orange roughy, red snapper, sea bass, striped bass,
    or whitefish

salt and freshly ground white pepper to taste

4 teaspoons lemon juice

1.   Preheat the oven to 400°F.

2.   In a medium nonstick skillet, heat the oil to medium, and sauté the shallots, celery, carrots, and apple for about 5 minutes, stirring often, until softened. Add the garlic and continue to cook, stirring for 30 seconds longer.

3.   Increase the heat to high, add the vermouth or wine, and cook for about 2 minutes. Add the parsley and dill, stir, remove from the heat, and set aside to cool slightly.

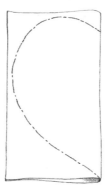

4. Cut 4 sheets of parchment paper into 15-x-20-inch rectangles. Fold each in half crosswise and cut the 15-x-10-inch rectangles into heart shapes with the fold running down the center. Open the hearts.

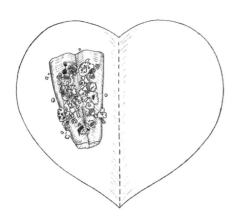

5. Place a fish fillet in the center of half of each heart. (If the fish is too long, cut it in half and place the pieces side by side.) Sprinkle the fish lightly with salt and pepper and distribute the vegetable mixture evenly among the 4 pieces of parchment. Sprinkle each with 1 teaspoon of the lemon juice and fold the heart over the fish and vegetables according to the following method: beginning at the top of the heart, seal the edges by folding over and crimping them all the way around. If the edges are not tightly sealed, the paper won't puff up and create the proper steam to keep the fish moist and juicy.

6. Place the packets on 2 cookie sheets and bake for 12 to 15 minutes, or until the "papillotes" are puffed and lightly browned.

7. Place the packets on individual plates, open, and serve immediately.

*V*ARIATION:

❖ To prepare the fish in aluminum foil packets, place the fish on 4 lightly oiled 14-x-16-inch squares of aluminum foil. Place the cooked vegetable mixture on top, fold over the foil envelope-style, and proceed with the recipe.

*C*OOK NOTE:

❖ When you buy fish, your nose is the most reliable gauge of freshness. The fish should smell like a fresh ocean breeze without a hint of ammonia-like odors. If you are selecting fish in packages at the supermarket, you can often detect a strong odor by smelling the package itself.

*D*O-AHEAD PREP:

❖ The vegetable topping can be prepared a day or two ahead and refrigerated in a covered container. The fish should be cooked just before serving.

Fish Fillets Veracruz Style

Serves: 4

*T*his is a variation on a recipe cooked at the Rancho La Puerta Spa in Tecate, California. Adding garlic with the tomatoes gives the dish a subtler flavor.

As a rule of thumb, cook fish ten minutes per inch at the thickest part of the fish.

1 pound fish fillets (sole, flounder, orange roughy, or other firm,
    fleshy white fish fillets)

1 tablespoon vegetable salt

½ teaspoon lemon juice

½ teaspoon Worcestershire sauce

⅛ teaspoon freshly ground pepper

1 tablespoon olive oil

½ cup sliced onion

1 green bell pepper, seeded and julienned

4 cups peeled, seeded, and chopped tomatoes

½ cup tomato puree

1 clove garlic, finely minced

8 black olives, pitted and halved

2 tablespoon capers, drained

1 tablespoon chopped fresh parsley

salt and freshly ground pepper to taste

*G*ARNISH: sprigs of watercress

1. Place the fish fillets in a single layer in an oven-proof dish. Sprinkle with the vegetable salt, lemon juice, Worcestershire sauce, and pepper. Set aside.

2. Preheat the oven to 350°F.

3. In a heavy nonstick saucepan, heat the olive oil over medium heat. Add the onion and green bell pepper and cook for about 4 to 5 minutes, or until softened and slightly translucent, stirring often.

4. Add the tomatoes, tomato puree, and garlic; bring to a boil. Cover, reduce the heat to medium, and cook for about 7 to 8 minutes, stirring occasionally. Add the olives, capers, parsley, and salt and pepper to taste; stir to combine, and cook uncovered for about 1 minute longer.

5.   Distribute the sauce evenly over the fish, cover the dish, and bake for 8 to 10 minutes, depending on the thickness of the fish.

6.   Serve immediately, garnished with sprigs of watercress.

*V*ARIATIONS:

❖   There are many vegetable salts on the market that can be used, but a mixture of salt, pepper, paprika, garlic powder, and onion powder will work as a substitute.

❖   If there is no time to peel the tomatoes, substitute drained ready-cut peeled tomatoes.

*C*OOK NOTE:

❖   An easy way to peel tomatoes is to drop them whole into boiling water and allow to sit for 1 minute. Remove from the water and the peel can easily be removed with a paring knife.

*D*O-AHEAD PREP:

❖   The sauce can be cooked a day in advance, covered, and chilled until ready to use. Allow the sauce to come to room temperature before using. The fish should be cooked just before serving.

Plaki (*Psari Plaki*)

Serves 8

*P*laki is a traditional Greek method of cooking fish, usually with onions, potatoes, tomatoes, parsley, lemon slices, and olive oil. The fish is arranged over lightly sautéed vegetables and then it is baked or poached. The result is a souplike mixture of vegetables and fish that is low in fat and sodium. The lemons get soft during the cooking process and can be eaten along with the fish, rind and all. A variety of fish fillets can be used for this dish, including catfish, flounder, halibut, John Dory, red snapper, sea bass, sole, and talapia.

4 teaspoons extra-virgin olive oil

1 large onion, thinly sliced

2 large ribs celery, thinly sliced

2 large carrots, peeled and thinly sliced

2 large medium white rose potatoes, thinly sliced

1 green or red bell pepper, seeded and julienned

2 large cloves garlic, finely minced

3 medium tomatoes, cored and roughly chopped

3 tablespoons freshly chopped parsley

1 teaspoon chopped fresh oregano, or ¼ teaspoon dried oregano, crumbled

freshly ground pepper to taste

⅔ cup dry white wine

½ cup Instant Fish Broth (see page 78), defatted chicken broth, or vegetable broth

1 bay leaf

2 pounds fish fillets

1 whole lemon, thinly sliced (including the rind), pits removed

3 tablespoons capers, rinsed and drained

*G*ARNISH: chopped fresh parsley

1. In a deep large nonstick, deep skillet, heat the oil and sauté the onion, celery, carrots, potatoes, and green bell pepper over medium-high heat, stirring often, until the onions and potatoes are translucent, about 5 to 6 minutes. Add the garlic and stir just to combine. Add the tomatoes, parsley, oregano, and pepper; increase the heat, add the wine, and continue to cook for about 3 minutes longer, or until some of the wine has evaporated. Add the broth and bay leaf, bring to a boil, reduce heat, cover, and simmer for 15 to 20 minutes, or until the vegetables are softened. Remove from the heat and set aside.

2. Preheat the oven to 350°F. Lightly coat a deep 9-x-12-inch baking pan that can accommodate the fish in a single layer with olive oil nonstick cooking spray.

3. Place the fish fillets in the prepared pan, place the lemon slices on top of the fish, sprinkle with the capers, top with the cooked vegetable mixture, and bake for about 30 to 35 minutes until soupy and the lemon slices have softened, basting occasionally.

4. Remove the bay leaf and serve hot in deep soup plates garnished with chopped parsley.

Cook Notes:

❖ The rule of thumb when cooking fish is 10 minutes per inch at the thickest point of the fish. Plaki is the exception to the rule; since this is a soup- or stew-type meal, the fish is cooked for a longer time.

❖ Do not store onions with potatoes. Onions release a gas that hastens the spoilage of potatoes.

Do-Ahead Prep:

❖ The base for the Plaki can be prepared through Step 1, earlier in the day, or even a day in advance, and chilled in a covered container until ready to use. The fish should not be cooked until just before serving.

Chilled Trout Fillets
with Creamy Dill Dressing

Serves: 4

*T*his chilled fish dish is easy to prepare a day in advance and is a refreshing and elegant entrée for a summer luncheon or supper.

*P*OACHING LIQUID:

1 cup Instant Fish Broth (see page 78), defatted chicken broth, or
    vegetable broth

¼ cup dry vermouth or white wine

1 leek, thoroughly washed and finely chopped (white part only)

1 thin slice lemon

¼ cup celery leaves

1½ tablespoons snipped fresh dill

6 peppercorns

½ bay leaf

4 to 6 trout fillets

1 cup Creamy Dill Dressing (see page 286)

*G*ARNISH: mixed greens, lemon wedges, cherry tomatoes, dill sprigs

1. In a large nonstick or nonreactive skillet that can accommodate the fish in a single layer, place the poaching liquid ingredients. Bring to a boil, reduce heat, cover, and simmer slowly for 10 minutes.

2. Add the trout fillets in a single layer, return to a boil, reduce the heat, cover, and simmer for 5 to 7 minutes, or until the fish is just flaky.

3. With a spatula, remove the fish from the liquid and place on a plate. Cover with plastic wrap and chill the fish for 4 to 6 hours or overnight.

4. Place a bed of mixed greens on a platter, attractively arrange the fish on top, garnish with lemon wedges, cherry tomatoes, and dill sprigs, and serve chilled or at room temperature topped with a layer of the Yogurt Dill Dressing.

*V*ARIATION:

❖ Orange roughy sea bass, flounder, tilapia, and other fish fillets can be substituted for the trout.

*D*O-AHEAD PREP:

❖ The trout is best cooked a day in advance and well chilled.

Fish Cioppino on a Bed of Linguine

Serves: 6 to 8

*C*ioppino is the San Francisco version of an Italian shellfish stew. It can be served as a complete meal in deep soup plates with lots of Italian bread for dunking. This lighter version uses only firm fleshy fish without the customary clams, mussels, and lobster and is served over a bed of linguine.

The best type of fish to use for this hearty stew is a dense, meaty, compact, less-flaky fish that will hold its shape like monkfish, all varieties of bass including Chilean sea bass and grouper, blackfish, halibut, orange roughy, mahimahi, red and black drum, and salmon. Flakier fish like cod or scrod can be used as well, but should be added at the last minute to prevent overcooking. It is best to use a combination of fish that are currently in season at the best available prices.

Since the clam juice and canned tomatoes have added salt, no extra salt is added to the cioppino.

4 teaspoons olive oil

1 large onion, finely chopped

2 leeks, thoroughly washed and finely chopped (white parts only), or use ½ cup finely chopped scallions

1 green bell pepper, seeded and finely chopped

1 large carrot, peeled and finely chopped

2 large cloves garlic, finely minced

1 cup dry white wine or dry vermouth

one 28-ounce can crushed tomatoes packed in puree

2 tablespoons freshly chopped parsley

1 tablespoon chopped fresh basil, or ½ teaspoon dried basil, crumbled

2 teaspoons chopped fresh oregano, or ½ teaspoon dried oregano, crumbled

2 teaspoons fresh lemon juice

1 bay leaf

freshly ground pepper to taste

1½ cup bottled clam juice or Instant Fish Broth (see page 78)

2 pounds firm, fleshy boned fish, cut into 2½-inch chunks

½ pound fresh or dried linguine

GARNISH: freshly chopped parsley and grated lemon rind

ACCOMPANIMENTS: toasted Italian, French, or sourdough bread slices

1. In a deep nonstick skillet or Dutch oven, heat the oil and sauté the onion, leeks, green bell pepper, and carrot over medium heat until soft, about 6 to 7 minutes. Add the garlic and stir to combine.

2. Increase the heat to high, add the wine, and cook for 2 to 3 minutes, stirring occasionally until most of the wine has evaporated. Add the tomatoes, parsley, basil, oregano, lemon juice, bay leaf, and pepper. Bring to a boil, reduce heat, cover, and simmer slowly for about 45 minutes.

3. When ready to cook the fish, heat the tomato base with the clam juice or fish broth over medium heat for about 3 to 4 minutes until piping hot. Add the fish, cover, and cook for about 6 to 7 minutes until tender and flaky, which is determined by the thickness of the fish.

4. Cook the linguine in boiling water until just al dente, drain, and place in the bottom of 6 to 8 soup plates. Remove the bay leaf, ladle the cioppino into the dishes, garnish with the parsley and grated lemon, and serve immediately accompanied by toasted Italian, French, or sourdough bread slices.

VARIATIONS:

❖ Red wine can be substituted for the white wine.

❖ If you are watching your sodium intake, substitute water or vegetable broth for the clam juice.

❖ If you like a thinner soup, add an extra 8-ounce bottle of clam juice to the cioppino.

COOK NOTE:

❖ If using a variety of fish with different thicknesses, cook the thicker fish for 2 to 3 minutes and then add the thinner fish fillets.

DO-AHEAD PREP:

❖ The base of the stew (prepared through Step 2) can be cooked several days in advance and refrigerated in a covered container, or it can be frozen for several months. Before adding the fish, make sure the base is simmering.

Santa Barbara Shrimp
with Spicy Lemon Garlic Sauce

Serves: 4

*T*his recipe was created by Nobu Matsuhisa, chef/proprietor of the Japanese restaurant Matsuhisa, located in Beverly Hills, Nobu in New York City, and Nobu London. His cuisine combines elements of Japanese and Peruvian cooking with his own unique style. Nobu's dishes are light, refreshing, and always exciting. The giant Santa Barbara shrimp used here come from California, but you can use any variety of extra-large shrimp or scampi available at your local fish market.

8 Santa Barbara shrimp or other very large shrimp

eight ¼-inch-thick slices of onion

3 tablespoons Japanese sake

2 tablespoons plus 1 teaspoon extra-virgin olive oil

2 tablespoons reduced-sodium soy sauce

½ teaspoon minced garlic

2 tablespoons lemon juice

1 teaspoon yuzu vinegar (see Cook Note)

pinch of cayenne pepper

*G*ARNISH: julienned strips of cooked beet, sprigs of cilantro

1. Lightly coat an outdoor or indoor grill, broiler, or a well-seasoned ridged stove-top grill pan with nonstick cooking spray and preheat to medium-high.

2. Butterfly the shrimp by making a deep inciscion in the back of the shrimp to devein and cut almost (but not quite) through to the underside. Spread the shrimp as flat as possible (like an open book). Rinse the shrimp and pat dry with paper towels. Place the shrimp and the onion on the grill and cook until just opaque at the thickest part of the shrimp, about 2 minutes.

3. In a small saucepan, heat the sake, olive oil, soy sauce, and garlic over medium-high heat until boiling. Remove the pan from the heat and add the lemon juice, yuzu vinegar, and cayenne.

4. Arrange 2 shrimp and 2 onion slices on each plate, drizzle with the sauce, garnish with the beet and cilantro, and serve immediately.

*V*ARIATION:

❖ Dry sherry can be substituted for the sake.

$\mathscr{C}$OOK NOTE:

❖   Yuzu vinegar is available at Asian groceries and health food stores. It is a tart seasoning made from the juice of the yuzu, a unique Japanese yellow citrus fruit. Since ancient times the yuzu has been respected as a "royal" fruit, gracing gardens and temple grounds and taking a central role in village celebrations. Yuzu vinegar is very versatile, adding a refreshing citrus flavor to salads and vegetables, soups, stews, and fish dishes, and can be used as a condiment or addition to sauces. If you can't find it, an equal amount of fresh lemon juice may be substituted.

$\mathscr{D}$O-AHEAD PREP:

❖   The ingredients can be readied earlier in the day, but the dish should be cooked just before serving.

Stir-Fried Szechuan Shrimp
and Asparagus

Serves: 4 to 6

*Y*ou don't need expensive jumbo shrimp for this recipe. Just use the medium ones and peel them yourself or ask the fishmonger who may have the time to peel the shrimp for you while you do the rest of your marketing.

1½ pounds fresh shrimp, peeled and deveined

2 tablespoons cornstarch

1 pound fresh asparagus

2 tablespoons minced scallion greens

1 teaspoon minced garlic

1 teaspoon minced ginger

SEASONING SAUCE:

½ cup defatted chicken broth

2 tablespoons reduced-sodium soy sauce

2 tablespoons dry sherry

1 tablespoon Asian-style sesame oil

1 tablespoon Chinese vinegar, Japanese vinegar, or balsamic
    vinegar

2 teaspoons sugar

2 teaspoons cornstarch

1 to 2 teaspoons hot bean paste, or to taste

2 tablespoons peanut oil

GARNISH: sprigs of cilantro

ACCOMPANIMENT: steamed white rice

1. Dust the shrimp lightly with cornstarch and set aside near cooking area.

2. Break off the tough, rubbery stalk ends of asparagus and discard. Cut the asparagus on the diagonal into 1-inch pieces and set aside near the cooking area along with the scallions, garlic, and ginger.

3. Combine the ingredients for the seasoning sauce and whisk until smooth.

4. Heat a nonstick wok or large skillet, add 1 tablespoon of the oil, and cook un-

til hot and just smoking. Add the asparagus and stir-fry for 3 to 4 minutes, or until just tender. Remove from the pan and set aside.

5. Add the remaining 1 tablespoon of the oil to the wok, heat, and then stir-fry the scallions, garlic, and ginger for 30 seconds. Add the shrimp and continue to stir-fry until they turn pink, about 2 to 3 minutes.

6. Return the asparagus to the pan, toss, pour in the sauce, stir well, cover, reduce heat to medium, and cook for about 1 to 2 minutes longer.

7. Serve immediately over steamed white rice.

𝒱ARIATION:

❖ Use any firm flesh white fish such as swordfish, halibut, or shark.

𝒞OOK NOTES:

❖ Hot bean paste is available at Asian groceries or some gourmet shops. If you cannot locate this item, add Tabasco Sauce to taste.

❖ The ideal way to store fresh gingerroot is unwrapped in the refrigerator or freezer; it will keep for up to 3 to 4 weeks. Do not wrap the ginger in plastic wrap or aluminum foil, which traps the moisture and may cause the ginger to form mold.

𝒟O-AHEAD PREP:

❖ The ingredients can be readied earlier in the day, but the dish should be cooked just before serving.

Shrimp Curry with Braised Cucumbers

Serves: 4

*T*his dish may surprise your guests if they've only seen cucumbers in salads or as part of a raw vegetable plate. Cucumbers absorb the flavor of the curry sauce and add an interesting texture to the dish.

As in most stir-fried dishes, the ingredients must be prepared in advance and placed in close proximity to the cooking area.

*S*AUCE:

¾ cup Instant Fish Broth (see page 78) or defatted chicken broth

1 tablespoon cornstarch mixed with 2 tablespoons cold water

1 tablespoon reduced-sodium soy sauce

1 teaspoon sugar

½ teaspoon Asian-style sesame oil

4 teaspoons peanut oil

4 scallions (green and white parts included), finely chopped

2 teaspoons finely minced garlic

1 teaspoon finely minced ginger

1 large European hothouse cucumber, split and cut into julienne strips, or 2 medium cucumbers, peeled, seeded, and cut into julienne strips

1 pound medium shrimp, peeled and deveined

2 to 3 teaspoons curry powder, or to taste

*G*ARNISH: toasted pine nuts and minced scallion greens

*A*CCOMPANIMENTS: steamed white or brown rice and Apricot Chutney (see page 53) or mango chutney

1. In a small bowl, whisk the sauce ingredients together and place near the cooking area.

2. In a nonstick wok or large skillet, heat 2 teaspoons of the oil over high heat and stir-fry the scallions, garlic, and ginger for 30 seconds. Add the cucumber and continue to stir-fry for 1 to 2 minutes or until just softened. Remove the cucumber from the pan and set aside.

3. Heat the remaining 2 teaspoons of the oil over high heat and stir-fry the shrimp over high heat, for about 2 to 3 minutes, or until they just turn pink. Add the curry powder and stir to combine. Add the sauce and stir; bring to a boil, return the cooked cucumbers, and continue to cook for 1 minute longer, or until warmed through.

4. Serve the curry hot over steamed white or brown rice accompanied by Apricot Chutney or mango chutney, and garnished with toasted pine nuts and minced scallion greens.

VARIATIONS:

❖ Bay scallops or halved sea scallops can be substituted for the shrimp but cooked only 1 minute, or until they turn opaque.

❖ The cucumbers can be cut into ½-inch circles.

❖ Zucchini can be substituted for the cucumbers.

COOK NOTE:

❖ Store cucumbers, unwashed, in a perforated plastic bag in the refrigerator.

DO-AHEAD PREP:

❖ The ingredients can be readied earlier in the day, but the dish should be cooked just before serving.

Stir-Fried Scallops with Black Bean Sauce

Serves: 4

*B*ay scallops are smaller than sea scallops and tend to be sweeter. Avoid the "fake" scallops, which are usually composed of inexpensive pollack and skate and give real scallops a bad name.

1 pound bay scallops or sea scallops, halved

1 sweet red, yellow, or green bell pepper, seeded and julienned

1 cup broccoli florets, washed and dried

*F*LAVORING INGREDIENTS:

4 teaspoons fermented black beans

2 scallions (green parts only), finely chopped

2 cloves garlic, finely chopped

1 quarter-size piece of ginger

*S*AUCE:

1 cup Instant Fish Broth (see page 78) or defatted chicken broth

2 tablespoons reduced-sodium soy sauce

1 tablespoon cornstarch mixed with 2 tablespoons cold water

1 tablespoon dry sherry

4 teaspoons peanut oil

*G*ARNISH: minced scallion greens

*A*CCOMPANIMENTS: steamed white rice or cooked noodles

1.　Rinse the scallops under cold running water. Blot dry on paper towels and place near the cooking area alongside the julienned red bell pepper and broccoli florets.

2.　In a small food processor or by hand, chop the black beans with the scallions, garlic, and ginger until just fine, and place on a plate near the cooking area.

3.　In a small bowl, combine the sauce ingredients, stir until smooth, and set near the cooking area.

4.　In a nonstick wok or large skillet, heat 3 teaspoons of the oil to high and stir-fry the red pepper and broccoli for 1 to 2 minutes, until just softened; add the scallops and continue to stir-fry until the scallops are just opaque, about 1 to 2 minutes. With a slotted spoon, remove the scallops and vegetables from the pan and set aside.

5. Add the remaining 1 teaspoon of the oil; add the flavoring ingredients and stir-fry for 30 seconds. Stir the sauce to make sure the cornstarch is thoroughly mixed, and then add the mixture; bring to a boil. Add the reserved scallops and vegetables and stir-fry for an additional minute to just heat through.

6. Serve the scallops hot over steamed white rice or cooked noodles garnished with minced scallion greens.

*V*ARIATIONS:

❖ 2-inch pieces of blanched green beans, asparagus tips, thick slices of celery, or other seasonal vegetables can be substituted for the broccoli florets.

❖ Peeled and deveined medium shrimp can be substituted for the scallops.

*C*OOK NOTES:

❖ Salted black beans or fermented black beans (not to be confused with black beans used in Western cooking) are small black soybeans that are preserved by a complicated process of fermenting, steaming, and combining with salt and spices. Black beans need to be crushed to release their aromatic flavor in cooking. Purchase the beans in plastic bags and store them for at least a year in an airtight container in the refrigerator or in a cool place away from light and heat.

❖ Select fresh white, plump scallops with no "fishy" odor. The scallops should be moist but not sitting in water.

*D*O-AHEAD PREP:

❖ The ingredients can be readied earlier in the day, but the dish should be cooked just before serving.

Spicy Clams in Tomato Sauce
with Cumin Flavor
Serves: 4 to 6

*U*se small-size hard-shelled clams for this dish, either the East Coast littlenecks or cherrystones or the West Coast Pacific littleneck or Puget Sound sweet butter clams.

The clams are easily cleaned by soaking them in water with cornmeal, cream of wheat, or semolina added. The clams take in the grain and spit it out with any sand that might be lurking inside.

3 pounds (about 24) small hard-shelled clams

1 teaspoon cornmeal, cream of wheat, or semolina

2 teaspoons olive oil

3 shallots, finely chopped

2 teaspoons finely minced garlic

1 teaspoon finely minced ginger

1 teaspoon seeded and diced jalapeño pepper, or to taste

½ teaspoon ground cumin

½ cup dry white wine or vermouth

one 14½-ounce can ready-cut diced canned tomatoes

½ cup clam broth, Instant Fish Broth (see page 78), or defatted chicken broth

salt and freshly ground pepper to taste

*G*ARNISH: chopped fresh cilantro

*A*CCOMPANIMENTS: Italian, French, or sourdough bread

1. Place the clams in a bowl with salted cold water to cover. Add the cornmeal and allow to sit for 10 minutes. Rinse the clams and place in a colander.

2. In a nonstick Dutch oven or deep saucepan, heat the oil over medium heat and sauté the shallots for 5 to 6 minutes, stirring often, until softened. Add the garlic, ginger, jalapeño pepper, and cumin and stir for 30 seconds.

3. Increase the heat to high, add the wine and cook, stirring occasionally until almost all the liquid has evaporated. Add the tomatoes, broth, and salt and pepper; bring to a boil, cover, reduce heat, and simmer for 10 minutes, stirring occasionally.

4.   Increase the heat to medium-high, carefully add the clams, cover again, and cook for 5 to 6 minutes, or until the clam shells have opened, shaking the pan occasionally.

5.   Discard any unopened clams and serve hot in deep soup plates, garnished with the cilantro and accompanied by thick warm slices of bread to dip in the liquid.

*V*ARIATION:

❖   Mussels can be substituted for the clams.

*C*OOK NOTES:

❖   When purchasing hard-shelled clams make sure the shells are tightly closed, which means the clam is alive and fresh. If a shell is slightly open, tap it lightly and if it doesn't snap shut that means the clam has died and should be tossed out. Also discard any clams with broken shells.

❖   Cumin, also known as *comino,* is a spice that dates from the Old Testament. It has a very distinctive and pronounced strong flavor so it should be used sparingly or it will dominate the flavor of the dish. If you can find the seeds, grind the cumin with a mortar and pestle since the flavorful oil escapes rapidly after grinding. Store cumin seeds away from the light in a cool, dark, dry place.

*D*O-AHEAD PREP:

❖   Do not clean the clams until ready to cook. The remaining ingredients can be readied earlier in the day, but the dish should be prepared at the last minute.

Meats

Grilled Flank Steak with Mustard Sauce
and Green Peppercorns

Meat Loaf with Porcini Mushrooms

Beef Burgundy with Porcini Mushrooms and Pearl Onions

Cajun Veal Chops

Braised Veal Brisket

Veal Ragout with Mushrooms and Ripe Olives

Grilled Osso Buco

Veal and Turkey Loaf with Sun-Dried Tomato Pesto

Rack of Lamb with Pistachio-Mint Crumb Crust
and Tangy Mint Sauce

Grilled Chinese Marinated Butterflied Leg of Lamb

Lamb and Golden Potato Stew with Baby Onions
and Baby Carrots

Braised Lamb Curry

Grilled Pork Tenderloin with Hoisin Mustard Glaze

Pork Chops with Sweet and Sour Sauce

Grilled Flank Steak with Mustard Sauce and Green Peppercorns

Serves: 6

*F*lank steak requires marinating to heighten both flavor and texture. Supermarkets carry small flank steaks, so it may be necessary to use two one-pound steaks to make this recipe.

2 pounds flank steak, trimmed of all visible fat

*M*ARINADE:

2 tablespoons olive oil

2 tablespoons balsamic vinegar

2 cloves garlic, finely minced

2 tablespoons grainy-style Dijon mustard

1 tablespoon Worcestershire sauce

salt and freshly ground pepper

*S*AUCE:

2 teaspoons olive oil

¼ cup finely chopped onion or shallot

2 tablespoons dry white wine or vermouth

⅓ cup defatted chicken or beef broth

2 tablespoons grainy-style Dijon mustard

1 teaspoon dry mustard

2 teaspoons green peppercorns

salt and freshly ground white pepper

2 tablespoons freshly chopped parsley

*G*ARNISH: sprigs of parsley

1. Place the steak in a large glass, ceramic, or other nonreactive dish, or a sealable plastic bag.

2. In a medium bowl, whisk the marinade ingredients together, pour over the meat, coat both sides, cover or seal, and allow to marinate at room temperature for 1 hour, or in the refrigerator for 3 to 4 hours.

3. Lightly coat an outdoor or indoor grill, broiler, or a well-seasoned ridged stove-top grill pan with nonstick cooking spray and preheat to medium-high.

4. Remove the steak from the marinade and grill for 5 minutes on each side or until cooked to the desired doneness, basting occasionally with the marinade. Transfer the meat to a carving board and allow to stand for 5 minutes before slicing.

5. In a small nonstick saucepan, heat the oil to medium and sauté the onion, stirring often, until softened and glazed, about 6 to 7 minutes.

6. Increase the heat to high, add the wine, and allow the liquid to evaporate. Add the broth and cook for 2 minutes longer, stirring often. Whisk in the remaining ingredients, except the parsley, until smooth. Remove from the heat, stir in the parsley, and place in a small bowl.

7. Slice the meat on a slant crosswise, against the grain, and serve garnished with the parsley and accompanied by the sauce.

*V*ARIATION:

❖ Skirt steak can be substituted for flank steak.

*C*OOK NOTES:

❖ It is important to slice the meat across the grain so that the meat will remain tender.

❖ Green peppercorns are the soft, underripe berries that are usually preserved in brine. They have a fresh flavor that's less pungent than the berry in its other forms.

*D*O-AHEAD PREP:

❖ The steak can be marinated overnight. The sauce can be prepared an hour in advance and reheated before serving.

Meat Loaf with Porcini Mushrooms

Serves: 8 to 10

This is comfort food at its finest, rich in childhood memories and redolent with strong flavors. I cook this dish in a fat-free meat loaf pan, which is available at gourmet shops. If you cannot find this type of pan, then cook the shaped loaf on a rack in a larger pan.

The loaf is sensational served cold the next day.

1 ounce dried porcini mushrooms

¾ cup quick-cooking oatmeal (not instant)

2 teaspoons olive oil

1 large onion, finely chopped

1 clove garlic, finely minced

1 pound very lean ground beef

1 lean turkey sausage, casing removed and finely chopped (optional)

2 tablespoons Dijon mustard, grainy style preferred

2 tablespoons freshly chopped parsley

2 tablespoons freshly chopped basil

2 tablespoons freshly grated Parmesan cheese

1 whole egg, lightly beaten

1 egg white, lightly beaten

salt and freshly ground pepper to taste

one 6-ounce can tomato paste

GARNISH: basil leaves

1. Soak the mushrooms in ½ cup hot water until softened, about 20 minutes. Strain the mushrooms, finely chop, and set aside. Strain the reserved mushroom liquid into a small bowl, stir in the oatmeal, and allow to sit at room temperature.

2. Preheat the oven to 350°F. Coat a 9-x-5-x-3-inch nonstick loaf pan with nonstick cooking spray.

3. In a small skillet, heat the oil and sauté the onion over medium-high heat, stirring often, until the onion is lightly golden, about 6 to 7 minutes. Add the garlic and stir to just combine the flavors, for 30 seconds. Remove the skillet from the heat, transfer the onions to a large bowl, and allow to cool slightly.

4.   Add the remaining ingredients to the onions, including the chopped mushrooms and oatmeal, mixing with your hands until well combined and place in the prepared loaf pan. Spread the tomato paste to cover the loaf.

5.   Bake for 1 hour. Remove the pan from the oven and allow it to sit for about 10 minutes to allow the flavors to develop and to make it easier to slice the loaf. Slice and serve the loaf garnished with basil leaves.

*C*OOK NOTE:

❖   A meat loaf cooked in a loaf pan will be juicier than one patted into a shape and cooked in a larger pan.

*D*O-AHEAD PREP:

❖   The meat loaf can be shaped earlier in the day, wrapped tightly, and refrigerated until ready to cook.

Beef Burgundy with Porcini Mushrooms and Pearl Onions

Serves: 6 to 8

*T*he flavor of the dried porcini mushrooms adds richness to the broth without added fat.

1 ounce dried porcini or mixed dried mushrooms

1 cup hot water

⅓ cup all-purpose flour

2 pounds lean beef, cut into 1½-inch cubes

1½ tablespoons olive oil

2 medium onions, finely chopped

¾ pound fresh mushrooms, stems removed, wiped clean and
    sliced

2 large cloves garlic, finely minced

1½ cups dry red wine

1½ cups defatted beef broth

bouquet garni (1 bay leaf and sprig each of fresh thyme, oregano,
    and parsley tied in cheesecloth)

salt and freshly ground pepper

1 pound small pearl onions, trimmed and peeled

*G*ARNISH: freshly chopped parsley

*A*CCOMPANIMENT: cooked broad noodles

1. Preheat the oven to 325°F.

2. Place the porcini mushrooms in a small bowl, cover with the hot water, and allow to soak for 20 minutes, until softened. Strain, reserve liquid, chop the mushrooms and set aside.

3. Place the flour in a resealable plastic bag. Add the beef, seal tightly, and shake. Remove the beef from the bag and shake off any excess flour.

4. In a large nonstick Dutch oven or large deep saucepan, heat the oil to medium-high, and sauté the beef cubes on all sides until golden brown. Remove, and set aside. (If your pan cannot hold the meat in one layer, sauté it in batches.)

5. Add the chopped onions and fresh mushrooms to the pan and continue to sauté over medium heat, for about 5 to 7 minutes, until softened, stirring often. Add the garlic and sauté for an additional 30 seconds.

6. Increase the heat to high, add the wine, and allow the liquid to reduce for 2 to 3 minutes, stirring often. Add the reserved beef, broth, reserved mushroom broth and porcini mushrooms, bouquet garni, and salt and pepper. Cover and place in preheated oven for 1½ hours, stirring every 30 minutes.

7. Add the small pearl onions, stir into the stew, cover, and return to the oven for an additional 30 to 40 minutes, or until the onions and meat are very tender.

8. Remove the herb bouquet and discard. Serve the stew hot over cooked broad noodles garnished with freshly chopped parsley.

*V*ARIATIONS:

❖ The stew can be cooked on top of the range at a very slow simmer instead of baking in the oven.

❖ Lamb or veal can be substituted for the beef.

*C*OOK NOTES:

❖ An easy way to peel onions is to make a tiny crisscross incision in the root end, drop them into boiling water for 1 to 2 minutes, drain, and plunge into a bowl of ice water. The peel will pop off easily.

❖ A bouquet garni is a bunch of herbs that are tied together or placed in a cheesecloth bag and used to flavor soups and stews. Tying or bagging the herbs allows for easy removal before serving.

❖ Porcini, the most celebrated Italian mushrooms, belong to the same species (*Boletus edulis*) as the mushrooms called cèpes in France or Steinpilze in Germany. Whatever the type of dried mushrooms you select, they should be soaked before using in hot, not boiling, water for at least 15 to 20 minutes, then drained. Strain the soaking liquid, which can be stored indefinitely in the refrigerator to add flavor to soups and stews.

*D*O-AHEAD PREP:

❖ This stew can be prepared several days in advance and chilled in a covered container or it can be frozen successfully for several months.

Cajun Veal Chops

Serves: 6

*C*ook these spicy chops on an outdoor grill for optimum flavor. The best way to grill meat outdoors is to sear it on both sides first and then continue to grill, turning often until cooked evenly.

6 loin veal chops, cut 1 inch thick

*M*ARINADE:

¼ cup olive oil

¼ cup fresh lime juice

2 cloves garlic, finely minced

1 thin slice ginger, finely minced

1 tablespoon chili powder

2 teaspoons dry mustard

1 teaspoon paprika

½ teaspoon mustard seeds

½ teaspoon cayenne pepper, or to taste

salt to taste

_G_ARNISH: sprigs of cilantro

1. Place the chops in a deep nonreactive dish or resealable plastic bag. In a food processor or blender, or by hand, combine the marinade ingredients and process until smooth. Pour the marinade over the chops, cover or seal tightly, and marinate for 1 hour at room temperature or 4 to 6 hours in refrigerator, turning occasionally. Bring the meat to room temperature before grilling.

2. Lightly coat an outdoor or indoor grill, broiler, or a well-seasoned ridged stove-top grill pan with nonstick cooking spray and preheat to medium-high.

3. Remove the chops from the marinade and grill until just pink on the inside, about 4 to 5 minutes per side, turning and basting often with the marinade. Do not overcook veal or it will toughen.

4. Serve the chops hot, garnished with sprigs of cilantro.

*V*ARIATION:

❖ Avocado or canola oil can be substituted for olive oil.

COOK NOTES:

❖ You get the most amount of juice from a lime if you squeeze it at room temperature.

❖ Resealable plastic bags are perfect for marinating foods. Place both the meat and the marinade in the bag, seal tightly, and you can turn the food easily without dirtying your hands.

DO-AHEAD PREP:

❖ The chops can be marinated overnight but should be grilled just before serving.

Braised Veal Brisket

Serves: 4 to 6

Veal brisket is actually the breast of veal with the bones removed. It is a lean cut of meat that becomes quite tender when marinated and then slowly braised. Veal brisket has a more subtle flavor than beef brisket; prepared in this way it makes a comforting but light dinner on a cold night.

two 1-pound veal briskets

1½ cups red wine

1½ tablespoons Worcestershire sauce

1 teaspoon freshly minced garlic

1 teaspoon freshly ground white pepper

1 bay leaf

2 tablespoons olive oil

1 large onion, roughly chopped

2 medium carrots, peeled and finely chopped

2 tablespoons all-purpose flour

1 teaspoon paprika

salt to taste

1 cup beer

½ cup chili sauce

GARNISH: parsley sprigs

ACCOMPANIMENTS: cooked noodles or steamed white rice

1.   Place the veal briskets in a resealable plastic bag. Add ¾ cup of the wine, Worcestershire sauce, ½ teaspoon of the garlic, white pepper, and bay leaf. Seal the bag tightly and turn several times to mix the ingredients; allow the briskets to marinate for 6 hours or overnight in the refrigerator.

2.   In a nonstick deep saucepan, heat 1 tablespoon of the oil to medium and sauté the onion and carrots for about 5 minutes, stirring often, until softened. Transfer the cooked vegetables to a bowl with a slotted spoon.

3.   Drain off the marinade from the meat and set aside. Pat the flour, paprika, and salt onto the meat. Heat the remaining 1 tablespoon oil in the pan and brown the seasoned meat over high heat until golden all over. Add the beer, the remaining ¾ cup wine, chili sauce, remaining ½ teaspoon garlic, and reserved vegetables and marinade. (The meat should be covered by the liquid.) Bring to a boil, cover, reduce heat, and simmer slowly, turning occasionally, for about 2½ hours or until very tender. Remove and discard the bay leaf.

4.   Remove the meat from the gravy, wrap it tightly in aluminum foil, place the gravy in a sealed container, and refrigerate both overnight.

5.   Skim the fat from the gravy and discard; slice the brisket and place in the gravy. Reheat the brisket on top of the range or in a 325°F oven until piping hot. Serve the meat and gravy accompanied by cooked noodles or steamed white rice, garnished with parsley.

𝒱ARIATION:

❖   Red wine can be substituted for the beer.

𝒞OOK NOTE:

❖   Since warm beer has more flavor, allow the beer to come to room temperature before adding to a recipe. The beer used can be fresh or flat, but flat beer is easier to measure. If you use fresh beer, do not include the foaming head in the measurement.

𝒟O-AHEAD PREP:

❖   Since brisket improves on standing, it is advisable to cook this dish at least one to two days in advance and refrigerate it covered until ready to reheat and serve. The meat can be sliced, returned to the gravy, and frozen. To reheat, defrost the night before, skim for fat, and place in a 325°F oven until piping hot.

Veal Ragout with Mushrooms and Ripe Olives

Serves: 10 to 12

*T*his is a great stew to prepare in advance and reheat for a fabulous and comforting fall or winter dinner party.

1½ ounce dried porcini mushrooms

4 pounds lean boneless veal stew meat, cut into 1½-inch pieces

¼ cup all-purpose flour

2 tablespoons olive oil

2 medium onions, finely chopped

¾ pound mushrooms, stems removed, wiped clean and thinly
    sliced

2 cloves garlic, finely minced

¾ cup dry vermouth or white wine

1 pound plum tomatoes, peeled, seeded, and roughly chopped or
    14½-ounce can ready-cut diced tomatoes, drained

1½ cups defatted chicken broth

1 tablespoon tomato paste

1 tablespoon grainy-style Dijon mustard

1 teaspoon currant jelly

1½ teaspoons finely chopped fresh thyme or ½ teaspoon dried
    thyme, crumbled

¼ teaspoon paprika

1 bay leaf

salt and freshly ground pepper to taste

12 pitted green olives

12 pitted black olives

*G*ARNISHES: chopped fresh Italian parsley and grated lemon
    rind

*A*CCOMPANIMENT: cooked broad noodles

1. Soak the porcini mushrooms in ¾ cup hot water for about 20 minutes, or until softened. Drain, chop mushrooms roughly, and strain and reserve the liquid.

2. Preheat the oven to 325°F.

3. Place the flour in a resealable plastic bag. Add the veal, seal tightly, and shake. Remove the veal from the bag and shake off any excess flour.

4. In a nonstick Dutch oven or large deep saucepan, heat 1½ tablespoons of the oil to medium-high and sauté the veal in batches, on all sides, until lightly browned. Remove the meat with a slotted spoon and set aside.

5. Add the remaining ½ tablespoon of olive oil and sauté the onions and fresh mushrooms, stirring often, until softened, about 5 to 7 minutes. Add the garlic and toss for 30 seconds.

6. Increase the heat to high, add the vermouth or wine, bring to a boil, and deglaze the pan, stirring constantly and scraping the browned particles into the sauce. Add the tomatoes, broth, tomato paste, mustard, currant jelly, thyme, paprika, bay leaf, and salt and pepper and stir to combine. Return the veal to the pan with the porcini and reserved mushroom liquid, bring to a boil, cover, and place in the preheated oven for 1½ hours or until the veal is tender.

7. Add the olives, stir to combine, and continue to bake for an additional 10 minutes.

8. Remove the bay leaf and discard; adjust the seasonings to taste. Serve the stew piping hot, over cooked broad noodles, garnished with chopped parsley and grated lemon.

*V*ARIATIONS:

❖ This dish can easily be prepared by cooking at a slow simmer on top of the range instead of in the oven.

❖ Beef or lamb can be substituted for the veal.

*C*OOK NOTES:

❖ Do not crumble bay leaves. Use them whole and always remember to remove them before serving.

❖ When storing extra-ripe black or green olives in the refrigerator, add a few tablespoons of vodka to the container. It keeps the olives fresh and imparts no change in flavor.

*D*O-AHEAD PREP:

❖ The stew can be prepared several days in advance and kept in a covered container in the refrigerator or it can be frozen successfully for several months.

Grilled Osso Buco

Serves: 6

*T*his recipe is a lightened variation of one served at the Al Forno restaurant in Providence, Rhode Island. The veal is grilled before braising, which not only eliminates fat but adds a wonderful flavor to the finished osso buco.

6 large veal shanks (ossi buchi), cut 1½ to 2 inches thick

1 tablespoon olive oil

2 ounces diced prosciutto

1 large onion, finely chopped

3 leeks, thoroughly washed and finely chopped (white parts only)

3 large carrots, peeled and finely chopped

3 large ribs celery, finely chopped

2 cups diced butternut squash (about a 2- to 3-pound squash), cut into 1-inch square pieces (Note: You can microwave the whole squash for 5 to 7 minutes to make cutting it easier.)

2½ teaspoons finely minced garlic

¾ cup dry white wine or vermouth

two 14½-ounce cans ready-cut tomatoes, including liquid

2 cups defatted chicken or beef broth

1 piece orange peel

1 piece lemon peel

½ teaspoon chopped fresh thyme leaves or ⅛ teaspoon dried thyme, crumbled

1 bay leaf

salt and freshly ground pepper to taste

*G*ARNISH: chopped parsley mixed with chopped lemon peel

1. Lightly coat an outdoor or indoor grill, broiler, or a well-seasoned ridged stove-top grill pan with nonstick cooking spray and preheat to medium-high.

2. Coat the veal shanks on all sides with olive oil nonstick cooking spray and grill for 4 minutes a side, or until well seared. Remove from the grill and set aside.

3. Preheat the oven to 325°F.

4. In a nonstick Dutch oven or large deep saucepan that will accommodate the veal in a single layer, heat the oil to medium and sauté the prosciutto for 2 minutes, stirring often. Add the onion, leeks, carrots, and celery and cook, stirring often, until the vegetables are softened, about 5 to 6 minutes. Add the squash, and cook for an additional 2 minutes. Add the garlic, and stir to combine for 30 seconds.

5. Increase the heat to high, add the wine, and cook until most of the liquid has been reduced. Add the remaining ingredients, place the grilled veal shanks in a single layer in the pan, bring to a boil, cover, and bake for about 1½ hours or until the meat is *very* tender.

6. Remove the bay leaf and orange and lemon peel and serve the meat and sauce garnished with a mixture of chopped parsley and lemon peel.

*V*ARIATION:

❖ The meat can be removed to a platter and the sauce pureed in a food mill.

*C*OOK NOTES:

❖ Osso buco, literally translated from Italian as "hole in the bone," is prepared from veal shank bones with the piece of bone in the middle, open and revealing a section of delicious marrow that is meant to be eaten with a special small fork.

❖ Make friends with the butcher and have him or her cut the shanks to order. Warn him or her not to remove the skin enveloping the shanks, which helps to hold them together. It is best to have the osso buco cut no more than 2 inches thick. The thicker pieces may look more impressive but they take too long to become tender.

*D*O-AHEAD PREP:

❖ Osso buco can be completely prepared a day or two in advance and chilled in a covered container until ready to cook. Remove any excess congealed fat and reheat the osso buco very slowly in a warm oven or at a slow simmer on top of the range. It may be necessary to add a little more broth if the dish has thickened on standing. Osso buco can also be frozen successfully for several months.

Veal and Turkey Loaf
with Sun-Dried Tomato Pesto

*T*here is very little fat remaining in the pan after cooking this flavorful and healthful loaf. Serve the loaf hot, at room temperature, or cold sliced with spicy mustard.

¾ cup sun-dried tomatoes, soaked in hot water to cover for 15 minutes

½ pound lean ground turkey

½ pound lean ground veal

1 small onion

¾ cup quick-cooking oatmeal (not instant)

one 6-ounce can tomato paste

1 whole egg

1 tablespoon grainy-style Dijon mustard

2 teaspoons finely minced garlic

1½ teaspoons Worcestershire sauce

¼ teaspoon celery seed

salt and freshly ground pepper to taste

*T*OPPING: 1 cup Sun-Dried Tomato Pesto (see page 58)

1. Preheat the oven to 350°F. Generously coat a 9-x-5-x-3-inch loaf pan with nonstick cooking spray.

2. Squeeze the moisture from the sun-dried tomatoes, cut them into 2 to 3 pieces, and set aside.

3. In a large bowl, place the turkey and veal. Grate the onion with a wide juicing grater or finely mince and mix with the meats.

4. Combine the remaining ingredients and mix with your hands until well blended. Layer half the mixture on the bottom of the pan, flatten evenly with a spatula, and place the soaked tomatoes on top. Place the remaining mixture over and coat the loaf with the tomato pesto.

5. Bake for 1 hour, remove from oven, place on platter, and serve hot, at room temperature, or cold.

*V*ARIATION:

❖ The loaf can be prepared with chicken instead of turkey, all turkey, or all veal.

*C*OOK NOTE:

❖ Other than the Scottish people, who have consumed vast quantities of oats for centuries, the rest of the world has used oats primarily to feed animals. Following the oat bran craze, we have been awakened to the benefits of grains, particularly oats. Oats are an excellent source of complex carbohydrates and both soluble and insoluble fiber. Oats contain about 50 percent more protein than bulgur wheat and twice as much as brown rice. Oats are a good source of iron and manganese, copper, folacin, vitamin E, and zinc. Though oats are higher in fat than other grains, the fat is 80 percent unsaturated.

*D*O-AHEAD PREP:

❖ The loaf can be shaped earlier in the day, covered, and chilled until ready to cook. The loaf can also be cooked earlier in the day, or even a day in advance, chilled, and reheated before serving.

Rack of Lamb with Pistachio-Mint Crumb Crust and Tangy Mint Sauce

Serves: 6

*E*ither the rib or loin lamb racks can be used for this delicious recipe. Have the butcher cut through the bone connecting the ribs so that the chops can be easily cut after roasting.

If fresh mint is unavailable, try making the sauce with any other fresh herb that is in abundant supply—basil, chives, dill, or even parsley. Avoid using dried herbs for this dish, which should be reserved for slow-cooked soups and stews.

> 2 racks of lamb (1½ to 2 pounds each), very well trimmed of all visible fat

*C*OATING INGREDIENTS:

1 cup dry white bread crumbs

3 tablespoons grainy-style Dijon mustard

2 tablespoons extra-virgin olive oil

2 tablespoons pistachio nuts, chopped

2 tablespoons finely chopped fresh mint

1 tablespoon finely chopped fresh parsley

1 tablespoon snipped fresh chives

2 teaspoons freshly minced garlic

2 teaspoons Worcestershire sauce

salt and freshly ground pepper to taste

*M*INT SAUCE:

¼ cup defatted chicken or beef broth

½ cup fresh mint, finely chopped

3 tablespoons raspberry (or other sweet-tasting) vinegar

2 tablespoons snipped fresh chives

1½ tablespoons extra-virgin olive oil

salt and freshly ground pepper to taste

*G*ARNISH: sprigs of mint

1. Preheat the oven to 425°F. Place the lamb fat-side up in a roasting pan.

2. Combine the coating ingredients in a bowl and mix until well combined. Pat the lamb dry with a paper towel and press the coating ingredients on top of the lamb, covering the surface.

3. Roast the lamb for 25 to 30 minutes, or until a meat thermometer registers 135°F for medium-rare. Remove the racks to a platter and allow to stand for 10 minutes.

4. Combine the mint sauce ingredients in a food processor and pulse until combined.

4. Carve the lamb into chops and serve hot, accompanied by the mint sauce and garnished with sprigs of mint.

*V*ARIATION:

❖ Substitute whole wheat bread crumbs for the dry white bread crumbs.

*C*OOK NOTES:

❖ Bunches of mint can be wrapped in foil and frozen. Just cut off what you need and chop.

❖ When buying racks of lamb inspect the rib bones. If they are pink, the lamb is young and more juicy and flavorful; if white, the lamb is more mature and will be tougher and more gamey in flavor.

*D*O-AHEAD PREP:

❖ The rack of lamb can be coated earlier in the day and kept refrigerated until ready to roast. Allow the lamb to sit at room temperature for one hour before cooking.

Grilled Chinese Marinated Butterflied Leg of Lamb

*B*utterflied leg of lamb is lamb that has been boned and left open so that the meat resembles a steak. It may look jagged and lopsided but after marinating and grilling, it is transformed into an incredible dish. This delicious recipe was inspired by a recipe in *Gourmet* magazine.

MARINADE:

½ cup hoisin sauce

⅓ cup finely minced scallions (green and white parts included)

3 tablespoons Asian-style sesame oil

3 tablespoons well-aged Chinese dark Chinkiang vinegar or balsamic vinegar

2 tablespoons Japanese vinegar

2 tablespoons reduced-sodium soy sauce

2 tablespoons minced fresh garlic

1 tablespoon minced fresh ginger

one 6- to 7-pound leg of lamb, boned, butterflied, with fell (tough outer skin) removed and well trimmed of any remaining fat

GARNISH: sprigs of mint or cilantro

1. Combine the marinade ingredients in a small bowl and whisk until smooth.

2. Place the lamb in a resealable plastic bag, pour in the marinade, seal the bag tightly, toss to coat the meat thoroughly, and refrigerate for 6 hours or overnight, turning occasionally. Allow the lamb to sit at room temperature for one hour before cooking.

3. Lightly coat an outdoor or indoor grill or broiler, with nonstick cooking spray and preheat to medium-high.

4. Drain the meat, reserving the marinade for basting, and grill or broil for about 15 minutes per side for medium rare, with an internal temperature of about 145°F., basting occasionally.

5. Allow the meat to rest for about 5 minutes and then slice on the bias and serve hot, garnished with sprigs of mint or cilantro.

Variations:

❖ The marinade can be used to flavor and tenderize rib or loin lamb chops.

❖ Leftover lamb is delicious served cold or at room temperature.

Do-ahead prep:

❖ The lamb can be marinated in sealed bags for up to 2 days in the refrigerator but should be cooked just before serving for optimum flavor.

Lamb and Golden Potato Stew with Baby Onions and Baby Carrots

Serves: 6 to 8

Yukon gold or yellow Finnish potatoes have a natural yellow buttery color and flavor that adds to the taste of the stew. If the Yukon Gold potatoes are unavailable, substitute small red potatoes. Instead of regular baby onions try the Italian pearl onions, called cipolline, which are sweet and flavorful, or use pearl or silver skin onions.

⅓ cup all-purpose flour

1½ pounds lean boneless leg or shoulder of lamb, trimmed of fat and cut into 1½-inch cubes

2½ tablespoons olive oil

2 medium onions, finely chopped

½ pound mushrooms, stems removed, wiped clean and sliced

3 large cloves garlic, finely minced

¾ cup dry red wine

3 cups defatted beef broth

1 cup crushed tomatoes packed in puree

bouquet garni (1 bay leaf and sprig each of fresh thyme, oregano, and parsley, tied in cheesecloth)

salt and freshly ground pepper

1¼ pounds small Yukon gold or yellow Finnish potatoes, scrubbed and quartered

1 pound baby onions, trimmed and peeled

one 16-ounce package peeled baby carrots

GARNISH: freshly chopped parsley

1. Place the flour in a resealable plastic bag, add the lamb, seal tightly, and shake well to coat the meat.

2. In a nonstick Dutch oven or large deep saucepan, heat 1½ tablespoons of the oil over medium-high heat and sauté the lamb cubes, in batches, until browned on all sides. Remove the lamb from the pan with a slotted spoon and set aside.

3. Add the remaining tablespoon of the oil to the pan and sauté the onions and mushrooms over medium heat, stirring often, for about about 5 to 7 minutes, or until softened. Add the garlic and continue to cook for 30 seconds. Increase the heat to high, add the wine, and allow the sauce to reduce for 2 to 3 minutes.

4. Return the lamb to pan, add the broth, tomatoes, bouquet garni, salt and pepper; bring to a boil, cover, reduce heat and simmer for 45 minutes, until meat is tender.

5. Add the potatoes and baby onions, stir, and return to the oven for an additional 25 minutes or until the potatoes are tender. Add the carrots and continue to cook an additional 10 to 15 minutes, or until the carrots are tender.

6. Remove the bouquet garni and taste the stew for seasoning, adjusting with salt and pepper as necessary. Serve the stew piping hot, in deep soup bowls, garnished with chopped parsley.

VARIATIONS:

❖ Lean beef can be substituted for the lamb.

❖ If tomatoes packed in puree are unavailable, use regular whole juice-packed tomatoes; chop, drain off most of the liquid, return the tomatoes to the can, and fill to the top with canned tomato puree.

COOK NOTE:

❖ The yellow Finnish potato is an all-purpose variety that works well for baking, boiling, frying, salads, and mashing. The Yukon gold potato, very similar to the Yellow Finnish potato, was created in Canada and is great for stews, steaming, or roasting.

DO-AHEAD PREP:

❖ This stew can be prepared several days in advance and chilled in a covered container, or can be frozen successfully for several months.

Braised Lamb Curry

Serves: 6

*C*urry can be an easy one-pot dish to serve for a party. Prepare it all well in advance, reheat it the day of the party, and serve it accompanied by lots of condiments. The sauce can be pureed as described in the recipe or served as a chunkier stew.

4 teaspoons olive oil

2 pounds completely trimmed lean lamb from the leg or shoulder, cut into 1-inch cubes

2 medium carrots, peeled and coarsely chopped

1 large onion, coarsely chopped

1 medium sweet potato, peeled and coarsely chopped

1 tart apple, peeled and coarsely chopped

2 cloves garlic, finely minced

1½ tablespoons curry powder, or more to taste

1 teaspoon ground cumin

pinch cayenne pepper

salt to taste

2 cups defatted beef or vegetable broth

1½ tablespoons tomato paste

1 tablespoon currant jelly

1 tablespoon lemon juice

*G*ARNISH: sprigs of cilantro

*A*CCOMPANIMENTS: condiments: chopped scallions, chopped cucumbers, chopped tomatoes, chopped pistachio nuts, chopped egg whites, raisins, shredded coconut, and Apricot Chutney (see page 53) or mango chutney, and steamed couscous or white rice

1. In a large nonstick Dutch oven or deep skillet, heat 2 teaspoons of the oil to high and sauté the lamb in batches, stirring often, until browned, about 3 minutes a batch. Remove the lamb and pan juices and set aside.

2. Reduce the heat to medium-high and add the remaining 2 teaspoons oil. Add the carrots, onion, sweet potato, and apple and sauté for about 5 to 6 minutes, stirring often until softened. Add the garlic, curry, cumin, cayenne pepper, and salt and stir to combine the flavors.

3.   Increase the heat to high and add the remaining ingredients including the reserved lamb and juices, bring to a boil, reduce heat to simmer, cover, and simmer for about 1 hour, until the meat is very tender. Allow to cool slightly.

4.   Remove the lamb with a slotted spoon and puree the sauce in a blender or food processor until smooth. Place both the lamb and the sauce back in the pan and reheat.

5.   Serve the curry with a variety of condiments such as chopped scallions, chopped cucumbers, chopped tomatoes, chopped pistachio nuts, chopped egg whites, raisins, shredded coconut, and Apricot Chutney or mango chutney, garnished with sprigs of cilantro, and served over a bed of steamed couscous or white rice.

VARIATION:

❖   Beef or pork can be substituted for the lamb. If using chicken, use the sauce base and reheat it gently with poached, cubed chicken. If using shrimp, poach it in the cooked sauce and serve when the shrimp are cooked through, about 3 minutes.

COOK NOTE:

❖   When adding curry to a recipe, start with less than the recipe calls for and gradually add more, tasting as you go along, until you get exactly the flavor you desire. Nothing can be done to correct a dish that has too much curry added.

DO-AHEAD PREP:

❖   It is actually advisable to prepare this lamb curry several days in advance and refrigerate until ready to reheat. It allows you a chance to defat the sauce after chilling and allows the flavors to develop. Lamb, beef, pork, or chicken curry freeze well for several months. If preparing shrimp curry just freeze the sauce and poach the shrimp just before serving to keep them from overcooking.

Grilled Pork Tenderloin
with Hoisin Mustard Glaze

Serves: 6

*P*ork tenderloin cooks quickly, renders little fat, and has a buttery-soft texture. Its subtle flavor pairs with a wide variety of sauces.

*M*ARINADE:

2 cloves garlic

1 quarter-sized piece of ginger

⅓ cup frozen orange juice

3 tablespoons reduced-sodium soy sauce

3 tablespoons hoisin sauce

2 tablespoons dry sherry

2 tablespoons grainy-style Dijon mustard

2 tablespoons honey

1 tablespoon balsamic vinegar

1 tablespoon Asian-style sesame oil

two ¾- to 1-pound pork tenderloins, well trimmed of fat

*G*ARNISH: sliced orange sections and sprigs of cilantro

1. In a small food processor, chop the garlic and ginger until minced. Add the remaining marinade ingredients and process until well mixed.

2. Place the tenderloins in a resealable plastic bag, add the marinade, seal tightly, and marinate for 3 to 4 hours in the refrigerator, turning occasionally. Let the pork stand at room temperature for 20 to 30 minutes before grilling.

3. Lightly coat an outdoor or indoor grill, or broiler with nonstick cooking spray and preheat to medium-high.

4. Remove the tenderloin from the marinade and grill the pork, turning often and basting with the marinade until browned on all sides and the inside is just cooked through, about 18 to 22 minutes or when a meat thermometer registers 150°F. Allow the meat to rest on a platter for 5 to 10 minutes.

5. In a small saucepan, bring the remaining marinade to a boil and set aside.

6. Slice the pork thinly on the diagonal, arrange overlapping slices on a platter in a curved pattern, pour the heated marinade over, and serve hot garnished with orange slices and sprigs of cilantro.

Variation:

❖ The pork can also be seared on all sides in a pan that has been coated with nonstick cooking spray and then roasted in a 350°F oven, until cooked through, about 10 to 15 minutes.

Cook Note:

❖ Select pork tenderloins that are deep pink, not gray or red. Trim the fat from the meat by pulling on it until you can separate it from the meat and then use a very sharp knife to cut it away. Use the tip of a knife to get under the silver-skin—a thin, tough, translucent membrane that covers most of the meat—and remove it.

Do-ahead Prep:

❖ Pork tenderloin is very delicate and should not be marinated longer than 4 hours. The marinade can be prepared a day in advance and refrigerated in a covered container.

Pork Chops with Sweet and Sour Sauce

Serves: 4

*P*ork is making a comeback. The long-maligned American hog is no longer as fat as a pig. Breeders have succeeded in slimming down their product, lowering the fat, cholesterol, and calories of the meat. This relatively inexpensive meat is also rich in essential nutrients, including protein, iron, zinc, and all the B vitamins, particularly thiamine, which is crucial to the nervous system.

3 tablespoons all-purpose flour

salt and freshly ground pepper to taste

4 lean loin or rib pork chops, cut ¾ inch thick

4 teaspoons olive oil

1 small onion, finely chopped

1 clove garlic, finely minced

⅓ cup hot defatted beef broth

2 tablespoons tomato paste

2 tablespoons cider or balsamic vinegar

1½ tablespoons light brown sugar

GARNISH: chopped fresh parsley

1. Place the flour in a resealable plastic bag. Add the pork chops, seal tightly, and shake. Remove the pork from the bag and shake off any excess flour.

2. In a large nonstick skillet, heat the oil to medium-high, and sauté the chops until golden brown on both sides, about 2 to 3 minutes a side. Remove the chops and set them aside.

3. Add the onion and garlic and cook over medium heat until they are softened, about 5 minutes. Discard any accumulated fat in skillet.

4. Add the broth, tomato paste, vinegar, and brown sugar and stir to combine. Return the chops to the pan, bring to a boil, cover, reduce heat, and simmer slowly for about 20 minutes; turn the chops and continue to cook for an additional 25 minutes, or until the chops are tender. (It may be necessary to add more broth. Check the liquid level periodically and add the broth when necessary.)

5. Taste, adjust seasonings with salt and pepper as necessary, and serve the chops garnished with the parsley.

$\mathscr{C}$OOK NOTES:

❖   Pork that is bought to be used the same day may be kept in the refrigerator in the store wrapping. To keep chops up to two days, place them on a rack in a covered dish in the coldest part of the refrigerator; the dish will collect the draining juices.

❖   Buy tomato paste in convenient tubes. Squeeze out just what you need and chill the remainder for other uses.

$\mathscr{D}$O-AHEAD PREP:

❖   The chops can be cooked a day in advance, chilled in a covered container, and reheated when ready to serve.

PASTA

Spaghetti with Turkey Meatballs

Pappardelle with Meat Sauce

Fettuccine with Turkey Sausages and Roasted
Red Peppers

Chinese Clams and Noodles

Spaghetti with Vegetables Chinoise

Farfalle with Caramelized Red Onion Sauce

Light Fettuccine Carbonara with Baby Peas

Fettuccine Primavera

Capellini with Spinach-Dill Pesto and Mixed Vegetables

Capellini with Canadian Bacon, Mushrooms, and Spinach

Fusilli with Japanese Eggplant, Leeks, and Spinach

Radiatore with Mexican Salsa

Confetti-Colored Orzo

Vegetarian Lasagne

Spaghetti with Turkey Meatballs

Serves: 6

*M*ost meatballs are prepared from fatty beef and fried in lots of oil. These turkey meatballs are prepared from lean turkey and roasted in a hot oven without added fat.

MEATBALLS:

½ pound lean ground white meat turkey

½ pound lean ground dark meat turkey

1 cup soft fresh bread crumbs

1 egg

¼ cup finely chopped onion

1 clove garlic, finely minced

2 tablespoons chopped fresh parsley

2 tablespoons chopped fresh basil

1 teaspoon Worcestershire sauce

salt and freshly ground pepper to taste

2 cups Marinara Sauce (see page 52)

1 pound spaghetti

GARNISH: freshly grated Parmesan cheese

1. Preheat the oven to 450°F. Lightly coat a large roasting pan or cookie sheet with nonstick cooking spray.

2. Combine the meatball ingredients with your hands, form into 1½-inch balls, and place them on the prepared pan.

3. Roast for about 20 minutes, shaking the pan occasionally, until browned on all sides.

4. Cook the spaghetti in boiling water until just al dente, drain, and immediately toss with the Marinara Sauce and the turkey meatballs.

5. Garnish lightly with grated cheese and serve immediately.

VARIATION:

❖ A good brand of bottled or packaged marinara sauce can be substituted for the fresh.

Pappardelle with Meat Sauce

Serves: 8

*T*uscany is famous for a wonderfully rustic dish called Pappardelle with Rabbit Sauce. In this version, I have replaced the rabbit with turkey sausage and ground veal or turkey and flavored it with dried porcini mushrooms. Pappardelle are wide noodles that adapt well to a thicker meat sauce.

1 ounce dried porcini mushrooms, soaked in 1 cup hot water for 20
   minutes

2 teaspoons olive oil

1 small onion, finely chopped

1 medium carrot, peeled and finely chopped

1 rib celery, finely chopped

½ pound lean turkey sausage, removed from casings

½ pound lean ground veal or turkey

1 cup dry red wine

one 28-ounce can crushed tomatoes packed in puree

½ teaspoon crushed red pepper flakes or to taste

salt and freshly ground pepper to taste

3 tablespoons chopped fresh parsley

1 pound pappardelle

*G*ARNISH: chopped fresh parsley and freshly grated Parmesan
   cheese

1.   Strain the mushrooms, squeeze them dry, and chop them into small pieces. Strain the liquid through a paper towel–lined sieve and set both aside.

2.   In a large nonstick skillet, heat the oil to medium, and sauté the onion, carrot, and celery, until softened, about 5 minutes, stirring often. Remove the vegetables with a slotted spoon and set aside.

3.   Increase the heat to high, add the sausage meat and ground veal or turkey and cook, making sure to break up the meat into small bits with a spatula, for about 4 minutes, or until it loses its pink color. Place the meat in a colander to drain off any accumulated fat. Wipe the pan clean with a paper towel and return the meat to the pan.

4.   Add the wine and cook until most of the liquid is evaporated. Add the reserved mushrooms and liquid, cooked vegetables, tomatoes, red pepper, and salt and pepper; bring to a boil, cover, reduce heat to a simmer, and cook for about 50 minutes to an hour, or until the sauce has reached a medium-thick consistency. If the sauce is not thickening, remove the lid of the pan halfway and continue to cook until slightly thickened.

5.   Cook the pasta in boiling water until just al dente. Drain.

6.   Toss the sauce with the hot pasta and serve immediately topped with chopped parsley and grated cheese.

*V*ARIATIONS:

❖   Fettuccine or other wide noodles can be substituted for the pappardelle.

❖   If tomatoes packed in puree are unavailable, use regular whole juice-packed tomatoes; chop, drain off most of the liquid, return the tomatoes to the can, and fill to the top with canned tomato puree.

*D*O-AHEAD PREP:

❖   The sauce can be prepared a day or two in advance and kept in a covered container in the refrigerator until ready to reheat. The pasta should not be cooked until just before serving.

Fettuccine with Turkey Sausages and Roasted Red Peppers

Serves: 6

*T*oday a healthful diet doesn't mean you have to give up sausages. Prepared with low-fat turkey or chicken, herbs, and spices, sausages make a simple pasta dish a satisfying meal.

½ pound Italian-style turkey sausages

12 ounces fettuccine

Marinara Sauce (see page 52)

1 red bell pepper, roasted, peeled, and roughly chopped (or use a roasted pepper from a jar, drained and chopped)

*G*ARNISH: freshly grated Parmesan cheese and chopped fresh parsley

1. Lightly coat an outdoor or indoor grill, broiler, or a well-seasoned ridged stove-top grill pan with nonstick cooking spray and preheat to medium-high.

2. Prick the sausages with a fork to release excess fat and grill or broil until well browned on all sides and cooked through. When cool enough to handle, cut into ½-inch slices.

3. Cook the pasta in boiling water until al dente. Drain and place in a large bowl. Heat the Marinara Sauce and toss with the red pepper and sausages.

4. Serve immediately garnished with the Parmesan cheese and chopped parsley.

*V*ARIATION:

❖ The sauce can be pureed if desired for a smoother consistency.

*C*OOK NOTE:

❖ To roast a pepper, place under the broiler or on a grill and roast until blackened and the skin has blistered. Place immediately in a brown paper bag or wrap it in foil and allow it to sit for about 10 minutes. Now the skin can easily be removed and discarded.

*D*O-AHEAD PREP:

❖ The ingredients can be readied well in advance but the pasta should not be cooked until just before serving.

Chinese Clams and Noodles

Serves: 4

*T*here are numerous ingredients in this delicious one-pot dinner, but once they are assembled, it takes only a few minutes to prepare. It is a variation on one from Chinese cooking expert Eileen Yin-Fei Lo.

Use small-size hard-shelled clams for this dish, either the East Coast littlenecks or cherrystones, or the West Coast Pacific littleneck or Puget Sound sweet butter clams.

*S*AUCE:

1 cup clam broth, Instant Fish Broth (see page 78), or defatted chicken broth

1 tablespoon oyster sauce

1 tablespoon reduced-sodium soy sauce

2 teaspoons cornstarch

1 teaspoon sugar

1 teaspoon Asian-style sesame oil

1 teaspoon dry sherry

12 ounces spaghetti

1 tablespoon plus 1 teaspoon peanut oil

1 quarter-size slice of fresh ginger, ¼ inch thick

24 small hard-shelled clams or small mussels, well scrubbed

1 medium onion, finely minced

one 14½-ounce can ready-cut tomatoes packed in puree

2 teaspoons finely minced garlic

1 teaspoon minced fresh jalapeño or ½ teaspoon dried red pepper

½ cup minced scallion greens

1. In a small bowl, combine the sauce ingredients; stir to combine and set near the cooking area.

2. Cook the pasta in boiling water until just al dente. Drain, run under cold water lightly, drain again, toss with 1 teaspoon of the peanut oil, and set aside.

3. In a separate pot, bring 8 cups of water and the ginger to a boil. Add the clams, cover, and return to the boil. Cook until the clams open, about 4 minutes. Drain, discard the liquid, and set the clams aside.

4. In a large nonstick wok or large skillet, heat the remaining 1 tablespoon of oil over high heat, swirling it to coat the wok. Add the onion and stir-fry for 2 minutes or until it begins to brown. Add the tomatoes, garlic, and jalapeño, and continue to cook for 2 minutes.

5. Add the reserved sauce and bring to a boil. Add the noodles and the clams and stir to coat well, about 1 to 2 minutes, until all the ingredients are hot. Toss in the scallions and serve immediately in deep soup bowls.

*V*ARIATIONS:

❖ 4 plum tomatoes, peeled, seeded, and chopped can be substituted for the canned tomatoes

❖ Mussels can be substituted for the clams. The common East Coast blue mussel (misnamed since it is actually black) will work well for this dish. There is also a beautifully colored mussel called a green-lipped mussel. This variety, imported from New Zealand, is farm-raised so it requires no cleaning.

❖ For added spiciness one teaspoon of hot bean paste or chili sauce with garlic can be substituted for the jalapeño pepper.

*C*OOK NOTES:

❖ The clams are easily cleaned by soaking them in water with 1 to 2 tablespoons of cornmeal added. The clams take in the cornmeal and spit it out with any sand that might be lurking inside.

❖ When purchasing hard-shelled clams make sure the shells are tightly closed, which means the clam is alive and fresh. If a shell is slightly open, tap it lightly and if it doesn't snap shut that means the clam has died and should be tossed out. Also discard any clams with broken shells.

*D*O-AHEAD PREP:

❖ Do not clean the clams until ready to cook. The noodles can be cooked about 1 hour ahead. The remaining ingredients can be readied but the complete dish should be prepared at the last minute.

Spaghetti with Vegetables Chinoise

Serves: 4

*T*his pasta dish is a melting pot, mixing the French and Italian styles of cooking with Chinese flavors.

1½ tablespoons peanut or olive oil

2 carrots, peeled and thinly sliced

2 medium zucchini, wiped clean and finely sliced

1 medium onion, thinly sliced

½ cup dry sherry

1 cup defatted chicken broth

2 tablespoons reduced-sodium soy sauce

2 cloves garlic, finely minced

2 teaspoons finely minced fresh ginger

salt and freshly ground pepper to taste

12 ounces spaghetti

1 to 2 tablespoons toasted sesame seeds

GARNISH: freshly chopped cilantro leaves

1. In a large nonstick skillet or wok, heat the oil to medium-high and sauté the carrots, zucchini, and onion for about 4 to 5 minutes, stirring often, until lightly golden.

2. Add the sherry and continue to cook over high heat until most of the liquid has evaporated. Add the broth, soy sauce, garlic, ginger, and salt and pepper, bring to a boil, cover, reduce heat, and simmer for 2 to 3 minutes, until the vegetables are tender.

3. Cook the spaghetti in boiling water until just al dente, drain, and toss with the sauce and sesame seeds.

4. Serve immediately garnished with freshly chopped cilantro.

VARIATIONS:

❖ Whole wheat fettuccine, linguine, capellini, or other types of pasta can be substituted for the spaghetti.

❖ Leftovers make a delicious chilled pasta salad with the addition of a few tablespoons of Chinese or Japanese vinegar.

❖   The ingredients can be prepped well in advance but the dish should be cooked just before serving.

Farfalle with Caramelized Red Onion Sauce

Serves: 4 to 6

*C*aramelized onions add a sweet taste to this easy-to-prepare pasta. The onion sauce also makes a fabulous topping for grilled poultry, meat, or even pizza.

    1 tablespoon olive oil
    3 large red onions, cut in half, sliced and broken into rings (about
        2 pounds)
    ½ pound mushrooms, stems removed, wiped clean and sliced
    ½ cup dry Marsala or red wine
    1 cup defatted chicken, beef, or vegetable broth
    salt and freshly ground pepper to taste
    12 ounces farfalle
    2 tablespoons grated Parmesan cheese

*G*ARNISH: freshly chopped parsley

1.   In a very large nonstick skillet or wok, heat the oil to medium-high, and sauté the onions and mushrooms, stirring often, about 15 to 20 minutes, or until the vegetables are lightly golden.

2.   Increase the heat to high, add the wine and cook for 1 to 2 minutes, or until most of the liquid has evaporated. Add the broth, reduce the heat to medium, and continue to cook, stirring occasionally, for about 3 to 4 minutes or until the sauce is slightly syrupy. Season with salt and pepper to taste.

3.   Cook the pasta in boiling water until just al dente. Drain, and toss with the onion sauce and the Parmesan cheese.

4.   Serve immediately, garnished with freshly chopped parsley.

❖   Penne, small ziti, fusilli, and other tubular pasta can be substituted for the far-falle.

❖   ¾ cup of thawed frozen tiny peas can be tossed in with the hot pasta.

*C*OOK NOTE:

❖   When chopping or slicing onions, use ski goggles to protect the eyes from tearing. As an alternative, freeze onions half an hour before slicing and the fumes will be lessened.

*D*O-AHEAD PREP:

❖   The sauce can be prepared a day or two in advance and refrigerated in a covered container until ready to cook the pasta. Reheat the sauce, toss with the hot pasta, and serve immediately.

Light Fettuccine Carbonara
with Baby Peas

Serves: 6

*F*ettuccine Carbonara is a rich traditional Italian dish that is very high in cholesterol-raising foods like bacon, eggs, cream, and cheese. In this lightened version I have substituted lower-fat prosciutto for the bacon, egg whites for most of the eggs, reduced the amount of Parmesan cheese, and have used lots of flavorful broth to add moisture without any cream.

2 teaspoons olive oil

3 ounces thinly sliced prosciutto, fat trimmed and finely chopped

4 shallots, peeled and finely chopped

2 cloves garlic, finely minced

¼ cup dry vermouth or white wine

¾ cup defatted chicken broth

1 cup frozen baby peas, thawed

12 ounces fettuccine

3 egg whites, removed from the refrigerator 15 minutes before using

1 whole egg, removed from the refrigerator 15 minutes before
    using
⅓ cup freshly grated Parmesan cheese
salt and freshly ground white pepper to taste

*G*ARNISH: freshly chopped parsley

1. In a medium nonstick skillet, heat the oil to medium and cook the prosciutto and shallots for about 5 minutes, stirring often, until golden. Add the garlic and stir for just 30 seconds.

2. Increase the heat to high and add the vermouth or white wine, stirring until most of the liquid has been absorbed. Add the broth, reduce heat to medium, and continue to stir until reduced and thickened about 5 minutes longer. Add the peas and stir to combine.

3. Cook the fettuccine in boiling water until just al dente.

4. Place the eggs and cheese in a large bowl and whisk until smooth.

5. Drain the pasta and return it to the hot pasta pot off the heat. Immediately add the egg and prosciutto mixtures and stir quickly to combine.

6. Season with salt and pepper, garnish with parsley, and serve immediately.

*V*ARIATION:

❖ Blanched asparagus tips can be substituted for the baby peas.

*C*OOK NOTES:

❖ Use only freshly cut prosciutto; even though it is air-dried, once it has been cut, air and heat are its enemies and can quickly diminish the flavor and texture. To store slices, wrap them airtight and chill up to 24 hours.

❖ Use good quality freshly grated Parmesan cheese. It has a stronger and more intense flavor than the pre-grated variety, so you can use less without sacrificing flavor.

*D*O-AHEAD PREP:

❖ The sauce in Step 2, without the peas, can be prepared an hour in advance.

Fettuccine Primavera

Serves: 6 to 8

Creamy sauces can be prepared in a lighter style by substituting low-fat milk for cream and using less butter in the preparation. Any combination of seasonal vegetables can be used in this dish, but remember to choose them for complementary tastes as well as color for a pretty presentation.

2 medium carrots, peeled and sliced

½ pound asparagus, fibrous tips removed and cut into 1-inch
   pieces on the diagonal

¾ cup fresh or frozen corn, thawed

1 pound fettuccine

⅓ cup all-purpose flour

1¾ cups 1% low-fat milk

1 tablespoon unsalted butter

1 small onion, finely chopped

1 teaspoon finely minced garlic

1¼ cups defatted chicken or vegetable broth

3 tablespoons freshly grated Parmesan cheese

2 tablespoons freshly chopped parsley

¼ teaspoon ground nutmeg

salt and freshly ground white pepper to taste

GARNISH: freshly chopped parsley

1. Bring a large pot of water to a boil, drop in the carrots, and cook for about 3 to 4 minutes; add the asparagus and cook for an additional 3 to 4 minutes, until just tender. Drain the vegetables in a colander, run under cold water, and allow to drain again. Add the corn and stir to combine.

2. Drop the pasta into boiling water and cook until just al dente.

3. In a medium nonstick saucepan, heat the butter to medium, and sauté the onion for about 5 to 6 minutes, stirring often, until softened. Add the garlic and stir to just combine.

4. In a medium bowl, whisk the flour with ¾ cup of the milk until smooth. Then whisk the flour mixture into the saucepan with the remaining milk and broth. Cook, stirring constantly, until the sauce thickens and just comes to a boil. Remove from the heat and stir in the cheese, parsley, nutmeg, and salt and pepper to taste, whisking until smooth. Reduce the heat to a simmer and continue to cook, stirring constantly for about 1 to 2 minutes, until the sauce is smooth. Add the well-drained vegetables and stir to heat through.

5. Drain the pasta, toss with the sauce, and serve immediately garnished with freshly chopped parsley.

$\mathcal{C}$OOK NOTES:

❖ Store asparagus as you would flowers with the stalks in a jug of cold water in the refrigerator.

❖ If time permits, peel the stalks of the asparagus with a vegetable peeler. It will make them more tender.

$\mathcal{D}$O-AHEAD PREP:

❖ The vegetables can be cooked a day in advance, dried well, and refrigerated in sealed bags. Bring the vegetables to room temperature before proceeding with the recipe.

Capellini with Spinach-Dill Pesto and Mixed Vegetables

Serves: 6

*P*esto is notoriously enriched with oil and cheese. This lighter version substitutes dill for the traditional basil and reduces the oil and cheese considerably. Steam a variety of vegetables or transform any leftovers into a delicious pasta dinner.

SPINACH-DILL PESTO:

2 cups firmly packed spinach leaves, well washed, dried, stems removed

3 tablespoons defatted chicken or vegetable broth

2 tablespoons olive oil

2 tablespoons snipped fresh dill

2 tablespoons lemon juice

2 cloves garlic

2 tablespoons pine nuts

2 tablespoons grated Parmesan cheese

salt and freshly ground white pepper to taste

12 ounces capellini

3 cups cooked mixed vegetables such as: steamed sliced carrots, sliced zucchini, broccoli florets, sliced mushrooms, chopped tomatoes, 1-inch pieces of asparagus, 1-inch pieces of green beans, at room temperature

freshly grated Parmesan cheese

1. In a food processor or blender, combine the pesto ingredients and process until smooth.

2. Cook the pasta in boiling water until just al dente. Drain.

3. Toss the hot pasta with the pesto, cooked vegetables, and cheese, and serve immediately.

VARIATION:

❖ Spaghetti, linguine, or fettuccine can be substituted for the capellini.

COOK NOTE:

❖ Since the water content of spinach is as high as 80 to 90 percent, it will wilt easily upon standing. Avoid washing this perishable green before storing, for even if well dried, some water still adheres to the leaves, causing them to rot. Store spinach, grit and all, in plastic bags until ready to use.

*D*O-AHEAD PREP:

❖   The pesto can be prepared up to a week in advance and kept in covered containers in the refrigerator or it can be frozen for several months. The pasta should not be cooked until just before serving.

Capellini with Canadian Bacon, Mushrooms, and Spinach

Serves: 4

*C*anadian bacon, with half the fat found in cured bacon, adds a smoky taste to this deeply flavored pasta dish.

1½ tablespoons olive oil

3 ounces Canadian bacon, finely chopped

1 medium onion, finely chopped

½ pound mushrooms, stems removed, wiped clean and thinly sliced

one 6-ounce package baby spinach leaves

2 cloves garlic, finely minced

1¼ cups defatted chicken broth

salt and freshly ground white pepper to taste

12 ounces capellini

2 egg whites, at room temperature

1 whole egg, at room temperature

3 tablespoons freshly grated Parmesan cheese

*G*ARNISH: freshly chopped parsley

1.   In a nonstick skillet, heat the oil to medium-high and sauté the Canadian bacon, onion, and mushrooms for about 5 to 7 minutes, stirring often, until lightly golden. Add the spinach and sauté until just wilted. Add the garlic and stir for 30 seconds. Add the broth and salt and pepper; bring to a boil, stirring often, until the mixture is slightly reduced, about 2 to 3 minutes.

2. In the meantime cook the capellini in boiling salted water until just al dente. Drain.

3. Return the cooked pasta to the pasta pot off the heat, add the spinach mixture, eggs, and cheese, and stir until well mixed.

4. Season with salt and pepper and serve immediately, garnished with parsley.

VARIATIONS:

❖ Proscuitto can be substituted for the Canadian bacon.

❖ If baby spinach is not available, substitute 7 to 8 ounces of fresh spinach leaves, coarse stems removed, washed and dried. To make it even easier, substitute half of a 10-ounce package of frozen chopped spinach, thawed and thoroughly squeezed dry.

COOK NOTE:

❖ Canadian bacon is a cured and smoked boneless meat taken from the lean, tender eye of the pork loin that is a closer kin to ham than it is to regular bacon. Though slightly more expensive than bacon, it is significantly leaner and adds a smoky flavor with less added fat.

DO-AHEAD PREP:

❖ The ingredients can be readied well in advance but the dish should be cooked just before serving.

Fusilli with Japanese Eggplant, Leeks, and Spinach

This is a wonderfully light supper dish, or luncheon entrée, accompanied by some crusty bread.

6 Japanese eggplants, sliced in half horizontally

12 ounces fusilli

2 teaspoons olive oil

3 leeks, thoroughly washed and thinly sliced (white parts only)

one 10-ounce package spinach, washed and stems removed

2 cloves garlic, finely minced

1¼ cups defatted chicken or vegetable broth

salt and freshly ground white pepper to taste

1 to 2 tablespoons freshly grated Parmesan cheese

*G*ARNISH: chopped fresh parsley

1. Lightly coat an outdoor or indoor grill, broiler, or a well-seasoned ridged stove-top grill pan with olive oil nonstick cooking spray and preheat to medium-high. Coat one side of the eggplants with the cooking spray and grill for 3 to 4 minutes. Spray the other side and continue to grill for 3 to 4 minutes longer or until golden brown. Cut into 1-inch pieces and set aside.

2. Cook the pasta in boiling water until al dente.

3. In a nonstick wok or large skillet, heat the oil over high heat and stir-fry the leeks for 1 to 2 minutes. Add the spinach and continue to stir-fry until just softened. Add the garlic and stir for 30 seconds. Add the broth, salt and pepper, and reserved eggplant; bring to a boil, and cook over high heat for 2 minutes.

4. Drain the pasta, toss with the cooked vegetables and cheese, and serve immediately garnished with chopped parsley.

*V*ARIATIONS:

❖ Regular eggplant, thinly sliced, can be substituted for the Japanese eggplant.

❖ Fusilli, the thin spindly, squiggly noodles, can be replaced with penne, farfalle, or small macaroni noodles.

*C*OOK NOTE:

❖   Japanese eggplants, and their lavender cousins, Chinese eggplants, are sweet, tender, relatively seedless, and require no lengthy salting or extra preparation before cooking. Asian eggplants are more perishable and should be used within days of purchase.

*D*O-AHEAD PREP:

❖   The vegetable sauce can be prepared a day in advance, refrigerated in a covered container, and brought to room temperature before using. The pasta should be cooked just before serving.

Radiatore with Mexican Salsa

Serves: 4 to 6

*R*adiatore, also known as pasta nuggets, is a ruffled pasta shaped like a car radiator. It's a great choice for a light sauce or salad because the ruffles catch all the flavor of the sauce or dressing.

Salsa makes an almost nonfat topping for pasta. The Mexican salsa in this recipe is easily prepared with canned tomatoes.

3 tablespoons finely chopped onion

3 tablespoons finely chopped fresh cilantro

2 cloves garlic, chopped

2 tablespoons finely chopped, seeded mild fresh green
  chile pepper

one 28-ounce can crushed tomatoes packed in puree,
  lightly drained

salt and freshly ground pepper to taste

12 ounces radiatore pasta

1 cup fresh or frozen corn, thawed

*G*ARNISH: chopped cilantro

1. In a food processor or blender, pulse the onion, cilantro, garlic, and chile pepper until just chopped. Do not over process.

2. Combine the chopped mixture with the tomatoes and salt and pepper and set aside until ready to use.

3. Cook the radiatore in boiling water until just al dente. Drain, toss the hot pasta with the frozen corn and the salsa until the vegetables are warmed by the hot pasta.

4. Serve immediately topped with chopped cilantro.

*V*ARIATIONS:

❖ Rotini, penne, fusilli, or farfalle can be substituted for the radiatore.

❖ Serve this spicy dish as a pasta salad the next day by adding some balsamic or red wine vinegar to taste.

❖ If tomatoes packed in puree are unavailable, use regular whole juice-packed tomatoes; chop, drain off most of the liquid, return the tomatoes to the can, and fill to the top with canned tomato puree.

*C*OOK NOTE:

❖ Cilantro is the Latin name for coriander, also known as Chinese parsley. Even though cilantro is purported to be the world's most widely used herb, there is definitely a love-hate relationship going on. If you love it, you really love it, but if you hate it (like my husband and son do), then the comments range from "It tastes like soap" to "Get that stuff off my tomatoes!"

*D*O-AHEAD PREP:

❖ The salsa can be prepared several days ahead, refrigerated in a covered container, and brought to room temperature before using. The pasta should not be cooked until just before serving.

Confetti-Colored Orzo

Serves: 6

*O*rzo is a rice-shaped pasta that makes a delicious dish when combined with colorful minced vegetables in a light broth. Serve orzo as a side dish with grilled meats or as a luncheon or supper dish—it's risotto without the stirring!

    1 tablespoon olive oil
    2 scallions (green and white parts included), finely chopped
    ½ cup minced sweet red bell pepper (½ medium pepper)
    ½ cup minced green bell pepper (½ medium pepper)
    ½ cup minced yellow bell pepper (½ medium pepper)
    ½ cup chopped carrots (1 medium carrot), peeled
    1½ cups orzo
    1½ teaspoons minced garlic
    3 cups defatted chicken or vegetable broth
    salt and freshly ground white pepper
    ½ cup chopped fresh Italian parsley
    2 tablespoons freshly grated Parmesan cheese
    2 tablespoons toasted pine nuts

1. In a large heavy nonstick saucepan, heat the oil over medium heat. Add the scallions, bell peppers, and carrots, and cook for 5 minutes, stirring often. Add the orzo and garlic, and sauté for 30 seconds, stirring constantly.

2. Add the broth and salt and pepper, bring to a boil, cover, reduce heat, and simmer for about 18 minutes, or until the orzo is tender and the liquid has been absorbed.

3. Remove from the heat, toss with the parsley, cheese, and nuts, and serve immediately.

*V*ARIATIONS:

❖ For an easier version use 1 whole red bell pepper and 1 whole yellow or green bell pepper and eliminate the carrots.

❖ Fresh chopped basil can be substituted for the parsley.

*C*OOK NOTE:

❖ It is best to chop the peppers by hand, not in the food processor, or they will become too watery.

❖   Although there is a lot of chopping involved in this recipe, much of it can be done a day in advance. The pasta should not be cooked until just before serving.

Vegetarian Lasagne

Serves: 8

$\mathcal{T}$his lasagne can be varied by selecting the freshest seasonal vegetables for the filling. Save time by doubling the recipe and freezing an extra pan for a future dinner party.

9 ounces (9 pieces) lasagne noodles

1 tablespoon olive oil

1 medium onion, finely chopped

½ pound mushrooms, stems removed, wiped clean and
    thinly sliced

2 medium zucchini, thinly sliced

½ pound spinach, stems removed, washed and dried

2 plum tomatoes, finely chopped

2 cloves garlic, finely minced

2 tablespoons chopped fresh parsley

2 tablespoons chopped fresh basil

salt and freshly ground pepper to taste

one 15-ounce container low-fat ricotta cheese

½ pound low-fat mozzarella cheese, shredded

¼ cup 1% low-fat milk

¼ cup freshly grated Parmesan cheese

⅛ teaspoon freshly ground nutmeg

salt and freshly ground white pepper

1.   Bring a large pot of water to a boil, add the lasagne noodles, and cook until just about tender, about 6 to 7 minutes. Place the noodles in a bowl of cold water to keep them from sticking.

2.   In a large nonstick skillet, heat the oil to medium, and sauté the onion and mushrooms for about 5 minutes, stirring often, until softened. Add the zucchini and continue to sauté for about 3 to 4 additional minutes, stirring often. Add the spinach

and tomatoes, and cook until the spinach softens and most of the liquid has evaporated, about 2 to 3 more minutes, stirring occasionally. Stir in the garlic, herbs, and salt and pepper and set aside.

3. In a medium bowl, combine the ricotta with the mozzarella, milk, and 2 tablespoons of the Parmesan cheese and stir until smooth. Season with nutmeg, salt and pepper, and set aside.

4. Preheat the oven to 425°F. Lightly coat a 9-x-13-inch baking dish with olive oil nonstick cooking spray.

5. Spread a thin layer of the vegetable mixture on the bottom of the pan. Top with 3 noodles and then another thin layer of vegetable mixture topped with a thin layer of cheese mixture. Repeat two times more ending with the cheese mixture and a sprinkling of the remaining 2 tablespoons Parmesan cheese on top.

6. Bake for 15 minutes or until golden and bubbly hot. Allow to cool slightly for about 5 to 7 minutes until the lasagne can be easily cut into squares and served.

*V*ARIATIONS:

❖ Oil-packed sun-dried tomatoes, wiped clean of oil and chopped, or rehydrated sun-dried tomatoes can be added with the garlic.

❖ Any seasonal vegetables can be substituted such as yellow squash, broccoli florets, asparagus, or even radicchio and arugula. Vary the fresh herbs according to taste.

*C*OOK NOTES:

❖ Store fresh basil as you would flowers. Trim the stems when you get home from the market and place them in a jar of water on your window sill. Change the water occasionally and trim the ends to keep the basil fresh and green.

❖ The Italian or flat-leaf parsley has more flavor than curly leaf parsley and is now readily available in supermarkets. Select bright-green leaves that show no sign of wilting. Wash the parsley, shake off excess water, and store it wrapped in paper towels and then in a plastic bag.

*D*O-AHEAD PREP:

❖ The lasagne can be prepared through Step 5, covered with plastic wrap, and refrigerated overnight or frozen for several weeks. It is advisable to bring the lasagne to room temperature before baking. The lasagne can also be baked, cooled, covered, and then frozen for several months. Thaw before reheating.

PIZZA

The perfect lover is one who turns into a pizza at 4 A.M.
—*Charles Pierce*

Basic Pizza Crust

Pizza Toppings

Pizza with Caramelized Onion and Mushrooms

Roasted Vegetables and Feta Cheese Pizza

Roasted Tomato, Basil, and Goat Cheese Pizza

Basic Pizza Crust

*M*y friend Anne Mayer has devised this very easy method of preparing pizza dough in the food processor. This same crust can be used for calzone or bread.

If you are really in a hurry substitute thawed frozen bread dough, which will make a nice crisp crust. One piece of frozen bread dough will yield two large or three small pizzas.

1 cup lukewarm water

2 teaspoons yeast

1½ teaspoons sugar

2½ cups plus 1 tablespoon flour

1 tablespoon cornmeal

1½ teaspoons salt

1.　Place the water, yeast, and sugar in the bowl of a food processor. Pulse for 1 second and allow to sit for 3 to 4 minutes until the yeast bubbles. (This step is called proofing the yeast.)

2.　Add 1 cup of the flour, the cornmeal, and the salt and process for a few seconds or until just blended. Add 1 additional cup of the flour and process for a few seconds until blended. Then add another tablespoon of the flour and process until that is blended. Continue to add the remaining flour, 1 tablespoon at a time, processing until the dough pulls apart from the sides of the bowl. At that point add just 1 more tablespoon of flour, process for 20 seconds, and then allow the dough to rest for 30 minutes in the bowl. After 30 minutes process the dough for an additional 10 seconds to knead it.

3.　When ready to bake the pizzas preheat the oven to 425°F. Lightly coat 1 large pizza pan or 2 small pizza pans with nonstick cooking spray.

4.　Remove the dough from the food processor. (Note: if the dough is too resistant, allow it to rest for 5 minutes longer to allow the gluten to relax.) Leave the dough whole for a large pizza and roll it into a 16- to 18-inch round. For small pizzas cut the dough in half with kitchen shears and roll the pieces into two 10- to 12-inch rounds.

5.　Place the pizza on the lower rack of the oven and bake for 8 minutes. (Note: the pizza may bubble up at this point but it is OK.) Remove the pizza from the oven, sprinkle on the toppings, return to the lower rack of the oven, and continue to bake for an additional 12 to 15 minutes, or until the toppings are cooked and the pizza is hot and crusty.

6. Serve immediately cut in slices.

*D*O-AHEAD PREP:

❖ The pizza dough can be tightly wrapped and frozen.

❖ For greater convenience, prepare several crusts at one time, cool, stack between pieces of wax paper, place in resealable plastic bags and freeze them for future use.

𝒫IZZA TOPPINGS

𝒯here are many varieties of pizza that are lower in fat and still quite delicious. The following variations should please inspire you to make your very own pizza at home.

Pizza with Caramelized Onion and Mushrooms

Yield: 1 large 16-inch pizza or 2 small 12-inch pizzas

1 tablespoon olive oil

3 large onions, thinly sliced

5 large mushrooms, stems removed, wiped clean, and thinly sliced

¼ teaspoon chopped fresh thyme or pinch of dried
thyme, crumbled

salt and freshly ground white pepper to taste

¼ cup freshly grated Parmesan cheese

1. In a heavy large nonstick skillet, heat the oil, add the onions, reduce the heat to low, cover, and cook the onions slowly for about 10 minutes, stirring occasionally, until the onions begin to turn golden. Add the mushrooms, increase the heat to medium-high, and continue to cook until caramelized. Add the thyme and salt and pepper and stir to mix the flavors.

2. Spread the onion mixture evenly over the partially baked pizza crust, sprinkle with the cheese, and bake for 12 to 15 minutes, or until hot and bubbly.

𝒞OOK NOTE:

❖ Onions should feel firm when pressed and should not have any powdery gray mold in sight. Store them for several months in a cool, dark, dry place with good air circulation.

𝒟O-AHEAD PREP:

❖ The onion mixture can be prepared several days in advance and kept in a covered container in the refrigerator.

Roasted Vegetables and Feta Cheese Pizza

**Yield: 1 large 16-inch pizza or
2 small 12-inch pizzas**

¾ cup Roasted Vegetable Spread (see page 31)

3 ounces feta cheese, crumbled

1. Coat the Roasted Vegetable Spread evenly over the partially baked pizza crust, sprinkle with the cheese, and bake for 12 to 15 minutes, or until hot and bubbly.

Cook Note:

❖ Because it is a crumbly cheese, leftover feta cheese can be frozen successfully for future use. Wrap the feta tightly in plastic wrap or foil and it will keep for about 2 months. Thaw the cheese thoroughly in the refrigerator before using.

Do-Ahead Prep:

❖ The spread can be prepared several days in advance and kept in a covered container in the refrigerator. The pizza should be topped just before baking.

Roasted Tomato, Basil, and Goat Cheese Pizza

**Yield: 1 large 16-inch pizza or
2 small 12-inch pizzas**

3 medium tomatoes, sliced in half horizontally

4 cloves garlic, unpeeled

salt and freshly ground pepper

3 ounces goat cheese

2 tablespoon chopped fresh basil

1. Preheat the oven to 425°F. Lightly coat a roasting pan with olive oil nonstick cooking spray.

2. In the prepared pan, place the tomatoes, cut-side up, alongside the garlic cloves. Coat the tomatoes and garlic with additional olive oil nonstick cooking spray, season with salt and pepper, and roast for 45 to 50 minutes, or until the garlic is golden brown and the tomato skins start to wrinkle and pull away from the pulp.

3. Squeeze the pulp from the garlic evenly over the partially baked pizza crust. Remove the skins from the tomatoes, which will pop right off in your hands, gently squeeze out the seeds, cut the tomatoes roughly, and distribute evenly on the crust. Top with the goat cheese and bake for 12 to 15 minutes, or until hot and bubbly.

4. Garnish with the basil and serve immediately.

*C*OOK NOTE:

❖ It is best to buy local varieties of tomatoes that are allowed to ripen on the vine before picking. These flavorful tomatoes have twice the vitamin C than the supermarket variety that are picked before ripening.

*D*O-AHEAD PREP:

❖ The pizza should be topped just before baking.

RICE & GRAINS

Tips for the Perfect Risotto

Light and Creamy Corn Risotto

Shrimp Risotto with Peas and Red Pepper

Light Fried Rice

Texmati Rice Pilaf with Sun-Dried Tomatoes, Peppers, and Pine Nuts

Hoppin' John

Mexican-Style Bulgur Pilaf

Custardy Cornbread

Grits Soufflé

Polenta Squares

Quinoa and Vegetable Pilaf

Couscous Provençale

Sourdough Stuffing with Apricots and Almonds

$\mathscr{T}$IPS FOR THE PERFECT RISOTTO

$\mathscr{R}$isotto is a wonderfully comforting rice dish that can be served as a light entrée, side dish, or luncheon centerpiece. Many cooks shy away from preparing risotto because it requires constant stirring. But, for an informal party, it is a perfect dish to get the guests involved and participating in the kitchen.

Although many risottos are prepared with butter and cheese, these lighter versions are made more delicious by adding intense flavorings such as dried porcini mushrooms; made richer and creamier by added purees of vegetables; and are made lighter by substituting a small amount of good olive oil in place of butter.

$\mathscr{T}$HE KEY INGREDIENTS

Riso or Rice: Risotto is prepared with a short-grain, highly glutinous rice grown in Italy. The main type of rice used for risotto is called Arborio. Arborio has special properties that allow it to absorb the flavors of the ingredients added to the dish and yet maintain an al dente texture in each individual grain. There are two other types of short-grain rice that can be used in risotto but are quite difficult to find in America: Carnaroli, valued for its firm texture, and Vialone Nano, which has shorter grains that yield a less creamy sauce and cook about five minutes more quickly than Arborio.

Soffritto: The mixture resulting when the butter or oil is sautéed with the minced onion, garlic, or celery to begin the risotto.

Brodo or Broth: The broth, wine, or other cooking liquid that is added in small increments, allowing the rice to absorb each addition fully before adding the remainder.

Condimenti: The additional flavorings such as meat, poultry, fish, vegetables, cheese, or whatever else is added to enhance the risotto and give it a distinct flavor.

$\mathscr{B}$ASICS FOR A LIGHT RISOTTO

❖ A heavy nonstick medium-size saucepan is the perfect size to cook the risotto. The nonstick surface will allow you to use less oil. If you cook the risotto in a pan that is too large, the rice and broth mixture will spread out and boil dry too quickly.

❖ The broth needs to be kept at a slow simmer, which maintains the constant cooking temperature of the risotto. Ladle the broth into the rice mixture in increments, allowing each addition to be absorbed fully before adding the next.

❖ Never wash the rice. The natural starch in Arborio rice keeps the risotto creamy.

❖ Chop the onions very fine so they do not overpower the other flavors in the risotto.

❖ Instead of using a measuring cup to add the half cupfuls of broth, try using a soup ladle, which is just about the correct measurement.

❖ If you are trying to reduce the amount of cheese, use a good imported Parmigiano Reggiano. A small amount of this aged cheese will add as much flavor as a large amount of domestic cheese.

❖ Toward the end of the cooking time, taste often to see if the rice is the correct texture. Some risottos cook more quickly than is specified so it is important to check to keep the rice al dente.

❖ Serve the risotto immediately. This is one dish that cannot be reheated!

❖ If time permits, keep the plates in a 200°F oven, which keeps the risotto from congealing on cold plates.

Light and Creamy Corn Risotto

Serves: 6 to 8

*T*his risotto is low in fat but the pureed corn gives a creamy consistency without added fats.

Check the Tips for the Perfect Risotto (see page 231) before proceeding with this recipe.

    4 ears fresh corn (white or yellow)
    3½ cups defatted chicken or vegetable broth
    2 teaspoons olive oil
    1 small onion, finely chopped
    1¼ cups Arborio or other short-grain rice suitable for risotto
    1 clove garlic, finely minced
    ¼ cup dry white wine or vermouth
    3 to 4 tablespoons freshly grated Parmesan cheese
    salt and freshly ground white pepper to taste

*G*ARNISH: chopped fresh parsley

1. Slice the corn off the cob and place it in a small bowl. Place half the corn in a food processor or blender and process until just smooth. Set aside.

2. Bring the broth to a simmer in a saucepan and keep it warm over very low heat.

3. In a deep large nonstick saucepan, heat the oil to medium and when hot, sauté the onion for about 4 to 5 minutes, stirring often, until just transparent. Add the rice and continue to sauté, coating with the mixture. Add the garlic and stir to combine.

4. Increase the heat, add the wine, and allow it to boil away, stirring often.

5. Add ½ cup of the broth to the rice and cook, stirring until the liquid is absorbed, about 3 to 4 minutes. Continue to cook, ladling in the broth ½ cup at a time, stirring constantly until each addition has been incorporated before adding the next. Cook until ½ cup of the broth remains, about 15 minutes longer.

6. Add the remaining broth, corn kernels, and corn puree and continue to stir for an additional 4 to 5 minutes or until the rice is just al dente and the corn is tender.

7. Stir in the cheese and salt and pepper and serve hot, garnished generously with chopped parsley.

$\mathcal{V}$ARIATION:

❖   2 tablespoons snipped fresh chives can be added with the fresh corn in Step 5.

$\mathcal{C}$OOK NOTES:

❖   The tip for selecting freshly picked corn is the stem. If it is a damp, pale, green, the corn has been freshly picked. After 24 hours, the stalk turns opaque and chalky and longer than that the stalk turns brown. As soon as the corn is picked, the sugar in the kernels starts to convert to starch, so the fresher the better!

❖   Fresh corn is an excellent source of soluble fiber, the kind believed to help lower blood cholesterol levels. All varieties are good sources of vitamin C, but only the yellow kernels contain small amounts of vitamin A in the form of beta-carotene.

$\mathcal{D}$O-AHEAD PREP:

❖   Serve the risotto immediately. This is one dish that cannot be reheated!

Shrimp Risotto with Peas
and Red Pepper

Serves: 6 to 8

*T*his risotto with shrimp and peas is a great main course dish for a luncheon or supper, accompanied by crusty bread and a light salad.

Check the Tips for the Perfect Risotto (see page 231) before proceeding with this recipe.

4½ to 5 cups defatted chicken or vegetable broth

1 tablespoon extra-virgin olive oil

1 large onion, finely chopped

8 medium mushrooms, stems removed, wiped clean and
    thinly sliced

½ sweet red bell pepper, seeded and finely chopped

1½ cups Arborio rice or other short-grain rice suitable for risotto

2 cloves garlic, finely minced

⅓ cup dry white wine or vermouth

1 pound small shrimp, deveined, and cut in half

½ cup frozen baby peas, thawed

salt and freshly ground white pepper to taste

2 tablespoons freshly grated Parmesan cheese

*G*ARNISH: chopped fresh Italian parsley

1. Bring the broth to a simmer in a saucepan and keep it warm over very low heat.

2. In a deep large nonstick saucepan, heat the oil to medium and when hot, sauté the onion and red bell pepper for about 5 to 6 minutes, stirring often, until just softened. Add the rice and continue to sauté, coating with the mixture. Add the garlic and stir to combine.

3. Increase the heat to high, add the wine, and cook, stirring constantly until all the liquid has been absorbed.

4. Add ½ cup of the broth to the rice and cook, stirring until absorbed, about 4 to 5 minutes. Continue to cook, ladling in the broth ½ cup at a time, stirring constantly until each addition has been incorporated before adding the next. Continue to cook, ladling in the broth ½ cup at a time, stirring constantly, for 15 minutes.

5. Add the shrimp and continue to cook, stirring and ladling in the broth for an additional 5 minutes or until the shrimp are cooked, the rice is al dente, and the liquid is absorbed.

6. After about 20 minutes, taste the rice to see if it is tender. When tender but still firm, add the peas and stir well. Season with salt and pepper, stir in the Parmesan cheese, garnish with the parsley, and serve immediately.

*V*ARIATIONS:

❖ Chopped fresh seeded tomatoes can be added with the peas if desired.

❖ A pinch of saffron threads soaked in the hot broth can be added.

*C*OOK NOTES:

❖ Tasting is your guide to a successful risotto. If the rice is too chewy and needs a little more cooking, add an additional ½ to 1 cup of hot liquid and continue to cook until al dente, still firm but tender.

❖ If using frozen shrimp, make sure to thaw them first before adding to the risotto. When purchasing frozen shrimp, make sure each shrimp has its own coat of ice, which means that each shrimp was frozen separately and that it was not thawed and then refrozen.

*D*O-AHEAD PREP:

❖ Serve the risotto immediately. This is one dish that cannot be reheated!

Light Fried Rice

Serves: 8

*F*ried rice is a great way to use up leftover rice and cooked vegetables. The eggs, seasonings, and rice remain the same, just vary the vegetables or even meat, fish, or poultry, by seasonality and availability.

Most Chinese restaurants use lots of oil to fry the rice, but here the amount has been reduced and I have added more egg whites in place of the traditional whole eggs.

2 whole eggs

2 egg whites

⅓ cup finely chopped scallion greens

½ teaspoon freshly minced ginger

1 teaspoon finely minced garlic

3 cups cold cooked rice

3 tablespoons reduced-sodium soy sauce

½ teaspoon sugar

½ cup bean sprouts

½ cup fresh or frozen corn kernels, thawed

½ cup frozen tiny peas, thawed

2½ tablespoons peanut oil

*G*ARNISH: 1 tablespoon toasted sesame seeds

1. Lightly beat the whole eggs with the egg whites and place them with the scallions, ginger, garlic, rice, soy sauce, sugar, sprouts, corn, and peas in small containers near the cooking area.

2. Heat a wok or large heavy skillet. Add ½ tablespoon of the peanut oil and when it is very hot, scramble the eggs and egg whites very loosely. Remove them and set aside.

3. Heat the remaining 2 tablespoons of the oil in the wok. When the oil is hot, stir-fry the scallions, garlic, and ginger for 30 seconds.

4. Add the rice and stir-fry until well mixed with the vegetables. Add the remaining ingredients, including the eggs, breaking them up to distribute evenly. Cook 1 to 2 minutes more to heat through. Sprinkle the sesame seeds over and serve immediately.

$\mathcal{V}$ARIATIONS:

❖ 5 egg whites can be substituted for 2 whole eggs and 2 egg whites.

❖ A 1-ounce package of shiitake mushrooms, soaked, stems removed, and chopped can be added with the vegetables.

❖ Additional vegetables or meats can be added to taste.

$\mathcal{D}$O-AHEAD PREP:

❖ The rice can be prepared a few hours in advance and reheated in the microwave oven. Leftover fried rice can be refrigerated in a covered container for 2 days and reheated. It can also be frozen.

Texmati Rice Pilaf with Sun-Dried Tomatoes, Peppers, and Pine Nuts

Serves: 6

*T*examti rice, also referred to as American basmati, is a hybrid of aromatic rice and regular long-grained varieties. It has the same nutty flavor but does not require the extra rinsing step necessary to prepare basmati.

1 tablespoon oil from a jar of oil-packed sun-dried tomatoes

3 large shallots, finely chopped

½ sweet red bell pepper, seeded and chopped

½ yellow bell pepper, seeded and chopped

1 cup Texmati white rice or rinsed basmati rice

4 oil-packed sun-dried tomatoes, blotted dry on paper towels
   and chopped

1 clove garlic, finely minced

1¾ cups defatted chicken or vegetable broth

salt and freshly ground pepper to taste

2 to 3 tablespoons toasted pine nuts

2 to 3 tablespoons Parmesan cheese

*G*ARNISH: freshly chopped parsley

1. In a deep nonstick saucepan, heat the oil to medium and sauté the shallots and bell peppers, stirring often, about 5 minutes, until softened.

2. Add the rice and toss to coat thoroughly. Add the sun-dried tomatoes and garlic and stir to combine. Add the broth and salt and pepper, bring to a boil, cover, reduce heat, and simmer for 20 minutes, without peeking.

3. Allow the rice to stand for 5 minutes, toss with the pine nuts and cheese, garnish with the parsley, and serve immediately.

*V*ARIATIONS:

❖ 1 whole red, yellow, or green bell pepper can be substituted for half the red and half the yellow bell pepper.

❖ Toasted almonds can be substituted for the pine nuts.

❖ Other aromatic rices such as Thai jasmine or jasmine rice can be used in this recipe but they will have a stickier texture.

$\mathcal{C}$OOK NOTES:

❖   Texmati, which is an American "basmati" or "aromatic" rice, is said to have come to America from Indochina via France in the early 1900s. This aromatic rice gives the same nutty, popcornlike flavor as basmati rice, but when the grains are cooked they are separate and similar to long-grain rice. In addition to Texmati, this aromatic rice is often found under the names "wild pecan rice" or "popcorn rice."

❖   The sun-dried tomatoes can be easily chopped with the aid of a kitchen scissors.

❖   The quick and easy way to toast pine nuts is to place them in a single layer on a baking sheet or in a toaster oven and bake them at 300°F for about 10 minutes, or until golden. Watch carefully to prevent burning.

$\mathcal{D}$O-AHEAD PREP:

❖   The rice can be cooked an hour in advance and reheated in a microwave oven.

Hoppin' John

Serves: 8

*B*lack-eyed peas, also called Southern peas or crowder peas, were thought to have originated in China. From there they traveled to Africa and the Arabic cultures, and then in the eighteenth century to the West through the African slave trade. Hoppin' John, a mixture of black-eyed peas and rice, is traditionally served on New Year's Day in the South to bring luck for the coming year.

4 cups water

1 cup dried black-eyed peas, rinsed and drained

2 teaspoons olive oil

½ cup finely chopped Canadian bacon (about 4 slices)

1 medium onion, finely chopped

1 small green bell pepper, chopped

1 clove garlic, minced

2 cups defatted chicken or beef broth

1 cup raw long-grain rice

½ teaspoon dried oregano, crumbled

salt to taste

pinch of cayenne pepper or to taste

*G*ARNISH: chopped parsley

1.   In a large saucepan, combine the water and black-eyed peas. Bring to a boil, reduce the heat, cover, and gently simmer for about 1 hour or until tender but not mushy. Drain the beans, discarding any excess liquid.

2.   In a deep large nonstick saucepan, heat the oil to medium and sauté the Canadian bacon for 2 to 3 minutes. Add the onion and green bell pepper and continue to sauté until softened. Add the garlic and stir to combine.

3.   Add the beans and remaining ingredients to the onions, bring to a boil, cover, reduce heat, and simmer slowly for about 25 minutes or until the rice is tender and the liquid is absorbed. If any liquid is remaining, remove the lid and cook uncovered until all the liquid is absorbed.

4.   Serve the beans hot, garnished with chopped parsley.

*V*ARIATIONS:

❖   A yellow or sweet red bell pepper can be substituted for the green bell pepper.

❖   Brown rice can be substituted for white rice, but increase the cooking time in Step 3 to at least 45 minutes.

𝒞ook notes:

❖   Store dried black-eyed peas in an airtight container in a cool, well-ventilated place for up to a year.

❖   Canadian bacon, which is smoked and cured pork tenderloin, is a leaner alternative to regular bacon. Called *back bacon* in Canada and England, it is more expensive than regular bacon but is leaner and precooked, which allows for less shrinkage and therefore less waste.

𝒟o-ahead prep:

❖   The beans can be cooked the day before and kept in a covered container in the refrigerator. The whole dish can also be cooked an hour or two in advance and reheated in the microwave oven.

Mexican-Style Bulgur Pilaf

Serves: 4 to 6

*T*here is more to bulgur than just tabbouleh, the Middle Eastern cracked wheat salad. This nutty high-fiber grain is a versatile side dish that complements a variety of main dishes.

2 teaspoons olive oil

1 small onion, finely chopped

1 green bell pepper, seeded and finely chopped

1 cup bulgur

1 teaspoon finely minced garlic

2 cups defatted chicken, beef, or vegetable broth

½ teaspoon chili powder

¼ teaspoon ground cumin

salt and freshly ground pepper to taste

one 4-ounce can diced mild green chiles, drained

one 2-ounce jar diced pimientos, drained

2 tablespoons chopped fresh parsley

*A*CCOMPANIMENT: Pico de Gallo (see page 59) or fresh salsa

1. In a heavy medium nonstick saucepan, heat the oil to medium and sauté the onion and green bell pepper for 5 to 6 minutes, stirring often, until softened. Add the bulgur and stir to coat the grains. Add the garlic and stir just to combine.

2. Add the broth, chili powder, cumin, and salt and pepper; bring to a boil, cover, reduce heat, and simmer slowly for about 20 minutes, or until the liquid is absorbed.

3. During the last few minutes of cooking, stir in the chiles, pimientos, and parsley, and continue to cook just until all the ingredients are heated through.

4. Serve the pilaf hot, accompanied by Pico de Gallo or fresh salsa.

*V*ARIATION:

❖ For a spicier version, a jalapeño pepper can be added with the onion and green bell pepper.

*C*OOK NOTE:

❖   Bulgur is not the same as cracked wheat. Both bulgur and cracked wheat are compounded of whole wheat berries but the similarity ends there. Cracked wheat is uncooked wheat that has been dried first and then cracked by coarse milling. Bulgur, on the other hand, is wheat that has been steamed, then dried before being crushed into various grinds.

*D*O-AHEAD PREP:

❖   The bulgur can be prepared an hour or two in advance and reheated in the microwave oven.

Custardy Cornbread

Serves: 6 to 8

I use this low-fat yet surprisingly rich tasting cornbread as a delicious side dish in place of pasta, rice, or potatoes.

- 1 cup stone-ground yellow or white cornmeal
- ¼ cup all-purpose flour
- 1 tablespoon sugar
- 1 teaspoon baking powder
- ½ teaspoon salt
- 1½ cups 1% low-fat milk
- 1 egg, lightly beaten
- 2 tablespoons unsalted butter

1. Preheat the oven to 400°F.

2. In a large mixing bowl, combine the cornmeal with the flour, sugar, baking powder, and salt. Add 1 cup of the milk and stir to combine. Add the egg and stir until well mixed.

3. Place the butter in an 8-inch square baking dish. Place the dish in the oven until the butter melts, about 1 to 2 minutes.

4. Pour the batter into the pan, pour the remaining ½ cup of milk over the top but do *not* stir. Bake the cornbread for 30 minutes, or until golden on top but still custardy on the inside.

5. Remove from the oven, allow to cool slightly, cut into squares, and serve hot.

*V*ARIATION:

❖ Chopped pimentos or diced green chiles can be added for a flavorful variation.

*C*OOK NOTES:

❖ Stone-ground cornmeal, which still contains most of the hull and the germ, can be found in most health food stores and many supermarkets.

❖ Store seldom-used packages of cornmeal in a sealed container or resealable plastic bag in the freezer.

*D*O-AHEAD PREP:

❖ The cornbread is at its most flavorful and has the best texture when baked just before eating.

Grits Soufflé

Serves: 4 to 6

This delicious and appealing side dish is a Southern treat. Although it's often referred to as a soufflé, it's more like a pudding.

Part-skim milk mozzarella or other flavorful part-skim milk cheeses can be substituted successfully for Jarlsberg Lite.

⅓ cup quick-cooking grits (not instant)

1½ cups water

pinch of salt

2 ounces (½ cup) grated Jarlsberg Lite or similar reduced fat,
    semisoft low-fat cheese

¼ cup 1% low-fat milk

2 tablespoons snipped fresh chives or chopped scallion greens

1 tablespoon freshly grated Parmesan cheese

1 tablespoon unsalted butter

1 egg, lightly beaten

¼ teaspoon minced garlic

Tabasco to taste

salt to taste

1. In a medium saucepan, combine the grits with the water and pinch of salt. Bring the ingredients to a boil, stirring frequently. Cover and allow to sit for 2 to 3 minutes. Remove from the heat, remove the cover, and allow to cool slightly.

2. Preheat the oven to 350°F. Coat an 8-inch-high round by 3-inch-high baking dish, or similar size ovenproof dish, with nonstick cooking spray.

3. Add the remaining ingredients to the cooked grits, stir until thoroughly mixed, and pour into prepared dish.

4. Bake for 35 to 40 minutes, or until lightly golden, and serve immediately.

VARIATION:

❖ Substitute ⅔ cup barley grits—a creamy, hot breakfast cereal prepared from pearled and cracked barley—for the hominy grits.

COOK NOTE:

❖ Grits is the term for finely ground hominy. Hominy is made from field corn: the corn kernels are bathed in a slaked lime or lye solution, which removes their tough skins and imparts a special flavor. Hominy is available in many forms. When dried and finely ground, it is known as grits, or more precisely hominy grits.

*D*O-AHEAD PREP:

❖ The grits can be assembled earlier in the day through Step 3, covered, and refrigerated until ready to bake. The cooked dish can also be reheated in the microwave oven.

Polenta Squares

Serves: 6 to 8

*P*olenta, a staple of northern Italy, is simply cornmeal mush. It can be eaten hot with a little butter or cooled until firm, cut into squares, and sautéed as it is in this recipe. Since instant polenta (precooked maize meal) is not readily available, I successfully prepare this recipe with cornmeal.

1½ cups defatted chicken or vegetable broth
¾ cup yellow cornmeal
2 tablespoons freshly grated Parmesan cheese
salt and freshly ground white pepper

1. Lightly coat an 8-inch square baking pan with olive oil nonstick cooking spray.

2. In a heavy medium nonstick saucepan, combine the broth and cornmeal, and whisk until smooth. Bring to a boil, stirring constantly over medium-high heat, and cook until thickened about 4 minutes. Remove from the heat, stir in the cheese and salt and pepper, and pour into the prepared pan; cover and chill for at least an hour or overnight.

3. Remove the polenta from the refrigerator and cut into 16 squares. Coat a large griddle with olive oil nonstick cooking spray and sauté the squares in two batches, over medium heat, until golden, for about 2 to 3 minutes per square. It may be necessary to coat the pan with additional spray after the first batch.

4. Serve hot as an accompaniment to stews, grilled meats, and poultry dishes.

$\mathcal{V}$ARIATIONS:

❖   1 to 2 tablespoons freshly chopped basil or rosemary can be added with the Parmesan cheese.

❖   If using instant polenta, follow the directions on the box and sauté according to the instructions.

$\mathcal{C}$OOK NOTES:

❖   Cornmeal is ground milled corn, either white or yellow. Yellow cornmeal has more nutrients than white.

❖   For an even easier method, pour the polenta into a nonstick muffin tin, chill it, flip the tin over, and neat, uniform, individual round servings fall out to be heated as above.

$\mathcal{D}$O-AHEAD PREP:

❖   The squares can be prepared, wrapped tightly, and chilled a day or two in advance. Cook just before serving.

Quinoa and Vegetable Pilaf

Serves: 4 to 6

Quinoa (pronounced *keen-wa*), dubbed the "supergrain of the future," originated in the Andes mountains of South America about 3000 B.C. when the Incas referred to it as "the mother grain." Quinoa is higher in protein than any other grain, has a balance of amino acids lacking in other grains, is a good source of calcium, is high in fiber, and has no cholesterol.

This side dish or lunch main course is easy to cook and can be assembled well in advance and reheated just before serving. Any leftovers? Just add a little vinaigrette and you have a quinoa salad.

1 cup quinoa

2 cups defatted chicken or vegetable broth

1 tablespoon olive oil

1 small onion, finely chopped

2 carrots, peeled and finely chopped

¼ cup green bell pepper, seeded and finely chopped

¼ cup sweet red bell pepper, seeded and finely chopped

1 large rib celery, finely chopped

1 teaspoon finely minced garlic

salt and freshly ground pepper

2 to 3 tablespoons freshly grated Parmesan cheese

GARNISH: 2 tablespoons toasted slivered almonds and chopped fresh parsley

1. Rinse the quinoa thoroughly, using a very fine mesh strainer. Drain well.

2. Place the quinoa and the broth in a medium saucepan and bring to a boil. Reduce the heat, cover, and simmer until all of the liquid is absorbed, about 15 minutes. You will know that the quinoa is done when all the grains have turned from white to transparent, and the spiral-like germ has separated.

3. In a medium nonstick skillet, heat the oil to medium; add the onion, carrots, bell peppers, and celery and cook for about 5 minutes, stirring often, until softened, but still crisp. Add the garlic and stir to just combine.

4. Add the cooked vegetables and salt and pepper to the hot quinoa, toss with the Parmesan cheese, and serve hot, garnished with the almonds and chopped fresh parsley.

*V*ARIATION:

❖ The vegetables can be varied according to seasonal availability.

*C*OOK NOTE:

❖ Most varieties of quinoa have a naturally occurring bitter-tasting coating on each grain. This coating is removed before packaging, but there may be a small amount of bitter residue or powder left on the grain. This can be removed simply by rinsing before cooking.

*D*O-AHEAD PREP:

❖ The pilaf can be prepared in advance and reheated in the microwave just before serving.

Couscous Provençale

*C*ouscous, a staple of North African cooking, is made from semolina that has been precooked and then dried. Although it would seem to be a pasta, it more resembles rice or grits than noodles. Unlike other pastas that are cooked in large quantities of water, couscous is cooked like rice, in a small amount of water that is absorbed during the cooking process.

It is perfectly acceptable to use the quick-cooking (also called instant or precooked) couscous, which can be prepared in only five or six minutes.

1 tablespoon extra-virgin olive oil

1 small onion, finely minced

1 clove garlic, finely minced

2 cups hot defatted chicken, beef, or vegetable broth

pinch of saffron threads soaked in 2 tablespoons of hot water for
     2 minutes

1 tablespoon minced fresh oregano or thyme

1 tablespoon minced fresh Italian parsley

6 oil-packed sun-dried tomatoes, blotted dry on paper towels
     and julienned

6 Niçoise olives, pitted and sliced

1 cup quick-cooking couscous

*G*ARNISH: 2 tablespoons toasted pistachio nuts, crushed

1. In a medium nonstick saucepan, heat the oil over medium heat, and sauté the onion, stirring often, for 5 to 6 minutes, or until softened. Add the garlic, and stir for 30 seconds.

2. Add the remaining ingredients, bring to a boil, cover, remove from the heat, and allow to sit for 6 to 7 minutes, or until the liquid has been absorbed.

3. Fluff with a fork, top with the nuts, and serve hot.

*V*ARIATIONS:

❖ Turn any leftovers into a delicious tabbouleh-like salad by tossing with a mixture of the following: 2 tablespoons of balsamic vinegar mixed with 2 teaspoons of olive oil, 1 tablespoon of Dijon mustard, and salt and pepper.

❖ If fresh basil or thyme are not available, substitute 2 tablespoons fresh parsley.

❖ Greek Kalamata olives can be substituted for the French Niçoise olives.

❖ Pine nuts can be substituted for the pistachio nuts.

𝒞ook NOTES:

❖ Saffron comes from the stigmas of the small purple crocus. Each flower only provides three stigmas that must be hand-picked and then dried. Not only is this process labor intensive, but it takes more than 14,000 of these tiny stigmas for each ounce of saffron. It's no wonder that saffron has been called the world's most expensive spice! Saffron comes in two forms: powdered and threads, which are actually the whole stigmas. Powdered saffron will lose its flavor more quickly than the threads and should be stored in a very cool, dark place for up to 6 months.

❖ Use a scissor to quickly and easily chop the sun-dried tomatoes.

𝒟o-AHEAD PREP:

❖ The dish can be cooked earlier in the day and reheated in a microwave oven.

Sourdough Stuffing with Apricots and Almonds

Yield: 8 cups to serve 10 to 12

*A*pple cider adds extra moisture to this low-fat stuffing. It's perfect for the holidays or when you have a craving for a comforting turkey dinner with all the trimmings.

½ cup apple cider or juice

1 cup dried apricots, chopped fine

1 pound sourdough bread, crusts removed, or 12 ounces egg
  bread with crusts left on, cut in ½-inch cubes (about 10 cups)

¼ cup slivered almonds

2 tablespoons vegetable oil

2 cups finely chopped onions

2 cups finely chopped celery

2 tablespoons finely chopped fresh parsley

1½ teaspoons finely chopped fresh thyme leaves, or ½ teaspoon
  dried thyme, crumbled

1 teaspoon finely chopped fresh sage or ½ teaspoon dried
  sage, crumbled

1 teaspoon finely chopped fresh oregano leaves or ½ teaspoon
  dried, crumbled

salt and freshly ground pepper to taste

¼ cup defatted chicken broth

1. In a small saucepan, heat the cider or juice until just boiling. Add the apricots, remove from the heat, and allow to stand at least 15 to 20 minutes to soften.

2. Preheat the oven to 375°F.

3. Spread the bread cubes and almonds on a baking sheet and bake for 7 minutes, stirring occasionally, or until lightly golden and crisp. Transfer to a large bowl.

4. Reduce the oven temperature to 350°F.

5. In a large nonstick skillet, heat the oil to medium, add the onions and celery, and cook, stirring often, about 5 to 7 minutes, until just tender. Stir in the parsley, thyme, sage, oregano, and salt and pepper. Pour over the bread cubes and almonds. Stir in the apricots and cider. Gradually stir in the chicken broth just until the stuffing mixture holds together.

6. Stuff the mixture in a turkey or bake in a covered 2½-quart baking dish that has been coated with nonstick cooking spray in a 350°F oven for 45 to 50 minutes, or until hot and the top is slightly crusty.

*V*ARIATION:

❖ Dried cherries, cranberries, or raisins can be substituted for the apricots.

*C*OOK NOTE:

❖ After the meal, promptly remove any leftover stuffing from the poultry cavity and tightly wrap and refrigerate both the bird and the stuffing separately to reduce the risk of food spoilage.

*D*O-AHEAD PREP:

❖ Chilled stuffing is easier to handle, so prepare the stuffing a day in advance and refrigerate it in a covered container. Remember not to stuff the bird until you are ready to put it in the oven!

VEGETABLES

❖ ❖ ❖ ❖ ❖ ❖ ❖

Steamed Vegetables with Fresh Herbs:
A Basic Primer

Vegetable Pasta

Warm Cannellini Beans with Sage

Grilled Green Beans with Peppers and Oregano

Brussels Sprouts with Chestnuts

Carrot and Corn Patties with Salsa

Roasted Summer Corn

Braised Onions with Sage

Gratin of Yukon Gold Potatoes

Crusty Light Mashed Potatoes with Roasted Garlic

Herb Roasted Potatoes and Onions

Oven-Roasted Cheese Fries

Light and Crispy Potato-Zucchini Pancakes

Light Sweet Potato Soufflé

Spinach and Rice Pie with Vegetables

Stir-Fried Spinach with Roasted Garlic

An avocado is also called an alligator pear. So, would a pear-shaped alligator be called an avocado . . . or just fat?
—Anonymous

Steamed Vegetables with Fresh Herbs:
A Basic Primer

Serves: 4 to 6

*S*teaming or cooking by moist heat is one of the best ways to preserve the nutrients in vegetables but there is a rule that should always be observed during the steaming process: keep the cooking time short! Cut thicker vegetables like carrots into small pieces so they will cook more quickly and softer vegetables like zucchini into large pieces so they will retain their crisp texture.

Use color as a key to testing when the vegetable is perfectly cooked. When the color is bright, test the vegetables with the tip of a sharp knife—they will pierce readily if done. When the vegetables are done, immediately uncover the steamer or pot to stop the cooking process. Remember, never allow them to sit in the pot, even if the heat has been turned off, or the vegetables will continue to cook and lose their crispness.

Since every vegetable requires a different steaming time, it is best to steam them separately or add faster-cooking vegetables after the slower ones have partially steamed. You can, however, steam vegetables and hold them cold as a preliminary step to many final preparations such as sautéing with a little butter or oil and seasonings.

In all steamers, the food is placed on a rack at least one inch above the boiling liquid and is not in direct contact with the liquid. The pan is covered to keep in the steam. Several types of steamers are available. The small French folding steamer rack can be set in the bottom of any deep, tightly covered saucepan, to become an inexpensive steamer. Chinese bamboo or metal steamers are convenient because the trays can be stacked and several different vegetables can be steamed at once and each removed according to its own cooking time. For cooking small amounts of vegetables, steamers can be improvised by setting a colander or strainer in a large tightly covered saucepan.

This is just a guideline to a basic steamed vegetable dish. Cauliflower can be substituted for the broccoli, kohlrabi, or Jerusalem artichokes for the turnips, or any variety or combination of vegetables can be assembled according to taste preferences. The vegetables in this recipe are cut up to allow for faster steaming but can be adjusted if a vegetable is to be cooked whole.

2 turnips

2 large carrots

1 parsnip

½ head broccoli

2 tablespoons snipped fresh dill

1 tablespoon freshly grated Parmesan cheese

salt and freshly ground white pepper to taste

1. Peel the turnips, slice off and discard the root ends, and cut into 1½-inch chunks. Steaming time for turnips is 10 to 12 minutes.

2. Wash and peel the carrots and parsnip lightly (many of the nutrients are in the peel), trim off the root and stem ends, and cut into 1½- to 2-inch pieces. Steaming time for carrots and parsnips is 8 to 10 minutes.

3. Wash the broccoli, slice off and discard the tough ends, and lightly peel the stalks. For even cooking, break the florets off and cut the stems into 1½-inch slices. Steaming time for broccoli is 6 to 8 minutes.

4. Steam the vegetables in tiers in a bamboo steamer, on a rack in a saucepan, or in an electric steamer, according to the cooking times specified. Begin with the turnips, then add the carrots and the parsnip, and finally the broccoli so that the vegetables are finished at the same time.

5. Toss the finished vegetables with the dill, Parmesan, salt and pepper and serve them immediately.

*V*ARIATIONS:

❖ Additional vegetable combinations:
    cabbage and potato seasoned with chives and caraway seeds
    artichokes and garlic seasoned with tarragon
    zucchini and crookneck squash seasoned with basil and Parmesan cheese
    acorn squash seasoned with cinnamon and nutmeg
    peas and corn seasoned with dill

Vegetable Pasta

Serves: 4

*W*ith the use of a food processor shredding disc you can cut vegetables into pastalike spaghetti strands that provide a healthful base for stews and sauces. The vegetables should be cut into pieces that will fit the width of the food processor feed tube.

> 1 large turnip, peeled and cut into 3-inch-long pieces
>
> 2 medium carrots, peeled and cut into 3-inch-long pieces
>
> 2 medium parsnips, peeled and cut into 3-inch-long pieces
>
> 2 large zucchini, washed and dried, trimmed, and cut into 3-inch-long pieces
>
> salt and freshly ground pepper to taste

1. Place the vegetables in batches in the top of the food processor and slice them into ribbons.

2. Bring a large pot of water to a boil. Drop the turnips, carrots, and parsnips in the water and cook for about 1 minute, or until tender. Add the zucchini and cook for an additional 30 seconds.

3. Drain, season with salt and pepper, and serve immediately.

*V*ARIATIONS:

❖ Vegetables can also be shredded with a hand-held mandoline or other slicing and shredding gadget.

❖ Cooked spaghetti squash can be added to the finished product.

❖ If to be used as a side dish, instead of as a base for sauce, toss the vegetable pasta with 1 to 2 tablespoons of grated Parmesan cheese.

*C*OOK NOTE:

❖ Turnips are the culinary Cinderellas of the vegetable world. They are an excellent source of vitamin C and retain 60 percent of this necessary vitamin even after cooking. Turnips are rich in potassium, calcium, and phosphorus. Turnips deteriorate rapidly so remove the leaves, which drain the juices from the roots, to allow them to stay fresher. Turnips will stay fresh in a perforated plastic bag in the vegetable crisper in the refrigerator for about a week.

*D*O-AHEAD PREP:

❖ The vegetables can be readied in advance but must be cooked at the very last minute.

Warm Cannellini Beans with Sage

Serves: 4 to 6

*A*nnie Somerville is the executive chef at Greens restaurant in San Francisco. This recipe, adapted from her book *Field of Greens* (Bantam 1993), transforms beans into a delicious side dish or comforting winter or fall luncheon treat.

2 cups dried cannellini beans (about 12 ounces), sorted and
  soaked overnight

6 cups water

1 bay leaf

2 sprigs winter savory or fresh thyme

2 whole fresh sage leaves plus 8 fresh sage leaves, chopped

1 tablespoon extra-virgin olive oil

1 medium yellow onion, cut into ½-inch pieces

salt and freshly ground pepper to taste

3 garlic cloves, finely chopped

⅓ cup dry white wine or vermouth

2 to 3 tablespoons water

½ tablespoon chopped fresh Italian parsley

*G*ARNISH: whole fresh sage leaves

1. Drain the soaked beans, rinse them well, and place them in a large saucepan. Add the water, bay leaf, savory, and the 2 whole sage leaves. Bring to a boil, reduce the heat, and simmer, uncovered, stirring occasionally until tender, about 35 to 40 minutes. Watch them closely during the last 5 to 10 minutes to make sure the skins have softened and the beans have opened but still hold their shape. Remove the herbs and bay leaf. Leave the beans in their broth.

2. In a large nonstick skillet, heat the oil to medium. Add the onion, salt and pepper, and sauté, stirring often, until the onion begins to soften, about 5 to 6 minutes. Add the garlic and remaining 8 chopped sage leaves and sauté for about 10 minutes, stirring occasionally. Increase the heat to high, add the wine or vermouth, and cook for a minute or two, until most of the liquid has been absorbed.

3. Add the beans and their broth to the onions. Lower the heat and cook uncovered for 20 minutes, adding a little water if needed to keep the beans saucy.

4. Add salt and pepper to taste, stir in the parsley, and serve hot, garnished with sage leaves.

*V*ARIATION:

❖ If fresh sage is unavailable, substitute dried sage, but since dried sage is more powerful than fresh, substitute only ½ teaspoon dried ground sage in Step 1 for the total of 10 fresh sage leaves.

*C*OOK NOTES:

❖ The use of sage in America is pretty much restricted to Thanksgiving and Christmas when the poultry seasoning is pulled from the shelf and sprinkled on the bird. But fresh sage can enhance many dishes including bean dishes, marinated cheese, grilled meats, and roasted poultry.

❖ Savory comes in two types: winter and summer, which are both relatives of the mint family. Savory acts as an herbal enhancer—its pungent flavor helps to bring out the best in other herbs such as the sage in this bean dish. Savory is actually known as the *bean herb* for two reasons: it intensifies the flavor of beans and its high tannin content is thought to make beans more digestible.

*D*O-AHEAD PREP:

❖ The beans can be done a day or two in advance, stored in a covered container in the refrigerator, and reheated when ready to serve.

Grilled Green Beans with Peppers and Oregano

Serves: 4 to 6

This easy-to-prepare summer treat uses fresh summer green beans and peppers that have been wrapped in foil and cooked over a hot grill. During the winter and fall, the vegetables can be roasted in a 375°F oven for 30 minutes.

    1½ pounds fresh green beans, washed and trimmed
    1 sweet red bell pepper, seeded and julienned
    1 sweet yellow bell pepper, seeded and julienned
    2 scallions (green and white parts included), finely chopped
    2 tablespoons dry white wine
    2 tablespoons defatted chicken or vegetable broth
    1 tablespoon balsamic vinegar
    2 teaspoons olive oil
    1 teaspoon chopped fresh oregano or ¼ teaspoon dried
        oregano, crumbled
    salt and freshly ground pepper to taste

1. Preheat a covered outdoor grill. Place a large 2-foot-square piece of heavy-duty aluminum foil on the counter and coat with olive oil nonstick cooking spray.

2. Place the green beans and red and yellow bell peppers in the center of the foil and sprinkle with the scallions. In a small bowl, combine the remaining ingredients, stir together, and drizzle evenly over the vegetables.

3. Seal the foil tightly and place on the grill. Place the lid on the grill and cook for about 15 to 20 minutes, or until the vegetables are tender.

4. Unwrap and serve hot.

VARIATIONS:

❖ Leeks or shallots can be substituted for the scallions.

❖ Haricots verts, the slender and delicate French beans, can be substituted for the green beans.

COOK NOTE:

❖ Green beans have very few calories and are a very good source of fiber, iron, potassium, vitamin A, and vitamin C.

❖   The foil packet can be assembled earlier in the day and kept in the refrigerator until ready to grill.

Brussels Sprouts with Chestnuts

Serves: 4

*C*hestnuts are delicious all year-round, not just for holiday dinners. They are low in calories and they have absolutely no fat! You no longer need to roast chestnuts and burn your hands trying to peel them. Just buy the jars of peeled roasted or steamed chestnuts, but make sure to avoid the cans of chestnuts packed in heavy syrup.

> 20 to 26 (1 to 1¼ pounds) small Brussels sprouts, washed, wilted
> or damaged leaves removed
> 1 cup defatted chicken or vegetable broth
> 1 cup water
> 1 cup peeled, roasted or steamed chestnuts
> 1 tablespoon unsalted butter
> 1 tablespoon snipped fresh chives or finely chopped
> scallion greens
> salt and freshly ground white pepper

1.   Cut off the bottom stems and any tough outer leaves of the Brussels sprouts and make a tiny crosswise incision at the base to speed up the cooking process.

2.   In a medium saucepan, bring the broth and water to a boil, add the Brussels sprouts, and boil for 2 minutes. Cover, reduce heat to medium-low, and cook for 5 minutes. Add the chestnuts and continue to cook for 1 minute longer, until the Brussels sprouts are tender and the chestnuts are heated through. (Do not overcook the Brussels sprouts or they will become mealy.)

3.   Drain, discard the liquid, toss the Brussels sprouts and chestnuts with the remaining ingredients, and serve hot.

*V*ariation:

❖   The Brussels sprouts can be steamed for 10 minutes in a vegetable steamer. The chestnuts can be added during the last 2 minutes of steaming and then tossed with the remaining ingredients and served.

$\mathcal{C}$ook Notes:

❖ Brussels sprouts are a good source of vitamins A and C, potassium, iron, and protein. They are highly perishable and should be used within 1 to 2 days of purchase.

❖ Chestnuts are highly perishable. Once they are peeled and cooled, store them in an airtight container in the refrigerator for up to three to four days, or freeze them for up to one year.

❖ If you still want to peel chestnuts the old-fashioned way, simply carve an X on the flat side of each chestnut. Put the chestnuts in a saucepan with water to cover, bring to a boil, and simmer for 15 to 20 minutes. Drain the chestnuts and when cool, the shell and inner peel should be easy to remove with your fingers. One pound of fresh chestnuts yields 2½ cups peeled.

$\mathcal{D}$o-ahead Prep:

❖ Do not cook the Brussels sprouts until just before serving to maintain their crunchy texture.

Carrot and Corn Patties with Salsa

Serves: 8 to 10

*T*hese light patties are a combination of a pancake and a croquette. They are versatile and can be used as both a starch and a vegetable side dish, a vegetarian luncheon dish, or a spectacular appetizer. Serve them with just a dollop of low-fat sour cream and accompany them with a fresh salsa.

4 teaspoons olive oil

6 medium carrots, peeled and finely chopped (about 2 cups)

2 leeks, thoroughly washed and diced (white parts only) (about 1½ cups)

1 cup fresh or frozen corn, thawed

1¼ cup low-fat, part-skim milk ricotta

¼ cup low-fat sour cream

½ cup all-purpose flour

½ teaspoon baking powder

3 egg whites

salt and freshly ground white pepper to taste

*G*ARNISH: dollop of low-fat sour cream and sprigs of cilantro

*A*CCOMPANIMENTS: Mango Salsa (see page 146), Pico de Gallo (see page 59), or Creamy Horseradish Dressing (see page 316)

1. In a medium nonstick skillet, heat 2 teaspoons of the oil and sauté the carrots and leeks over medium heat, stirring often, until softened, about 5 minutes. Add the corn and continue to cook for an additional 2 to 3 minutes, until all the vegetables are softened.

2. Place the vegetable mixture in a large bowl, add the remaining ingredients, and stir until combined. The consistency should be like a thick pancake batter.

3. Preheat the oven to 200°F.

4. Heat a nonstick griddle or a large nonstick skillet over medium heat, add the remaining 2 teaspoons of the oil, and when hot drop the batter by large tablespoons. Press the batter down in the middle to make an even patty and sauté for 2 minutes a side or until crisp and golden on the outside and cooked through on the inside. Remove the finished ones to a platter, keep warm in the oven, and finish off the batter, spraying the pan generously with olive oil nonstick cooking spray as necessary.

5. Serve the patties garnished with a dollop of low-fat sour cream and sprigs of cilantro and accompanied by Mango Salsa, Pico de Gallo, or Creamy Horseradish Dressing.

*V*ARIATION:

❖ Zucchini or yellow crookneck squash can be substituted for the carrots.

*C*OOK NOTES:

❖ Do not store carrots and apples together. Apples release a gas that gives carrots a bitter taste.

❖ Carrot greens draw moisture from the carrots so remove them as soon as you get home from the market and store them in a plastic bag in the crisper section of the refrigerator.

*D*O-AHEAD PREP:

❖ The pancakes are at their optimum flavor when served just after baking, but they can be reheated for about 4 to 5 minutes in a 350°F oven.

Roasted Summer Corn

Serves: 4 to 6

*C*orn is the summer vegetable of choice—the perfect vegetable for an outdoor barbecue. When bought locally, fresh corn is sweet, crisp, and tender.

Corn is a high-fiber, high-carbohydrate food with a fair source of vitamin A (if the corn is yellow). It is low in fat and low in sodium and contains traces of iron, vitamin C, and some of the B vitamins. The secret to keeping corn low fat is to roast or grill it flavored with fresh herbs and seasonings. It is so delicious this way, it needs no butter. This method is not only easy to prepare (no big pots to wash!) but creates a juicy ear of corn without any sogginess.

> 6 fresh ears of corn
> salt and freshly ground white pepper to taste
> 1 tablespoon chopped fresh basil
> 1 tablespoon snipped fresh chives

1. Preheat the oven to 400°F.

2. Loosen the husks from the corn, but do not pull them away entirely. Remove the silk and discard. Run the kernels under cold water and sprinkle each ear with salt, freshly ground white pepper, and the fresh herbs. Pull the husks back into place. Run the ear under cold water all over and place on a baking sheet.

3. Bake the ears for about 30 minutes, turning once, or until the kernels are tender.

4. Husk and serve hot.

*V*ARIATIONS:

❖ Other fresh herbs can be used: cilantro, dill, thyme, oregano, or a mixture of some or all of these.

❖ To cook on the outdoor grill, preheat the grill to medium-high. Prepare the corn the same way as for roasting and place the dampened ears on the grill. Cook for about 15 minutes, turning every 5 minutes, or until the husks are charred and the kernels are tender. You can also remove the husks entirely and lay the bare ears of corn right on the grill to cook for about 4 to 5 minutes, turning often.

*C*OOK NOTES:

❖ Buy ears of corn with fresh, snug, bright green husks and dark brown silk at the end. The ears should be filled to the tip, with no rows of missing kernels. The stem ends should not be too discolored or dried out. There should be no signs of decay.

❖ The sugar in standard yellow or white corn begins converting to starch minutes after the ear is picked. Not so with the newest sweet-corn hybrids on the market, which are bred to keep their sweetness for several weeks.

*D*O-AHEAD PREP:

❖ The corn can be prepared several hours in advance and kept in the refrigerator until ready to dampen and roast.

Braised Onions with Sage

Serves: 8

*N*o more creamed onions! This light and delicious vegetable side dish is the perfect accompaniment to a Thanksgiving feast, holiday meal, or any wintery dinner.

The cooking time varies with the size of the onions. Taste is your best guide to when the onion is tender.

2 teaspoons olive oil
24 small boiling onions, peeled and trimmed but left whole
2 tablespoons all-purpose flour
1 cup defatted chicken, beef, or vegetable broth
3 whole fresh sage leaves or ½ teaspoon ground dried sage
salt and freshly ground pepper

*G*ARNISH: chopped fresh parsley

1. In a medium nonstick saucepan, heat the oil to medium-high and sauté the onions, stirring often, until golden, for about 5 minutes.

2. Add the flour and stir until lightly browned, about 2 minutes. Gradually add the broth, stirring until smooth. Add the sage and salt and pepper, reduce heat, cover, and simmer for about 35 minutes, or until the onions are tender.

3. Remove from the heat, discard the sage leaves if using the fresh ones, and serve hot garnished with chopped parsley.

*V*ARIATION:

❖ 1 teaspoon chopped fresh thyme leaves or ¼ teaspoon dried thyme, crumbled, can be substituted for the sage.

❖　An easy way to peel onions is to make a tiny crisscross incision in the root end of each onion, drop them into boiling water for 1 to 2 minutes, drain, and plunge them into a bowl of ice water. The peel will easily pop off.

*D*O-AHEAD PREP:

❖　The onions can be prepared a day or two in advance and refrigerated in a covered container. Reheat in a microwave oven or on top of the range.

Gratin of Yukon Gold Potatoes

Serves: 4 to 6

*Y*ukon gold or yellow Finnish potatoes add extra natural buttery flavor to this gratin but you can easily substitute russet potatoes. There is no need to peel the potato since the skin adds additional texture and nutrients.

2 pounds Yukon gold or yellow Finnish potatoes, scrubbed clean
　　and thinly sliced
1 large onion, thinly sliced
1 clove garlic, finely minced
3 tablespoons all-purpose flour
½ cup grated Jarlsberg Lite or other light Swiss cheese
salt and freshly ground pepper to taste
1⅓ cups defatted chicken or vegetable broth
3 tablespoons freshly grated Parmesan cheese

1.　Preheat the oven to 375°F. Generously coat a 1½-quart flat oval gratin, or similar shaped baking dish, with olive oil nonstick cooking spray.

2.　In a large bowl, toss the potatoes, onion, and garlic with the flour, cheese, and salt and pepper until well coated.

3.　Layer the potatoes and onion slices in the prepared baking dish. Lightly spray the potatoes with olive oil nonstick cooking spray, pour the chicken or vegetable broth over the potatoes, and bake for 1¼ hours.

4.　Sprinkle the top evenly with the Parmesan cheese, and continue to bake for an additional 15 to 20 minutes, or until the potatoes are tender and the top is golden brown.

*V*ARIATION:

❖ Reduced-fat cheddar, Monterey Jack, or Muenster cheese can be substituted for the Swiss.

*C*OOK NOTES:

❖ Do not store potatoes with onions. Onions release a gas that hastens the spoilage of potatoes.

❖ Select Yukon gold or yellow Finnish potatoes that are firm and except for some black scabs, they should be free of blemishes or sprouts. Store the potatoes in a cool dark place, not in the refrigerator, where the starch converts to sugar and the nutrient value is reduced.

*D*O-AHEAD PREP:

❖ The finished dish can be cooked an hour earlier and reheated in a microwave.

Crusty Light Baked Mashed Potatoes with Roasted Garlic

Serves: 4 to 6

*M*ashed potatoes are definitely comfort food and these light ones give you all the stroking without the guilt! Do *not* use a food processor or the potatoes will become gluey in texture.

 2 large white rose or other thin-skinned potatoes
 1 tablespoon unsalted butter
 ½ cup 1% low-fat milk
 4 to 6 cloves roasted garlic (see Cook Note, below)
 salt and freshly ground white pepper to taste
 paprika to taste
 seasoning salt to taste

GARNISH: sprigs of watercress

1. Place the potatoes in a medium saucepan, cover with water, and bring to a boil. Cover, reduce the heat, and simmer for about 45 minutes, or until tender. Remove the potatoes and peel easily by holding them with thick rubber gloves.

2. Cut the cooked potatoes into large chunks, place in the bowl of an electric mixer, or using a hand mixer, mash the potatoes with the butter, milk, roasted garlic, and salt and pepper until smooth and whipped.

3. Preheat the oven to 350°F. Generously coat a small baking dish with nonstick cooking spray.

4. Place the mashed potatoes in the prepared pan, sprinkle lightly with the paprika and seasoning salt, and bake for 30 minutes, or until golden on top.

5. Serve hot, garnished with watercress.

VARIATION:

❖ The potatoes can be whipped and served as is without additional baking.

COOK NOTES:

❖ To roast garlic: preheat the oven to 275°F. Lightly coat a small baking sheet with olive oil nonstick cooking spray. Place the unpeeled garlic cloves on the baking sheet in a single layer and bake for about 35 to 40 minutes, or until very soft. Remove from the oven and allow to cool slightly. Squeeze the garlic from their skins (they will come out very easily) and use as directed.

❖ One often sees the sign NEW POTATOES in the supermarket. These are not any special variety, but are spuds picked before they've matured. New potatoes are best boiled or steamed. They have a high sugar content, so they brown excessively when fried. They have a high water content so they make greasy, limp fries.

*D*O-AHEAD PREP:

❖ The potatoes can be mashed earlier in the day, placed in the baking dish, and refrigerated until ready to bake.

Herb Roasted Potatoes and Onions

Serves: 6 to 8

*T*his dish takes a while to cook, but once in the oven, requires only a little basting, allowing you to easily concentrate on the other parts of the meal. The herbs can be varied according to the accompanying dish.

> 12 small white rose potatoes
>
> 12 small boiling onions (golf-ball size), peeled
>
> 6 sprigs fresh rosemary, thyme, oregano, or a combination of
>   all three
>
> salt, freshly ground pepper, and paprika to taste
>
> paprika
>
> 2 tablespoons olive oil
>
> 1½ tablespoons balsamic vinegar
>
> **GARNISH:** fresh herb sprigs

1.   Preheat the oven to 375°F. Lightly coat a large roasting pan with olive oil nonstick cooking spray.

2.   Slice the potatoes in half and arrange them with the onions in the pan in a single layer. Bury the herbs among the vegetables and sprinkle with salt and pepper and paprika.

3.   In a small bowl, mix the oil and vinegar together and brush on the vegetables. Place the pan in the oven and roast for about 1 to 1¼ hours, or until the vegetables are golden brown, basting occasionally.

4.   Remove from the oven, place on a platter, garnish with fresh herbs, and serve hot.

VARIATIONS:

❖   If small onions and potatoes are unavailable, substitute larger ones, but cut them in half.

❖   Baby Yukon gold or yellow Finnish potatoes have a wonderful natural buttery flavor and moist flesh that work well in this recipe.

COOK NOTE:

❖   Potatoes should be stored in a cool, well-ventilated place that's dark and humid but not wet. Do not store potatoes in the refrigerator where the natural starch will convert to sugar causing an overly sweet taste.

*D*O-AHEAD PREP:

❖ The potatoes can be cooked an hour or two in advance and reheated just before serving.

Oven-Roasted Cheese Fries

Serves: 3 to 4

*F*rench fries don't need to be heavy and greasy! These crispy fries are flavorful, low in fat, and easy to prepare. It is best to use Parmesan cheese that has been finely ground.

> 1½ pounds baking potatoes, cut into thin strips about ¼ inch wide
> 3 tablespoons finely ground Parmesan cheese
> salt and freshly ground white pepper to taste

1. Preheat the oven to 400°F. Lightly coat a baking pan with nonstick cooking spray.

2. Place the potato slices in a resealable plastic bag, add the cheese and salt and pepper, seal the bag, and shake to thoroughly coat the slices.

3. Place the potatoes in a single layer in the prepared pan and bake for about 15 to 20 minutes, or until golden. Turn, sprinkle lightly with salt and pepper, and continue to bake for about 15 to 20 minutes, or until they are crisp and golden all over.

4. Serve the potatoes immediately.

*V*ARIATION:

❖ Substitute Yukon gold, yellow Finnish, or even sweet potatoes for the baking potatoes.

*C*OOK NOTE:

❖ If you are a potato connoisseur, you may choose to test your tubers for mealiness. Mealy, soft potatoes, best for making French fries, mashing, and baking, are denser than the waxy ones preferred for salad, boiled, and scalloped potatoes. Put unpeeled, raw potatoes in a solution of one pound salt and one gallon water. The mealy potatoes will sink, the waxy ones will float.

*D*O-AHEAD PREP:

❖ It is best to slice the potatoes just before baking to prevent discoloration. The cheese fries must be served immediately to prevent sogginess.

Light and Crispy
Potato-Zucchini Pancakes

Serves: 4 to 6

*P*otato pancakes have come a long way since Grandma's time. This light version is crispy and delicious and you won't miss the fat.

¼ cup chopped scallions (green and white parts included)

2 tablespoons freshly snipped dill

1 whole egg, lightly beaten

1 egg white, lightly beaten

2 tablespoons all-purpose flour

½ teaspoon baking powder

salt and freshly ground white pepper to taste

2 medium zucchini (about ½ pound), washed, wiped dry, ends trimmed

2 medium baking potatoes (about 1 pound)

2 tablespoons olive or canola oil

*G*ARNISH: low-fat sour cream and snipped fresh chives or chopped scallion greens

1. In a large bowl, combine the scallions, dill, egg, egg white, flour, baking powder, and salt and pepper and stir until well mixed.

2. Grate the zucchini in a food processor fitted with the small shredding blade, or grate by hand. Place the zucchini between layers of paper towels, squeeze dry, and stir into the other ingredients.

3. Peel the potatoes, immediately grate them in the food processor or by hand, and blot dry on paper towels. Add the potatoes to the bowl and stir until the batter is smooth.

4. Preheat the oven to 425°F. Line a baking sheet with aluminum foil.

5. In a nonstick griddle pan, heat 1 tablespoon of the oil over medium-high heat. When hot, add the batter by large spoonfuls (4 to 5 pancakes per batch), and cook for about 3 to 4 minutes per side, or until golden, lightly flattening them after flipping. Drain the pancakes on paper towels while cooking the second batch. Continue to use up the batter, adding the remaining tablespoon of oil before cooking the last 4 patties.

6. Place the browned pancakes on prepared baking sheet and bake for 10 to 15 minutes or until crisp.

7. Serve the pancakes hot garnished with a dollop of low-fat sour cream and snipped fresh chives or scallion greens.

*V*ARIATION:

❖ Yellow crookneck or pattypan squash can be substituted for the zucchini.

*C*OOK NOTES:

❖ To keep the pancakes crispy, make sure all the moisture is squeezed out of both the zucchini and the potatoes.

❖ Select crisp zucchini that have a dark green glossy skin. Gently prod the blossom end (the end opposite the stem end) to make sure it is hard; a soft blossom end is a sign of overripeness. Avoid very large zucchini, which are seedy and have little flavor.

❖ If you don't have time to blot the potatoes dry, grate them into a salad spinner and spin them dry.

*D*O-AHEAD PREP:

❖ The pancakes are at their optimum flavor when served just after baking, but they can be reheated in a 425°F oven for about 4 to 5 minutes.

Light Sweet Potato Soufflé

Serves: 10 to 12

*Y*ou will reduce both the fat and the calories in any holiday or festive dinner with this lightened version of a traditional sweet potato pudding. Cream has been set aside in favor of 1% milk, eggs have been replaced with egg whites, and both the butter and the amounts of sugar have been greatly reduced. The result is amazingly smooth and delicious, and qualifies as serious comfort food material.

> 5½ pounds large sweet potatoes or yams
>
> 2 tablespoons unsalted butter
>
> ¾ cup 1% milk, warmed
>
> 3 egg whites
>
> ½ cup dark brown sugar, firmly packed
>
> 2 teaspoons grated orange rind
>
> ½ teaspoon grated nutmeg
>
> salt to taste

OPTIONAL TOPPING: 2 cups minimarshmallows

1. Bake, boil, or microwave the potatoes until soft. Peel and place them in the bowl of an electric mixer.

2. Preheat the oven to 350°F. Coat a large 2-quart casserole or rectangular or oval baking dish with nonstick cooking spray.

3. Beat the cooked potatoes with the butter. Add the warmed milk, egg whites, sugar, orange rind, nutmeg and salt and continue to beat until smooth.

4. Pour the mixture into the prepared casserole and bake for 40 minutes.

5. For an extra added treat with no added fat, top the casserole with mini-marshmallows and return it to the oven for 3 to 4 minutes, or until just golden, watching carefully to avoid burning.

6. Serve hot.

VARIATION:

❖ A pinch of ground cinnamon and nutmeg can be added if desired.

COOK NOTES:

❖ The best way to prepare this dish is with an electric mixer. A food processor will overmix the potatoes, causing them to become gluey and pasty.

❖ What we buy under the label "yams" are actually sweet potatoes, in two varieties: a dry-fleshed yellow one with a pale brown outer skin, and a moist-fleshed orange one with a reddish-colored outer skin. The latter variety is best suited for this recipe.

❖ Once opened, immediately store brown sugar in an airtight container where it will keep fresh and soft. If brown sugar has hardened, put it in the food processor until the sugar is soft and smooth.

*D*O-AHEAD PREP:

❖ The sweet potatoes can be cooked, poured in the prepared casserole, covered, and refrigerated for 1 to 2 days before baking. The cooked casserole can also be cooked a few hours ahead and reheated in a microwave oven.

Spinach and Rice Pie with Vegetables

Serves: 4 to 6

*M*y friend Donna Cassutt serves this pizzalike vegetarian entrée for a buffet, light supper, or as a luncheon dish.

2 teaspoons olive oil

1 medium onion, thinly sliced

¼ pound mushrooms, stems removed, wiped clean and
    thinly sliced

1 clove garlic, finely minced

½ pound fresh spinach, stems removed, well washed, dried, and
    cut into strips

2 tablespoons freshly grated Parmesan cheese

salt and freshly ground pepper to taste

3 cups white rice cooked in defatted chicken or vegetable broth

1 egg white

3 tomatoes, sliced

½ cup shredded low-fat Muenster, Swiss, Monterey Jack, or
    mozzarella cheese

1. In a heavy large nonstick skillet, heat the oil to medium-high and sauté the onion and mushrooms for 6 to 7 minutes, stirring often, until golden. Add the garlic and stir for 30 seconds. Remove from the heat, stir in the spinach, 1 tablespoon of the Parmesan, the salt and pepper, and set aside.

2. Preheat the oven to 450°F. Lightly coat a 12-inch pizza pan or 7-x-11-inch pan with nonstick cooking spray.

3. Combine the rice, egg white, and the remaining 1 tablespoon of Parmesan cheese in a bowl. Press the rice mixture into the bottom of the prepared pan and bake for 4 minutes.

4. Top with the spinach mixture, distribute the tomatoes evenly over the top, and bake on the top rack of the oven, for an additional 9 minutes. Top with the cheese and bake for 2 minutes or until hot and bubbly.

*V*ARIATIONS:

❖ If available, use a 6-ounce package of baby spinach, which requires no washing or removal of stems.

❖ Brown rice can be substituted for the white rice.

𝒞ook notes:

❖ Never cook spinach in an aluminum pot or it will darken the greens and give them a metallic flavor.

❖ Use a stainless steel knife when cutting spinach, never carbon steel, which will discolor both the spinach and the knife.

𝒟o-ahead prep:

❖ The pie can be cooked earlier in the day, covered tightly, and then reheated, but it is best served freshly baked.

Stir-Fried Spinach with Roasted Garlic

Serves: 4

*I*f fresh baby spinach leaves are available use them, since you do not have to remove the stems and they have a lovely and delicate flavor.

> 4 large cloves garlic (unpeeled)
> 1 tablespoon olive oil
> 1 pound fresh baby spinach or regular spinach, stems removed, well washed and dried
> salt and freshly ground pepper to taste

1. Preheat the oven to 275°F. Lightly coat a small roasting pan with olive oil nonstick cooking spray.

2. Place the garlic cloves in the pan and roast slowly until soft, about 40 to 45 minutes. When cooked, allow them to cool slightly, squeeze the garlic from the peel, chop finely, and set aside.

3. Heat a nonstick wok over high heat with the oil and when hot, add the spinach and stir-fry for 1 to 2 minutes until just wilted. Add the roasted garlic, stir to combine, and serve immediately.

*V*ARIATION:

❖ For a quicker way to cook the garlic, roast at 400°F for 20 minutes but watch carefully to prevent burning.

*C*OOK NOTES:

❖ Do not wash spinach before storing. Even if the spinach is dried, some water lurks on the leaves, causing them to rot. Store spinach, grit and all, in your vegetable bin, for 3 to 4 days, in plastic bags in the refrigerator.

❖ Never serve spinach in a silver bowl, which will react with the acid in the spinach.

*D*O-AHEAD PREP:

❖ It is best to stir-fry the spinach at the last minute to keep the optimum green color. The garlic can be roasted earlier in the day.

SALADS

❖ ❖ ❖ ❖ ❖ ❖

Basic Light Vinaigrette

Thai Salad with Lemon Dressing

Light Caesar Salad

Mixed Green Salad with Creamy Dill Dressing

Roasted Asparagus with Warm Vinaigrette

Tuscan White Bean Salad with Chopped Arugula

Celery Root and Apple Salad

Corn Salad

Cucumber, Tomato, and Feta Salad with Mint Vinaigrette

Fennel and Red Onion Salad

Warm Chinese Green Bean Salad with Toasted Sesame Seeds

New Potato and Green Bean Salad

Spaghetti Squash Salad with Lemon-Basil Vinaigrette

Black Bean, Quinoa, and Corn Salad with Tomato

Southwestern Tabbouleh

Chilled Sesame Noodles with Vegetables

Chinese Chicken Salad

Curried Chicken Salad

Tex-Mex Salad with Grilled Chicken

Grilled Tuna Salade Niçoise

Shrimp Salad with Watercress and Creamy Horseradish Dressing

Fresh Crab Salad with Lime-Cilantro Vinaigrette

Basic Light Vinaigrette

Serves: 4

*T*his basic vinaigrette can be used on all types of mixed green salads or can be used as a marinade for poultry or meats.

> 2½ tablespoons olive oil
>
> 1½ tablespoons balsamic or red wine vinegar
>
> 1 teaspoon grainy-style Dijon mustard
>
> pinch of sugar
>
> salt and freshly ground pepper to taste

1. In a small bowl, whisk the ingredients until smooth. Chill in a glass jar until ready to use.

VARIATIONS:

Use any of the following to vary the dressing flavors according to the salad ingredients used.

❖ Substitute lemon juice for the vinegar.

❖ Add 1 teaspoon crushed garlic or shallots, which can easily be done in a mini-food processor.

❖ Add fresh herbs such as 1½ tablespoons minced chives, parsley, tarragon, dill, basil, or a combination of herbs.

❖ Add 1 teaspoon chopped capers or cornichons (sour pickles).

❖ Add ½ teaspoon Worcestershire to taste.

❖ Add ½ teaspoon curry powder to taste.

❖ Add 1 tablespoon freshly grated Parmesan, crumbled feta, or Roquefort cheese to taste.

DO-AHEAD PREP:

❖ The dressing can be prepared 3 to 4 days in advance and chilled in a glass jar in the refrigerator until ready to use. Remember to bring the dressing to room temperature and shake well before tossing with the greens.

Thai Salad with Lemon Dressing

Serves: 6 to 8

The dressing for this refreshing salad is made creamy with plain nonfat or low-fat yogurt and herbs.

2 large heads Boston lettuce, core removed, washed and dried

1 large European hothouse cucumber, split and coarsely chopped, or 2 medium cucumbers, peeled, seeded, and coarsely chopped

1 head radicchio, core removed, washed and dried

LEMON THAI DRESSING:

½ cup nonfat or low-fat plain yogurt

1 tablespoon fresh lemon juice

2 teaspoons reduced-fat mayonnaise

1 teaspoon reduced-sodium soy sauce

2 teaspoons freshly snipped chives

1 teaspoon minced cilantro

¼ teaspoon minced garlic

¼ teaspoon grated fresh ginger

salt and freshly ground pepper to taste

3 tablespoons toasted sesame seeds

GARNISH: sprigs of cilantro

1. Place the lettuces, cucumber, and radicchio in a bowl and chill until ready to use.

2. Combine the dressing ingredients in a small bowl and whisk until smooth. Chill in a glass jar until ready to serve.

3. At serving time, drizzle the dressing over the salad greens, toss with the sesame seeds, garnish with the cilantro, and serve immediately.

VARIATION:

❖ If radicchio is unavailable, substitute an extra head of Boston lettuce. Romaine and other lettuces can be substituted for the Boston lettuce.

COOK NOTES:

❖ Looser heads of crisp lettuce like Boston or butter lettuce are more perishable than romaine or iceberg and last only a few days in the refrigerator.

❖   European cucumbers, also known as English, burpless, greenhouse, hothouse, and seedless cucumbers, are about 12 to 15 inches in length with thin skins and very few seeds.

*D*O-AHEAD PREP:

❖   The greens and dressing can be readied in advance and chilled but the salad should be tossed at the last minute.

Light Caesar Salad

Serves: 4

*Y*ou know how much fun it is to see a Caesar salad prepared with a great flourish at your table. What you don't know is that most Caesar salads contain about thirty-five to forty-five grams of fat! In this healthful version, I have eliminated the egg with its extra cholesterol and fat. I have also reduced the amount of both oil and cheese and have added baked sourdough croutons, in place of the traditional fried ones.

> 1 cup ½-inch sourdough bread cubes (about 2 slices)
>
> 1 clove garlic, crushed through a press
>
> salt and freshly ground black pepper
>
> 1 head romaine lettuce
>
> 1 clove garlic, pressed or finely chopped
>
> 1 teaspoon anchovy paste
>
> 2 tablespoons extra-virgin olive oil
>
> 3 tablespoons fresh lemon juice
>
> 1 teaspoon Dijon mustard
>
> 2 tablespoons freshly grated Parmesan cheese

*G*ARNISH: Freshly cracked black pepper

1.   Preheat the oven to 350°F. Lightly coat a small baking sheet with olive oil nonstick cooking spray.

2.   In a large resealable plastic bag, combine the bread cubes with the garlic and salt and pepper. Seal the bag tightly and shake to coat the bread cubes evenly.

3. Place the bread in a single layer on the prepared baking sheet and bake about 12 minutes, shaking occasionally to turn, or until they are lightly golden. Set aside.

4. Wash and dry the lettuce, break it into small pieces, and set it aside or chill it wrapped in paper towels until ready to use.

5. In a wooden salad bowl, place the garlic and anchovy paste. Add salt and pepper and whisk together with a fork.

6. Add the oil, lemon juice, and mustard and continue to whisk until combined. Add the crisp lettuce, Parmesan cheese, and croutons, and toss with the dressing and reserved croutons.

7. Sprinkle with additional cracked pepper and serve immediately.

*V*ARIATIONS:

❖ Italian or French bread can be substituted for the sourdough.

❖ To save time use packaged preservative-free low-fat croutons that are now available at many markets.

❖ Chopped, drained, and mashed anchovies can be substituted for the anchovy paste.

*C*OOK NOTES:

❖ Romaine lettuce has long deep green very crisp leaves that branch out from a white base. Romaine has twice the potassium and folic acid, six times as much vitamin C and eight times as much beta-carotene as iceberg lettuce.

❖ Do not store romaine or any other lettuce with fruits such as apples or bananas, which release a natural ethylene gas causing the greens to decay rapidly.

*D*O-AHEAD PREP:

❖ The greens can be washed and prepped earlier in the day and kept wrapped in paper towels in the refrigerator. The salad must be tossed at the very last minute.

Mixed Green Salad with
Creamy Dill Dressing

Serves: 8

*T*he yogurt cheese makes this dressing extra-rich and creamy.
Purchase the mixed salad greens in the supermarket or combine a mixture of baby or regular romaine, spinach, radicchio, arugula, chicory, Boston or butter lettuce, sorrel, or other types of field greens.

*D*RESSING:

¾ cup nonfat or low-fat Yogurt Cheese (see page 50)

2 tablespoons minced scallions (green and white
    parts included)

1½ tablespoons snipped fresh dill

2 cornichons (sour pickles), finely chopped (optional)

1 tablespoon lemon juice

2 teaspoons grainy-style Dijon mustard

pinch of sugar

salt and freshly ground white pepper to taste

8 to 10 cups mixed salad greens

1. Fold the dressing ingredients together in a large bowl and chill in a covered container until ready to use.

2. Place the greens in a large salad bowl, toss with the dressing and serve immediately.

*V*ARIATIONS:

❖ The dressing can be used as a dip with crudités.

❖ If you can't locate cornichons, substitute 2 to 3 tablespoons of dill pickle relish.

*C*OOK NOTES:

❖ Fresh dill is used in Scandinavian dishes like gravlax, Eastern European borschts, Indian raitas, and Greek salads. The distinctive flavor of fresh dill in no way translates to its dried form. Fresh dill loses its fragrance during heating and is at its optimum when used in chilled salads such as this one.

❖ Cornichons are French gherkins—tart, crisp pickles prepared from minicucumbers. They are a traditional accompaniment to pâtés but add a delicious flavor to salad dressings.

*D*o-ahead prep:

❖ The dressing can be prepared several days in advance and refrigerated in a covered container. Remember to pour off any accumulated water that may have collected on standing and adjust the seasonings after chilling.

Roasted Asparagus with Warm Vinaigrette

Serves: 6

*P*repare this salad during the spring and early summer months when asparagus are plentiful and reasonably priced. By peeling the stems of the asparagus, the vegetable cooks evenly and the texture is improved.

> 1½ pounds fresh asparagus, ends trimmed
> 2 tablespoons lemon juice
> 2 teaspoons extra-virgin olive oil
> salt and freshly ground pepper to taste

1. Preheat the oven to 475°F. Select a large attractive baking dish that can accommodate the asparagus in a single layer and coat it with olive oil nonstick cooking spray.

2. Peel the stems of the asparagus with a vegetable peeler and discard the trimmings or reserve them for a vegetable broth.

3. Place the asparagus in the prepared pan and roast for 10 to 12 minutes, depending on their thickness, turning once.

4. In a separate bowl, whisk the lemon juice with the oil and salt and pepper. Pour the vinaigrette over the hot asparagus and serve immediately.

*V*ARIATION:

❖ Balsamic vinegar can be substituted for the lemon juice.

❖ 1 teaspoon grated lemon peel can be added to the vinaigrette.

*C*OOK NOTES:

❖ Select asparagus that have firm, bright green spears with compact tips.

❖ Asparagus may be stored in a plastic bag in the crisper drawer of the refrigerator or they may be stored upright with the stems in water. Trim the stalk end about ½ inch and stand the asparagus upright in a few inches of cold water, covering the tips loosely with a plastic bag.

❖ Extra-virgin olive oil (the highest grade, the most expensive, and least acidic type of olive oil) is extracted from olives in a cold-press process. Because of its intense aroma and flavor, it is best used at the end of cooking or just before serving to enhance the dish.

*D*O-AHEAD PREP:

❖ The asparagus can be peeled and readied but the dish should not be cooked until just before serving to preserve flavor, color, and texture.

Tuscan White Bean Salad
with Chopped Arugula

Serves: 6

his recipe is simple to whip together with canned beans, but for the best taste and texture, you can cook white beans from scratch.

3½ cups cooked white beans (two 15-ounce cans cannellini or
    northern white beans, rinsed and drained)
¼ cup drained and chopped pimiento
2 scallions (green and white parts included), finely chopped
1 cup firmly packed arugula leaves, finely chopped
2 tablespoons chopped Italian parsley

BASIL VINAIGRETTE:

¼ cup lemon juice
2½ tablespoons extra-virgin olive oil
2 cloves garlic, finely minced
2 tablespoons capers, drained and chopped
2 tablespoons chopped fresh basil
1 teaspoon Dijon mustard, grainy-style preferred
salt and freshly ground pepper to taste

ACCOMPANIMENT: mixed baby greens

1. In a medium bowl, combine the beans with the remaining salad ingredients and gently toss.

2. In a small food processor or by hand, combine the vinaigrette ingredients until smooth.

3. Gently toss the beans with the vinaigrette to coat well, cover, and chill for about 1 hour.

4. Adjust the seasonings with salt and pepper, place the beans on a bed of mixed greens, and serve chilled or at room temperature.

VARIATIONS:

❖ To cook the dried beans, place them in a large pot, cover them with water by at least 3 inches, and soak overnight. Drain the water off, cover again with fresh cold water, bring to a boil, cover, reduce the heat, and simmer slowly for about 1 hour, or until the beans are tender. Drain.

❖ Roasted red bell pepper can be substituted for the pimiento.

𝒞OOK NOTES:

❖ Arugula, also called rocket or roquette, is a peppery salad green similar in look and taste to the dandelion green. Select bunches with small leaves that have a bright green color. Avoid any yellow leaves with thick stems, which are bitter tasting. Refrigerate the arugula in a perforated plastic bag in the vegetable drawer of the refrigerator.

❖ Canned beans should always be rinsed to remove excess salt.

𝒟O-AHEAD PREP:

❖ The bean salad can be prepared through Step 3 and refrigerated in a covered container overnight.

Celery Root and Apple Salad

Serves: 8

Celery root, also known as celeriac, is a big bulbous vegetable with fibrous brown skin, which actually is the root of a special celery cultivated for its root. The flavor is both mellow and earthy—a cross between celery and parsley.

Both the apples and the celery root can easily be shredded in the food processor with a coarse blade.

Dressing:

1 cup plain low-fat or nonfat yogurt

2 tablespoons low-fat mayonnaise

1 tablespoon cider vinegar

1 tablespoon sugar

1 teaspoon grainy-style Dijon mustard

½ teaspoon celery seeds

¼ teaspoon cayenne pepper or to taste

salt to taste

3 tablespoons lemon juice

2 medium-size tart green apples (Granny Smith, Pippin, or Fuji), peeled and coarsely shredded

2½ pounds celery root, peeled and coarsely shredded

Garnish: apple slices dipped in lemon juice

1. Combine the dressing ingredients in a large bowl and whisk until smooth.

2. Place the lemon juice in a medium bowl. Immediately add the apples and celery root and toss. Add the apples and celery root to the dressing, mix thoroughly, cover with plastic wrap, and chill for an hour.

3. Garnish the salad with the sliced apples just before serving.

Variations:

❖ Jicama can be substituted for the celery root.

❖ The dressing can be prepared in a food processor or blender.

Cook Notes:

❖ Select firm celery roots without soft spots and refrigerate them in plastic bags for about a week.

❖   Shredded apples and celery root discolor very quickly so shred them directly into the lemon juice in the bowl, or toss them with the lemon juice immediately after shredding.

*D*O-AHEAD PREP:

❖   Do not prepare this salad more than 2 hours ahead since the celery root and apples will discolor.

Corn Salad

Serves: 4

I don't know why people say "as American as apple pie," when it really should be "as American as corn-on-the-cob." Corn has been the most important crop in the Americas as far back as records exist, and even before, when it was called maize.

Leftover fresh summer corn makes a fabulous light and easy salad combined with peppers, cilantro, and a light citrus vinaigrette.

> 3 ears fresh corn, cooked, and the kernels removed
> ¼ cup diced sweet red bell peppers
> ¼ cup diced green bell peppers
> 2 scallions, finely chopped (green and white parts included)
> 2 tablespoons lime juice
> 1½ tablespoons corn oil
> 1½ tablespoons chopped fresh cilantro
> pinch of sugar
> salt and freshly ground pepper

*G*ARNISH: lettuce leaves, sliced black olives

1.   Place the corn in a bowl with the bell peppers and scallions.

2.   Combine the lime juice, oil, cilantro, sugar, and salt and pepper in a small jar and shake until smooth.

3.   Toss the corn with the dressing and serve immediately, mounded on top of lettuce leaves and garnished with black olives, or chill for 1 to 2 hours and serve cold.

*V*ARIATION:

❖   Frozen corn can be used, cooked only a few minutes, cooled, and drained well.

$\mathcal{C}$OOK NOTES:

❖ Always buy corn locally. Since the freshness deteriorates, eat corn as soon as possible after buying (within 24 hours) or the natural sugar converts to starch and the corn loses its sweetness. Store corn in the refrigerator in a single layer until it is to be cooked. If the corn is stacked, the heat will "cook" the corn.

❖ To cut the corn kernels from the cob, hold the ear of corn securely in one hand with the stem end resting on the bottom of the counter. Using the tip of a sharp knife, start at the top of the ear and cut down along the cob rotating the ear and cutting downward until all the kernels are removed. One ear of corn will yield about ½ cup of corn kernels.

$\mathcal{D}$O-AHEAD PREP:

❖ The salad can be prepared the day before and refrigerated in a covered container, but remember to adjust the seasonings before serving.

Cucumber, Tomato, and Feta Salad
with Mint Vinaigrette

Serves: 6

*O*ne of my favorite pre-theater haunts in Manhattan is Joe Allen's restaurant, which serves a refreshing salad that inspired this dish.

1 large European hothouse cucumber, split and coarsely chopped,
    or 2 medium cucumbers, peeled, seeded, and coarsely
    chopped

1 pint basket of cherry tomatoes, stems removed and halved

6 Kalamata, Niçoise, or black olives, pitted
    and roughly chopped

2 ounces low-fat feta cheese, crumbled

*M*INT VINAIGRETTE:

3 tablespoons lemon juice

2 tablespoons olive oil

1 tablespoon balsamic vinegar

2 tablespoons chopped fresh mint leaves

2 teaspoons snipped fresh dill

salt and freshly ground pepper to taste

*G*ARNISH: fresh mint leaves

1. In a large bowl, place the salad ingredients and toss together.

2. In a small food processor or by hand, combine the vinaigrette ingredients until smooth.

3. Gently toss the salad with the vinaigrette and serve garnished with fresh mint leaves.

*V*ARIATIONS:

❖ 2 ripe chopped tomatoes can substituted for the cherry tomatoes.

❖ If fresh mint is unavailable, use 2 tablespoons of snipped fresh dill as a substitute.

❖ If low-fat feta cheese is unavailable, substitute 1½ ounces of regular feta cheese.

$\mathcal{C}$OOK NOTES:

❖ There is more to mint than jelly or juleps. Fresh mint can be added to salads or used in vinegars, teas, salsas, and as a garnish for grilled meats. The most common type of mint available in markets today is spearmint, which is the subtlest to use in cooking. Mint is very easy to grow, so you might want to try out your green thumb on some of the new interesting varieties including lemon, orange, pineapple, bergamot, or peppermint.

❖ Feta is the Greek sheep or goat's cheese that is cured and stored in its own salty brine. To reduce the sodium content, drain, rinse in fresh cold water, dry with paper towels, and then crumble into your dish.

$\mathcal{D}$O-AHEAD PREP:

❖ The salad and dressing can be prepared separately and refrigerated in covered containers until ready to toss and serve.

Fennel and Red Onion Salad

Serves: 4

*U*ntil most recently fennel was used mostly in Italy and France, but today fennel is enjoying a new popularity in America. It's a great weight-loss vegetable since it has only 30 calories in 3½ ounces. Fennel is rich in vitamin A and is a good source of potassium and calcium. The Greeks called it marathon from their verb *maraino*, meaning "to grow thin."

It is best to let the salad come to room temperature for about 30 minutes before serving.

1 medium fennel bulb (about 2 pounds), trimmed

2 navel oranges, peeled and sliced

1 small red onion, very thinly sliced

1 head leaf lettuce, washed and dried

DRESSING:

3 tablespoons lemon juice

2 tablespoons olive oil

1 clove garlic

2 teaspoons Dijon mustard

salt and freshly ground white pepper

GARNISH: feathery tops of the fennel

1. Cut the feathery tops from the fennel and set them aside for the dressing. Chop 2 tablespoons of the tops and reserve separately. Trim the root ends and thinly slice the fennel. Place the fennel, orange slices, and red onion slices in a large bowl, cover, and chill until ready to serve.

2. Place the dressing ingredients plus the 2 tablespoons reserved, chopped feathery tops of the fennel in a food processor and blend until smooth. Chill in a covered container until ready to use.

3. When ready to serve, toss the salad ingredients with the dressing and serve immediately, garnished with the feathery tops.

COOK NOTES:

❖ Select fresh fennel bulbs that are solid and crisp. They should be firm, with no more than one coarse outer branch at each side of the bulb, and with at least 10-inch tops that ensure succulence. The color of the bulb should be a very pale greenish-white with fresh-looking green tops. Avoid all bulbs that are soft or have brownish-edged bases and stalks with wilted tops. Bunches that show flowers in the central seed stems are overly mature.

❖　Store fennel in a perforated plastic bag in the refrigerator for 3 to 4 days. Do not wash until ready to use.

$\mathcal{D}$O-AHEAD PREP:

❖　Since cut navel oranges turn bitter after sitting for a few hours, they should be sliced at the last minute along with the onions, which are too strong to prepare in advance. The dressing can be prepared and chilled in a covered container and then tossed with the salad ingredients just before serving.

Warm Chinese Green Bean Salad
with Toasted Sesame Seeds

Serves: 4 to 6

*T*his salad is best served warm but can be cooled and served at room temperature as well.

1 pound green beans, washed

DRESSING:

3 tablespoons Chinese or Japanese rice vinegar

2 tablespoons finely snipped chives

2 teaspoons reduced-sodium soy sauce

2 teaspoons Asian-style sesame oil

1 teaspoon finely minced ginger

1 teaspoon honey

salt and freshly ground pepper to taste

2 teaspoons peanut oil

2 tablespoons toasted sesame seeds

GARNISH: chopped pimientos

1. Trim the green beans and cut in 1-inch pieces. Blanch the beans by dropping them into boiling water and cooking them for 2 minutes. Drain and rinse under cold water; drain thoroughly.

2. Combine the dressing ingredients in a small bowl and whisk until smooth.

3. In a nonstick wok or large nonstick skillet, heat the peanut oil and stir-fry the green beans for about 2 minutes, until just tender, stirring constantly.

4. Place the beans in a bowl, toss with the dressing and sesame seeds, garnish with the pimientos, and serve immediately.

VARIATION:

❖ Asparagus can be substituted for the green beans.

COOK NOTE:

❖ Try growing a chive plant on your window sill so that you can snip them anytime for use as a garnish and flavor enhancer. If you buy chives in the market, select a bunch that is not wilted, wrap them in wet paper towel, and then store them in a plastic bag in the refrigerator. If you have any leftovers, snip them into a container and freeze them for future use.

*D*O-AHEAD PREP:

❖ The beans can be blanched a day ahead and chilled in a covered container until ready to stir-fry. The sauce can be prepared earlier in the day, brought to room temperature, and whisked just before tossing with the stir-fried beans.

New Potato and Green Bean Salad
Serves: 8

*M*ost potato salads are laden with mayonnaise dressings but this lighter one is a refreshing addition to a summer menu.

    1 pound tiny new or red potatoes, cut in half
    2 cloves garlic, crushed but still intact
    1 pound green beans, washed and trimmed
    12 small pitted black olives
    2 tablespoons capers
    2 tablespoons freshly chopped parsley
    1 head red leaf lettuce, washed and dried

*D*RESSING:

    ¼ cup defatted chicken or vegetable broth
    3 tablespoons lemon juice
    2½ tablespoons olive oil
    2 tablespoons snipped fresh dill
    1 tablespoon grainy-style Dijon mustard
    1 clove garlic, finely minced
    salt and freshly ground pepper to taste

*G*ARNISH: chopped pimientos

1. Cook the potatoes with the smashed garlic in boiling water for about 20 minutes, or until just fork tender. Drain water, discard garlic, and cool.

2. Cook the green beans in boiling water for about 4 minutes, until just tender, drain, and immediately run under cold water. Thoroughly drain again and place in a large bowl.

3. In a food processor or by hand, combine the dressing ingredients and blend until smooth. Pour over the green beans, add the olives, capers, and parsley, and toss well. Add the potatoes and gently toss to combine.

4. Arrange the lettuce leaves attractively on a serving platter, place the potatoes and green beans on top, garnish with the pimientos and serve at room temperature for optimum flavor.

*V*ARIATIONS:

❖ Asparagus can be substituted for the green beans.

❖ If small new potatoes are not available, substitute large ones, and quarter them.

*C*OOK NOTE:

❖ Once you have opened a can of olives, transfer them and their liquid to a glass jar or plastic container and store them in the refrigerator.

*D*O-AHEAD PREP:

❖ The potatoes and green beans can be cooked a day in advance and chilled in covered containers until ready to serve. The dressing can be prepared 1 to 2 days in advance, but do not put the dressing on until just before serving or the beans will lose their bright green color. It is best to allow the vegetables to come to room temperature before serving.

Spaghetti Squash Salad
with Lemon-Basil Vinaigrette

Serves: 8

Spaghetti squash, also called vegetable spaghetti, diet spaghetti, Manchurian squash, cucuzzi, suzza melon, and calabush, is an oval-shaped yellow vegetable. It takes its name from the texture of its cooked flesh, which resembles crunchy spaghetti strands.

> one 4-pound spaghetti squash
> 2 scallions (green and white parts included), finely chopped
> 1 sweet red bell pepper, seeded and finely chopped

LEMON-BASIL VINAIGRETTE:

> ¼ cup lemon juice
> 2 tablespoons chopped fresh basil
> 1½ tablespoons olive oil
> 2 teaspoons Dijon mustard
> 1 teaspoon finely chopped lemon rind
> salt and freshly ground pepper to taste

GARNISH: basil leaves

ACCOMPANIMENT: lettuce leaves

1. Preheat the oven to 350°F.

2. Prick the spaghetti squash with a fork and bake for 40 minutes. Turn and continue to bake for an additional 40 to 50 minutes, or until softened.

3. Cut the squash in half, remove and discard the seeds, and scrape the inside with a fork to remove the spaghetti-like strands. Allow the cooked squash to cool slightly and then place the strands in a bowl with the scallions and red bell pepper.

4. In a small food processor or by hand, combine the vinaigrette ingredients until smooth. Pour the vinaigrette over the squash and vegetables, toss well, cover, and chill for 2 hours, or until ready to serve.

5. Taste and adjust with salt and pepper, mound the salad on a lettuce-lined platter, garnish with basil leaves, and serve chilled or at room temperature.

VARIATION:

❖ Spaghetti squash can be microwaved whole but remember to pierce it in several places with a fork to avoid it bursting open. Cook the squash for about 8 minutes, turn it over and cook it for another 8 minutes, or until softened.

$\mathcal{C}$OOK NOTES:

❖ Although spaghetti squash is classified as a winter squash, because of its hard shell, its stringy strands taste best with the same seasonings used on summer squashes like zucchini.

❖ Spaghetti squash is available year-round but the peak season is early fall through the winter. Select hard and smooth squash with an even, pale yellow color. Avoid squash that are greenish, which indicates they are immature, or ones with bruises or damaged spots. Store spaghetti squash at room temperature for about 4 to 6 weeks.

$\mathcal{D}$O-AHEAD PREP:

❖ The salad can be prepared a day in advance and refrigerated in a covered container. Remember to adjust the seasonings with salt and pepper before serving since cold diminishes the intensity of the flavors.

Black Bean, Quinoa, and Corn Salad
with Tomato

Serves: 4

*T*his colorful salad combines black beans, quinoa, corn, and tomatoes, all ingredients native to the Americas. If you use vegetable broth, it makes a vegetarian entrée that's high in protein.

1 cup fresh or frozen corn, thawed

½ cup defatted chicken or vegetable broth

¼ cup quinoa, rinsed thoroughly

½ teaspoon ground cumin

*D*RESSING:

3 tablespoons fresh lemon juice

2 tablespoons extra-virgin olive oil

2 tablespoons minced cilantro

2 tablespoons scallions (green and white parts included),
    finely chopped

½ teaspoon minced garlic

salt and freshly ground pepper to taste

½ cup cooked black beans

1 medium tomato, seeded and diced

*G*ARNISH: cilantro sprigs

1.   In a small saucepan, place the corn, broth, quinoa, and cumin. Bring to a boil, cover, reduce heat, and simmer until the quinoa has absorbed the liquid, about 10 to 15 minutes. Transfer the quinoa to a large nonreactive bowl and cool slightly.

2.   In a small screw-topped jar combine the dressing ingredients. Shake well and set aside.

3.   Add the beans and tomatoes to the corn and quinoa, toss with the dressing, cover well, and chill for 2 to 4 hours or until ready to serve.

4.   Taste, adjust the seasoning with salt and pepper, and serve the salad chilled or at room temperature, garnished with the cilantro.

*V*ARIATION:

❖   Bulgur can be substituted for the quinoa.

$\mathcal{C}$OOK NOTES:

❖   Quinoa expands about 4 times when cooked. Before cooking, always rinse the grain well to remove a slightly bitter coating. Quinoa is high in protein—16 percent compared with 7½ percent for rice—and is even a little higher in protein than soy. Because it is low in gluten, it can be enjoyed by many who cannot tolerate wheat products.

❖   To cook black beans: rinse the beans and pick them over; cover with water and soak for 4 hours or overnight. Drain, place the beans in a large pot, and cover again with water. Bring to a boil and reduce to a simmer. Skim for a few minutes to remove any foam, and cook, partly covered, for about 50 minutes, until the beans are tender but still hold their shape. Drain and cool.

$\mathcal{D}$O-AHEAD PREP:

❖   The salad can be prepared a day in advance, covered, and refrigerated overnight.

Southwestern Tabbouleh

Serves: 6

*T*abbouleh, or tabbouli, is a wheat pilaf salad prepared with the Middle-Eastern cracked wheat grain called bulgur. In a traditional tabbouleh the bulgur is marinated with fresh mint, lemon juice, and spices resulting in a salad that is both high in fiber and low in fat. This Southwestern version adds hot peppers and spices for added zip. For best results, use fine-grain bulgur.

2 cups boiling water

1 cup fine-grain bulgur

½ cup chopped fresh cilantro

⅓ cup chopped fresh parsley

3 scallions (green and white parts included), finely chopped

2 small tomatoes, seeded and chopped

1 yellow, red, or green bell pepper, seeded and
    coarsely chopped

1 teaspoon jalapeño pepper, seeded, and finely minced

1 teaspoon finely minced garlic

2 tablespoons lemon juice

2 tablespoons red wine vinegar

1 tablespoon olive oil

¼ teaspoon ground coriander

¼ teaspoon ground cumin

⅛ teaspoon ground chili powder

salt to taste

*G*ARNISH: 2 tablespoons toasted pine nuts, halved cherry
    tomatoes, and sprigs of cilantro

1. In a medium bowl, pour the boiling water over the bulgur to cover. Allow the wheat to stand for 25 to 30 minutes, or until the bulgur is light and fluffy. Drain through a fine mesh strainer, pushing out any excess water.

2. In a large bowl, place the soaked bulgur. Add the remaining ingredients and toss well. Cover and refrigerate for 2 hours or overnight.

3. Taste, adjust the seasonings with salt and pepper, and serve chilled or at room temperature, topped with the pine nuts, halved cherry tomatoes, and sprigs of cilantro.

$\mathcal{V}$ARIATION:

❖ For a less spicy version, omit the jalapeño pepper.

$\mathcal{C}$OOK NOTES:

❖ Bulgur is a processed form of cracked wheat that is produced by a method that is similar to that used for converted rice. The whole wheat kernels are steam-cooked and dried, then the grain is cracked into three different granulations. The coarsest grain is used for pilaf, the medium is used for cereal, while the finest is used in tabbouleh and other salads.

❖ Bulgur is available in health food stores and many supermarkets. Once opened it should be stored in an airtight container in a cool, dry place where it will last for 6 months, or it can be stored in the freezer indefinitely.

$\mathcal{D}$O-AHEAD PREP:

❖ Tabbouleh is best prepared a day in advance to allow the flavors to blend.

Chilled Sesame Noodles with Vegetables

Serves: 6 to 8

*C*old noodles with spicy peanut sauce are a great lunch dish or can be served as part of a summer buffet.

12 ounces spaghetti

½ teaspoon sesame oil

1 large zucchini, shredded (about 1 cup)

3 radishes, trimmed and shredded

2 scallions, green parts only

DRESSING:

2 teaspoons chopped ginger

2 cloves garlic, finely minced

¼ cup fresh lime juice

2 tablespoons peanut butter

1½ tablespoons honey

2 teaspoons Asian-style sesame oil

1 teaspoon chili paste with garlic (or to taste)

2 tablespoons toasted sesame seeds

GARNISH: scallion greens

1. Drop the spaghetti into boiling water and cook until al dente, drain well, and toss with the ½ teaspoon sesame oil.

2. Place the cooked noodles in a serving bowl and top with the zucchini, radishes, and scallions.

3. In a small food processor, chop the ginger and garlic until just minced. Add the remaining dressing ingredients and process until smooth.

4. Pour the dressing over the noodles and vegetables, top with the sesame seeds, toss, and serve immediately garnished with the scallion greens.

VARIATIONS:

❖ Hot chili oil can be substituted for the chili paste.

❖ Other shredded seasonal vegetables can be added to taste.

Cook NOTE:

❖ Since you are only using the green part of the scallion, use the remaining part to make a beautiful scallion brush garnish. Trim the root end and top part leaving a 2½- to 3-inch piece. With a sharp paring knife make many crisscross incisions in each end. Soak the scallion in cold water for several hours and it will "flower."

Do-AHEAD PREP:

❖ The sauce can be readied a day in advance and kept in a covered container in the refrigerator. The noodles can be prepared through Step 1 an hour or two in advance and kept at room temperature. Do not assemble the salad until just before serving or the noodles may become gummy.

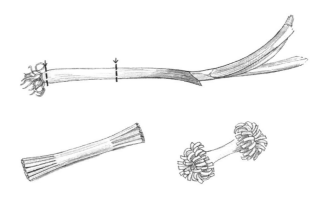

Chinese Chicken Salad

Serves: 4 to 6

he Los Angeles Times recently did an analysis of the nutritional content of Chinese chicken salad served at local restaurants. I was amazed to find that the average calorie count was about 900 per serving and the average fat content was about 45 grams! This lightened version dispenses with fried noodles and oily dressings but yields delicious results.

3 cups shredded cooked chicken

3 cups shredded iceberg lettuce

2 scallions (green and white parts included), finely chopped

DRESSING:

3 tablespoons Chinese or Japanese rice vinegar

2 tablespoons peanut oil

2 tablespoons soy sauce

2 tablespoons sugar

2 teaspoons Asian-style sesame oil

¼ teaspoon dry mustard

2 tablespoons toasted sesame seeds

2 tablespoons toasted pine nuts

2 tablespoons preserved red ginger, diced

GARNISH: cilantro sprigs

1. Place the chicken, lettuce, and scallions in a large bowl.

2. Whisk the dressing ingredients together and toss with the chicken and lettuce to combine.

3. Top with the remaining ingredients and serve immediately garnished with cilantro.

VARIATIONS:

❖ Toasted almonds can be substituted for the pine nuts.

❖ Sliced or chopped water chestnuts or blanched snow pea pods or baby bok choy can be added to the salad.

Cook NOTES:

❖ Preserved ginger, also called pickled ginger, is used in Asian cooking as a tangy garnish. Whole, sliced, or shredded peeled gingerroot is preserved in brine, rice wine, or rice vinegar where it naturally acquires a light pink color. Often red food coloring is added to enhance the color turning it into "red ginger," which is used as a garnish in Chinese cooking. This item is available at Asian grocery stores, by mail order (see page 387), or at many supermarkets.

❖ The Chinese poach chicken for salad by cooking it "white cut" style, which is extremely moist and flavorful. In a pot large enough to cover the chicken with liquid, bring 2 quarts of water or chicken broth to a boil. Add a whole cut-up chicken, 3 whole scallions or a quartered onion, and slice of fresh ginger: bring to a boil again, cover tightly, reduce heat to medium, and cook without peeking for 15 minutes. Remove from the heat and allow the chicken to cool in the liquid for an additional 25 minutes. Strain the broth and reserve for another use. Remove the skin and bones and discard.

Do-AHEAD PREP:

❖ The ingredients can be readied a day in advance and kept in covered containers in the refrigerator. The salad should be tossed at the last minute.

Curried Chicken Salad

Serves: 4 to 6

*C*hicken salad is traditionally prepared with high-fat mayonnaise or sour cream. Here I use low-fat yogurt cheese and low-fat mayonnaise plus flavorful curry powder to create a perfect dish for lunch or light supper.

- 4 cups cooked chicken or turkey, cubed or shredded
- ½ cup drained, chopped water chestnuts
- 2 tablespoons chopped scallions, white part only (reserve the greens for garnish)

DRESSING:

- ¾ cup nonfat or low-fat Yogurt Cheese (see page 50)
- 2 tablespoons low-fat mayonnaise
- 1 tablespoon chopped fresh chives
- 1 teaspoon grainy-style Dijon mustard
- ½ to 1 teaspoon curry powder, or more to taste
- pinch of paprika
- salt and freshly ground white pepper to taste

GARNISH: chopped scallions, cold asparagus, sliced tomatoes

ACCOMPANIMENT: fresh rye bread slices

1. Place the chicken in a large bowl and add the water chestnuts and scallions.

2. In a separate bowl, combine the dressing ingredients, whisk until smooth, and toss with the chicken mixture. Cover and chill for 1 to 2 hours.

3. Serve the salad on a platter garnished with chopped scallions, cold asparagus, sliced tomatoes, and accompanied by fresh rye bread slices.

VARIATIONS:

- ❖ Chopped peeled jicama can be substituted for the water chestnuts.
- ❖ ½ cup nonfat or low-fat plain yogurt plus ¼ cup low-fat sour cream can be substituted for the Yogurt Cheese.

COOK NOTE:

- ❖ Water chestnuts are Chinese root vegetables that remain crisp and crunchy even after cooking. Water chestnuts supply some iron, potassium, and fiber plus a modicum of B vitamins. They are extremely low in calories and sodium, and contain zero fat or cholesterol.

𝒟O-AHEAD PREP:

❖   The salad can be prepared a day in advance and chilled in a covered container until ready to use. Remember to adjust seasonings with salt and pepper just before serving.

Tex-Mex Salad with Grilled Chicken

Serves: 6

𝒯his salad makes a wonderful summer supper and can be varied according to the whims of your guests. Grilled shrimp can be substituted for the chicken and additional vegetables can be added to taste.

The marinade doubles as a dressing so you save extra steps in the preparation.

ℳARINADE/DRESSING:

½ teaspoon grated lime rind

3 tablespoons lime juice

2½ tablespoons olive oil

2 tablespoons tomato or vegetable juice

2 tablespoons chopped fresh cilantro

¼ teaspoon ground coriander

¼ teaspoon ground cumin

¼ teaspoon ground chili powder

salt and freshly ground pepper to taste

1 whole skinless, boneless chicken breast, halved, pounded to
　　uniform thickness

3 cups shredded iceberg lettuce

2 pints cherry tomatoes, halved

one 16-ounce can fat-free or low-fat refried beans

½ cup cooked and cooled fresh or frozen corn, or canned corn,
　　rinsed and drained

½ ripe avocado, peeled and diced

3 scallions (green and white parts included), finely chopped

GARNISH: 2 to 3 tablespoons low-fat sour cream, 2 to 3 tablespoons Pico de Gallo (see page 59) or fresh tomato salsa, and sprigs of cilantro

1. Combine the marinade/dressing ingredients in a small bowl and whisk together. Place one-third of the mixture in a large bowl, add the chicken, cover the container, and marinate at room temperature for 30 minutes or in the refrigerator for 2 to 3 hours.

2. Lightly coat an outdoor or indoor grill, broiler, or a well-seasoned ridged stove-top grill pan with nonstick cooking spray and preheat to medium-high.

3. Grill the chicken for about 3 minutes per side, or until just tender, basting with the marinade. Do not overcook. Allow to cool slightly.

4. In a wide shallow bowl, attractively layer the lettuce, tomatoes, refried beans, corn, avocado, and scallions. Thinly slice the chicken into strips and arrange on top.

5. Stir the reserved dressing ingredients together, drizzle over the salad, and serve immediately garnished with a dollop of sour cream, Pico de Gallo or fresh tomato salsa, and sprigs of cilantro.

VARIATION:

❖ Other possible additions to this salad include: chopped black olives, canned chiles, and roasted red bell peppers.

COOK NOTES:

❖ Cumin is the small, amber-colored seed of a plant in the parsley family often known by its Spanish name, *comino*. Cumin is used in many Mexican and Tex-Mex dishes, Indian cuisine, and the dishes of North Africa.

❖ Purchase spices in small quantities and date them. Judge the freshness of spices by color and aroma. When fresh, most spices are bright in color and have a strong aroma. As a general rule, replace old spices once a year and store them away from heat.

DO-AHEAD PREP:

❖ The salad ingredients and dressing can be prepared a day in advance and chilled in covered containers until ready to serve. It is best to toss the salad at the last minute.

Grilled Tuna Salade Niçoise

*S*alade Niçoise is a traditional French dish consisting of tuna, green beans, potatoes, olives, tomatoes, red onion, and egg. In this version, I use fresh tuna, which is grilled, and the dressing is lightened by replacing some of the oil with broth.

> 8 tiny red potatoes
> ½ pound green beans, ends trimmed

*D*RESSING:

> 2½ tablespoons extra-virgin olive oil
> 2 tablespoons defatted chicken or vegetable broth
> 1½ tablespoons red wine vinegar
> 1½ tablespoons lemon juice
> 1½ teaspoons grainy-style Dijon mustard
> 1 clove garlic
> ½ teaspoon anchovy paste
> salt and freshly ground black pepper to taste

> ½ pound fresh ahi tuna
> 1 head leaf lettuce (red and green combined if possible)
> 3 ripe plum tomatoes or small ripe tomatoes, thinly sliced
> 1 small red or white sweet onion cut into rings
> 2 hard-cooked eggs, peeled and cut into wedges
> 1 tablespoon capers, drained

1. Peel a band around the center of the potatoes and steam for 15 minutes or cook in a microwave for 5 to 7 minutes, or until just fork tender.

2. Drop the beans in boiling salted water and when they return to a boil, cook for 2 to 3 minutes, or until fork tender. Drain and immediately run under cold water. Drain again and blot dry.

3. Combine the dressing ingredients in a food processor, blender, or by hand, and process until smooth.

4. Lightly coat an outdoor or indoor grill, broiler, or a well-seasoned ridged stove-top grill pan with nonstick cooking spray and preheat to medium-high.

5. Grill the tuna according to degree of doneness and slice.

6. In an attractive salad bowl, arrange the lettuce on the bottom and top with the tomatoes, onion rings, egg wedges, potatoes, green beans, tuna, and a sprinkling of capers.

7. Drizzle with the dressing and serve immediately.

Variations:

❖ If ahi tuna is too expensive, substitute salmon or other firm fleshy fish that can be easily grilled.

❖ Snow peas or snap peas can be substituted for the green beans.

Cook Note:

❖ The good news is that baking soda added to the cooking water for green beans intensifies the green color. The bad news is that it also leaches out precious nutrients.

Do-ahead Prep:

❖ All the salad ingredients, except the tomatoes, can be readied a day in advance and kept in covered containers in the refrigerator until ready to serve. The tomatoes should be added to the salad at the last minute to prevent the greens from becoming soggy and the dressing drizzled over just before serving.

Shrimp Salad with Watercress and Creamy Horseradish Dressing

Serves: 6

*T*his light buttermilk-based dressing can be used as a dip, as an accompanying sauce for Carrot and Corn Patties (see page 264), or as it is here, a piquant salad dressing that is perfect for chilled cooked shrimp, crab, or even lobster.

DRESSING:

⅓ cup low-fat buttermilk

2 tablespoons low-fat sour cream

1½ tablespoons tomato paste

1 tablespoon snipped chives or chopped scallion greens

1 teaspoon grainy-style Dijon mustard

1 teaspoon white horseradish

¼ teaspoon Worcestershire sauce

salt and freshly ground white pepper to taste

2 large heads Boston or butter lettuce, washed, dried, and broken into pieces

1 pound watercress (about 2 bunches), washed and broken into bite-size pieces

1 large European hothouse cucumber, or 2 medium cucumbers, peeled, seeded, and thinly sliced

¾ pound cooked medium shrimp or bay shrimp

1. In a small bowl, combine the dressing ingredients, and whisk until smooth.

2. Place the lettuce, watercress, cucumber and shrimp in a large bowl, toss with the dressing, and serve immediately.

VARIATION:

❖ Cold cooked crab meat, lobster, or even cooked firm-fleshed fish can be substituted for the shrimp.

COOK NOTES:

❖ Bottled horseradish is prepared from grated horseradish root mixed with vinegar, which acts as a preservative. It is available in white, or in red, which is tinted with beet juice. Store prepared horseradish in the refrigerator for about 6 weeks to 2 months, but after that time it loses its pungency and color.

❖ European cucumbers, also known as English, burpless, greenhouse, hothouse, and seedless cucumbers, are about 12 to 15 inches in length with thin skins, very few seeds, and require no peeling.

*D*O-AHEAD PREP:

❖ The salad ingredients and dressing can be prepared in advance and kept in covered containers in the refrigerator until ready to serve. It is best to toss the salad at the last minute.

Fresh Crab Salad
with Lime-Cilantro Vinaigrette

Serves: 4 to 6

*T*his light, refreshing salad can be served as a main course or as a starter for an elegant meal.

2 cups fresh mixed salad greens

12 cherry tomatoes, halved

½ cup cooked fresh or frozen corn, cooled

½ cup cooked fresh or frozen peas, cooled

¾ pound fresh crabmeat, picked over and flaked

*C*ILANTRO-LIME VINAIGRETTE:

3 tablespoons fresh lime juice

2 tablespoons olive oil

1 tablespoons rice vinegar

½ teaspoon Asian-style sesame oil

1½ teaspoons chopped fresh cilantro

1 teaspoon reduced-sodium soy sauce

1 teaspoon sugar

½ teaspoon finely minced garlic

salt and freshly ground pepper to taste

*G*ARNISH: 2 tablespoons toasted sesame seeds, sprigs of cilantro

1. In a large salad bowl, place the salad greens. Attractively arrange the toma-oes, corn, and peas on top. Mound the crab in the center and chill until ready to serve.

2. In a small food processor, blender, or screw-topped jar, combine the cilantro-lime vinaigrette ingredients and process or shake until smooth. Chill in a covered container until ready to serve.

3. Drizzle the dressing over the salad and serve chilled, garnished with the toasted sesame seeds and sprigs of cilantro.

*V*ARIATIONS:

❖ Fresh crabmeat is sold as lump (choice chunks of body meat, which is the most expensive), backfin (small pieces of body meat), and flake (white meat from the body and other parts sold in flakes). Any of these meats will work well in this salad.

❖ You can use the meat from an Alaskan king crab, which will be colorful and delicious in the salad.

*C*OOK NOTES:

❖ Once purchased, cooked crabmeat should be kept refrigerated and used within 2 days.

❖ Limes are more perishable than lemons and should be refrigerated after buying, where they will keep for 4 to 6 weeks.

*D*O-AHEAD PREP:

❖ The salad can be prepared a few hours before and chilled in a covered container until ready to use. If preparing earlier in the day, add the crab at the last minute. The dressing can be prepared a few days in advance and chilled in a covered container until ready to use. Bring the dressing to room temperature at least 20 minutes before serving.

BREADS

Popovers

Southern Comfort Corn Sticks

Black Olive and Cheese Biscuits

Scallion-Dill Muffins

Presto Focaccia

Cranberry-Orange Scones

Kiwi Christmas Bread

Blueberry-Orange Muffins with Crunchy Granola Topping

Pumpkin-Cornmeal Spice Muffins

Banana-Oatmeal Muffins

Lemon Poppy Seed Muffins

Spa Muffins

It is better to have loafed and lost than never to have loafed at all.
—James Thurber

Popovers

Yield: 10 popovers

I find that the best method of baking popovers is to start them in a cold oven. These light and airy puffy treats are low in fat and can be eaten with jelly, preserves, honey, or just by themselves.

  1 cup all-purpose flour
  1 cup 1% low-fat milk
  2 egg whites, at room temperature
  1 egg, at room temperature
  1 tablespoon unsalted butter, melted
  ¼ teaspoon salt

ACCOMPANIMENTS: jelly, preserves, or honey

1. Place all the ingredients in a large bowl and whisk until just combined but not overbeaten.

2. Very generously coat a nonstick popover pan, muffin pan, or custard cups with nonstick cooking spray. Fill the popover cups halfway with the batter, place them in a cold oven, turn the heat to 450°F, and bake for 20 minutes.

3. Reduce the heat to 350°F and continue to bake for an additional 15 to 20 minutes. Test one popover to see if it is done by removing it from the pan with a sharp knife. The popovers are ready when they are crisp on the outside and moist on the inside.

4. Remove from the pan and serve immediately accompanied by jelly, preserves, or honey.

VARIATION:

❖ Unfiltered honey, which is now sold as a creamy spread, makes a wonderful accompaniment to the popovers.

COOK NOTES:

❖ Always buy eggs from a refrigerated case since they will rapidly deteriorate at room temperature.

❖ As an egg ages, moisture escapes through the shell and the air pocket enlarges. To test for freshness shake the egg. A fresh one should feel heavy and well filled. Another test is to float the egg in a bowl of cold water—if it floats it is older and filled with more air.

O-AHEAD PREP:

❖ The popovers must be prepared and baked just before serving.

Southern Comfort Corn Sticks

Yield: 24 corn sticks or 16 squares

*C*orn sticks do not have to be high in fat. This lightened version uses corn kernels to give them a moister texture. The corn sticks are best baked in cast-iron corn stick pans, but they can also be baked in nonstick madeleine pans or a seasoned cast-iron skillet and then cut into wedges or squares.

- 1 cup yellow cornmeal
- 1 cup all-purpose flour
- 2 teaspoons baking powder
- ½ teaspoon salt
- 2 eggs
- 1 cup 1% low-fat milk
- ¼ cup vegetable oil
- ¼ cup honey
- ½ cup fresh or frozen corn, thawed

1. Preheat the oven to 400°F . Lightly coat 2 to 3 large corn stick pans with non-stick coating spray.

2. In a medium bowl, combine the cornmeal, flour, baking powder, and salt. In a separate bowl, beat the eggs with the milk, oil, and honey.

3. Add the cornmeal to the egg mixture and stir until just moistened. Add the corn, stirring to distribute it in the batter. Gently spoon the batter into the prepared pans, and bake for about 20 minutes, or until an inserted knife comes out clean.

4. Remove the corn sticks from the pan, cool for 2 to 3 minutes, turn out onto a rack, allow to cool slightly, and serve.

VARIATION:

❖ If preparing cornbread, bake in a cast-iron skillet or a 9-inch square baking pan at 400°F for about 25 minutes. Remove the pan from the oven, cool on a rack, and when cool enough to handle cut into wedges or squares and serve.

❖   To measure sticky liquids such as honey, wash out the measuring cup with very hot water first, and then measure the honey.

𝒟o-ᴀʜᴇᴀᴅ ᴘʀᴇᴘ:

❖   The corn sticks can be prepared a day in advance, kept in an airtight container, and warmed just before serving. The corn sticks can also be frozen in a sealed container or plastic bag for 2 to 3 months.

Black Olive and Cheese Biscuits

Yield: Sixteen 1½-inch biscuits

𝒯he word *biscuit* originally meant "twice cooked" (*bis* means "twice" and *cuire* means "to cook"). In most European countries, biscuit refers to a sweet confection. In France it means a spongecake. In Italy (*biscotti*) and England, a biscuit is a crisp and sweet cookie. But, in America, the word means a quick bread usually served for breakfast or as a side dish—and one that is made with lots of butter.

This lightened biscuit uses one-third of the shortening in a traditional recipe, and is enriched with low-fat buttermilk and enhanced with pungent olive and cheese flavors.

> 1¾ cups all-purpose flour
>
> 2 teaspoons baking powder
>
> ½ teaspoon baking soda
>
> ½ teaspoon salt
>
> 2 tablespoons unsalted chilled butter, diced
>
> ⅔ cup low-fat buttermilk
>
> 2 tablespoons freshly grated Parmesan cheese
>
> 4 black or Kalamata olives, pitted and finely chopped

1.   Preheat the oven to 400°F.

2.   In a food processor, combine the flour with the baking powder, baking soda, and salt and process to just combine. Add the butter and pulse until a coarse meal is formed. Add the buttermilk and cheese and process until just mixed. Add the olives and pulse for a few seconds to combine until a slightly sticky dough is formed.

3.   Turn the dough out on a lightly floured surface and with lightly floured hands knead it 3 or 4 times. Roll the dough out to ½-inch thickness and cut rounds with a small 1½-inch biscuit cutter or similar size cookie cutter. Lightly coat the biscuits with butter-flavored nonstick cooking spray.

4.   Place the biscuits on an ungreased baking sheet and bake for 15 minutes or until lightly golden.

5.   Remove from the oven and serve piping hot.

*V*ARIATION:

❖   For a sweet biscuit omit the cheese and olives and add ½ cup raisins, currants, dried cherries, or dried blueberries.

*C*OOK NOTES:

❖   Pit olives as you would remove the skin from a garlic clove. With the flat side of a knife, strike the olive firmly. The olive will split and the pit can easily be removed.

❖   To preserve the olives remaining in the jar, add a tablespoon or two of vodka, which imparts no change of flavor but keeps the olives fresher. Once opened, store the olives in the refrigerator.

*D*O-AHEAD PREP:

❖   The biscuits can be prepared a day in advance, kept in an airtight container, and warmed just before serving. The biscuits can also be frozen in sealed containers or plastic bags for 2 to 3 months.

Scallion-Dill Muffins

**Yield: 24 mini-muffins or
8 to 10 regular muffins**

*T*hese savory mini-muffins make an unusual and tasty addition to a low-fat brunch bread basket or a delicious accompaniment for soups and stews.

2 cups all-purpose flour

2 teaspoons baking powder

½ teaspoon baking soda

½ teaspoon salt

½ teaspoon freshly ground white pepper

1 egg

1 cup low-fat buttermilk

¼ cup vegetable oil

3 scallions (green and white parts included), finely chopped

1½ tablespoons snipped fresh dill

1½ tablespoons freshly grated Parmesan cheese

1. Preheat the oven to 400°F. Lightly coat twelve 2½-inch muffin cups with non-stick cooking spray or line them with fluted paper or foil baking muffin cups.

2. In a large bowl, combine the flour with the baking powder, baking soda, salt, and pepper and stir well.

3. In a separate medium bowl, whisk the egg with the remaining ingredients until smooth. Add the egg mixture to the dry ingredients and stir until just combined.

4. Fill the muffin cups ¾ full and bake for 20 to 25 minutes or until golden and an inserted knife comes out clean.

5. Remove the tin from the oven and cool slightly on a wire rack. Turn the muffins out into a basket and serve them warm or at room temperature.

*V*ARIATION:

❖ Chopped fresh basil can be substituted for the dill.

*C*OOK NOTE:

❖ If you don't have buttermilk on hand for use in baking, use this easy substitute. For each cup of buttermilk, place 1 tablespoon of lemon juice or white vinegar in a glass measuring cup and add enough cold low-fat milk to make 1 cup. Stir and allow to stand for 5 minutes before using.

❖ The muffins can be prepared a day in advance, kept in an airtight container, and warmed just before serving. The muffins can also be frozen in a sealed container or plastic bag for 2 to 3 months.

Presto Focaccia

Serves: 6 to 8

*F*rozen bread dough can be used to create a variety of breadstuffs, including this focaccia. If rosemary is not your favorite herb, try this bread with chives, basil, dill, sage, oregano, marjoram, or thyme.

one 1-pound frozen bread dough or pizza dough, thawed

2 tablespoons extra-virgin olive oil

1 tablespoon chopped fresh rosemary leaves

1. Place the thawed dough in a bowl, add 1 tablespoon of the oil and the rosemary to the dough, and knead until well combined. Place the dough on a floured board and roll out into a large rectangular shape, about 12 inches by 8 inches. Place on an ungreased baking sheet and allow to rest in a draft-free area for about 45 minutes.

2. Preheat the oven to 400°F.

3. Push down on the dough with your fingers to create indentations, brush with the remaining tablespoon of the oil, and bake about 10 to 12 minutes, or until lightly golden.

4. Serve warm, cut into squares.

*D*o-AHEAD PREP:

❖ The focaccia can be baked, cooled, cut into squares, and frozen in a sealed plastic bag for later use. Defrost and reheat in a toaster oven until crisp.

Cranberry-Orange Scones

Yield: 8 large or 12 small scones

A scone is a Scottish tea cake that is similar to a baking powder biscuit but with added sugar and, occasionally, dried fruits and spices. Originally scones were browned on a griddle and then split and lavished with butter.

Low-fat vanilla yogurt replaces much of the fat in these scrumptious breakfast treats, which also can be served as part of an afternoon tea.

2½ cups all-purpose flour

¼ cup plus 1 tablespoon firmly packed brown sugar

2 teaspoons baking powder

½ teaspoon baking soda

pinch of salt

3 tablespoons chilled unsalted butter, diced

one 8-ounce container vanilla-flavored low-fat or nonfat yogurt

1 egg

2 tablespoons frozen orange juice concentrate, thawed

2 teaspoons grated orange rind

¾ cup dried cranberries

*G*LAZE:

1 egg, lightly beaten with 1 tablespoon water

*A*CCOMPANIMENTS: Light English Creamy Topping (see page 51) or fruit preserves

1. Preheat the oven to 400°F. Lightly coat a baking sheet with butter-flavored nonstick cooking spray.

2. In a food processor, combine the flour with ¼ cup of the brown sugar, baking powder, baking soda, and salt; process for a few seconds. Add the butter and pulse until the mixture resembles coarse meal. Add the yogurt, egg, orange concentrate, and orange rind and continue to pulse until just moistened. The dough will be slightly sticky.

3. Place the dough in a bowl and stir in the cranberries.

4. Turn the dough out onto a lightly floured work surface and with lightly floured hands pat the dough into a 9- to 10-inch circle; cut the dough into 8 large or 12 small wedges.

5. Brush the tops of the scones with the egg glaze. Push the remaining brown sugar through a strainer sprinkling it lightly over the tops of the scones. Transfer the scones to the prepared baking sheet and bake for 12 to 15 minutes, or until golden.

6. Remove the baked scones from the oven, allow them to cool slightly, and serve them warm or at room temperature accompanied by Light English Creamy Topping or fruit preserves.

*V*ARIATION:

❖ Vary both the dried fruits and the flavorings; try lemon and dried blueberry scones, lime and dried cherry scones, or orange and currant scones.

*C*OOK NOTES:

❖ The best way to store brown sugar once it is opened is to place it immediately in a sealed airtight container. If it is too late and your brown sugar has turned into a concrete block, process it in a food processor or blender and it will return to its original granular texture.

❖ Baking powder's potency diminishes with age and it loses its efficiency as a leavening agent. To test to see if the supply is still good, place ½ teaspoon of baking powder in ¼ cup of hot tap water. If the baking powder is still fresh, the water will actively bubble. If there's no reaction, it is time to buy a new supply.

❖ As with all scone or biscuit batters, you must be prepared to have a sticky dough that needs to be shaped on a floured board with floured hands.

*D*O-AHEAD PREP:

❖ The scones can be prepared a day in advance, kept in an airtight container, and warmed just before serving. The scones can also be frozen in a sealed container or plastic bag for 2 to 3 months.

Kiwi Christmas Bread

Yield: One 9-x-5-x-3-inch loaf

I got the original version of this recipe at a local farmers' produce market from a kiwi grower who serves this moist and delicious bread year-round for dessert, lunch, or even breakfast. This lightened version makes a wonderful holiday gift.

- ¼ cup vegetable oil
- ¾ cup sugar
- 1 whole egg
- 2 egg whites, lightly beaten
- 1 cup ripe kiwifruit pulp (about 3 medium kiwi), peeled and mashed with a fork
- ½ teaspoon pure vanilla extract
- 1 drop green food coloring (optional)
- 2 cups all-purpose flour
- ½ teaspoon baking powder
- ½ teaspoon baking soda
- two 3-ounce packages dried cranberries

1. Preheat the oven to 350°F. Coat a 9-x-5-x-3-inch loaf pan with nonstick cooking spray. Place a layer of parchment or waxed paper on the bottom of the pan and lightly coat the paper with the spray.

2. In a large bowl, beat the oil and sugar together until well mixed. Add the egg and egg whites and continue to beat well until incorporated into the mixture. Add the kiwi pulp, vanilla, and green food coloring and beat well until smooth.

3. In a medium bowl, combine the flour with the baking powder, baking soda, and cranberries; stir to combine and coat the dried fruit.

4. Add the flour mixture to the kiwifruit mixture and stir until just combined.

5. Pour into the prepared pan and bake for 1 hour, or until inserted knife comes out clean.

6. Allow the bread to cool slightly, turn out onto a wire rack, remove the parchment or waxed paper, and thoroughly cool.

7. Serve the bread in overlapping slices on a platter.

*V*ARIATION:

❖ Dried cherries or strawberries can be substituted for the cranberries.

Cook notes:

❖ Kiwifruit is unusually high in ascorbic acid, about twice that in oranges. An average kiwifruit supplies more than the daily requirement for vitamin C, as well as other vitamins and minerals. Kiwifruit also contains an enzyme called actinidin, which is a natural digestive aid and can even be used as a meat tenderizer.

❖ A ripe kiwifruit should be soft to the touch like a peach. If not ripe, place in a brown bag or fruit ripener with an apple. Apples release a gas that accelerates the ripening process.

Do-ahead prep:

❖ The bread can be prepared a day in advance, kept in an airtight container, and warmed just before serving. The bread can also be tightly wrapped and frozen for 2 to 3 months.

Blueberry-Orange Muffins
with Crunchy Granola Topping

**Yield: 24 mini-muffins or
8 to 10 regular muffins**

*T*hese mini-muffins are delicious as a breakfast snack or part of a bread basket for lunch. You can use fresh, frozen, or even dried blueberries.

¾ cup fresh blueberries, rinsed and drained, thawed frozen blueberries, drained, or ¾ cup dried blueberres

1½ cups plus 2 tablespoons all-purpose flour

2 teaspoons baking powder

½ teaspoon ground cinnamon

¼ teaspoon salt

1 egg

¾ cup 1% low-fat milk

¼ cup vegetable oil

3 tablespoons honey

2 tablespoons fresh orange juice

2 teaspoons freshly grated orange rind

*G*RANOLA TOPPING:

¼ cup low-fat granola

2 tablespoons brown sugar

½ teaspoon ground cinnamon

1. Preheat the oven to 375°F. Lightly coat twelve 2½-inch muffin cups with non-stick cooking spray or line them with fluted paper or foil baking muffin cups.

2. Dust the blueberries with 2 tablespoons of the flour and set aside.

3. In a large bowl, combine the remaining 1½ cups of the flour with the baking powder, cinnamon, and salt, and mix well.

4. In a medium bowl, whisk the egg with the remaining ingredients until smooth. Add the egg mixture to the dry ingredients and stir until just combined.

5. Gently fold in the blueberries and fill the muffin tins two-thirds full.

6. In a small bowl combine the topping ingredients, evenly sprinkle over the muffins, and bake for 18 to 20 minutes or until an inserted knife comes out clean.

7. Remove from the oven and cool slightly on a wire rack. Turn out into a basket and serve warm or at room temperature.

Variations:

❖ The same amount of dried cranberries, cherries, raisins, or currants can be substituted for the fresh berries.

❖ Lemon juice and grated lemon rind can be substituted for the orange.

Cook Notes:

❖ Select uniform, firm, plump blueberries with a dark blue color and silvery bloom, which is the natural protective wax on the berry. Avoid containers of blueberries with any signs of decay that will spread quickly.

❖ Do not wash blueberries until just before using them. Store them covered with plastic wrap in the crisper section of the refrigerator.

❖ When blueberries are in season, freeze several boxes in a single layer on cookie sheets. Once frozen, transfer the berries to a resealable freezer bag and use as needed.

Do-ahead prep:

❖ The muffins can be prepared a day in advance, kept in an airtight container, and warmed just before serving. The muffins can also be frozen in a sealed container or plastic bag for 2 to 3 months.

Pumpkin-Cornmeal Spice Muffins

Yield: 12 muffins

*T*hese muffins make a delicious treat for breakfast or a wonderful side dish for the holidays.

1 cup all-purpose flour

⅔ cup cornmeal

¼ cup firmly packed brown sugar

2 teaspoons baking powder

1 teaspoon pumpkin pie spice

½ teaspoon baking soda

pinch of salt

1 whole egg

2 egg whites

1 cup canned pumpkin

1 cup low-fat buttermilk

¼ cup vegetable oil

1 teaspoon grated orange rind

1. Preheat the oven to 400°F. Lightly coat twelve 2½-inch muffin cups with non-stick cooking spray or line them with fluted paper or foil baking muffin cups.

2. In a large bowl, combine the flour, cornmeal, brown sugar, baking powder, pumpkin pie spice, baking soda, and salt.

3. In a medium bowl, whisk the remaining ingredients until smooth. Add this mixture to the dry ingredients and stir until just combined, but not overmixed.

4. Fill the prepared muffin cups three-quarters full, and bake for about 22 to 25 minutes, or until the tops are lightly golden and an inserted knife comes out clean.

5. Remove from the oven and cool slightly on a wire rack. Transfer the muffins from the tin to the rack, cool slightly, and serve warm or at room temperature.

*V*ARIATION:

❖ If pumpkin pie spice is not available substitute a mixture of ¼ teaspoon ground cinnamon, ⅛ teaspoon ground nutmeg, a pinch of ground allspice, a pinch of ground ginger, and a pinch of ground cloves.

$\mathscr{C}$OOK NOTES:

❖ Use an ice-cream scoop to fill the muffin cups easily with the perfect amount of batter.

❖ Commercially sold buttermilk is a cultured low-fat product, not the by-product of butter making. If you've run out of buttermilk for use in baking, add 2 tablespoons vinegar or lemon juice to 2 cups low-fat milk and allow to stand and thicken for 5 minutes.

$\mathscr{D}$O-AHEAD PREP:

❖ The muffins can be prepared a day in advance, kept in an airtight container, and warmed just before serving. The muffins can also be frozen in a sealed container or plastic bag for 2 to 3 months.

Banana-Oatmeal Muffins

Yield: 12 muffins

*T*hese high-fiber muffins are a great breakfast or brunch addition Make them in double batches and freeze them for quick snacks on the run.

1 cup all-purpose flour

½ cup whole wheat flour

1 cup quick-cooking oats (not instant)

½ cup plus 2 tablespoons firmly packed brown sugar

2 teaspoons baking powder

½ teaspoon baking soda

½ teaspoon ground cinnamon

¼ teaspoon salt

1 whole egg

1 egg white

1 cup low-fat buttermilk

¼ cup vegetable oil

2 very ripe bananas, mashed with a fork (about 1⅛ cups)

1.   Preheat the oven to 375°F. Lightly coat twelve 2½-inch muffin cups with non-stick cooking spray or line them with fluted paper or foil baking muffin cups.

2.   In a large bowl, combine the flours with the oats, ½ cup of the brown sugar, baking powder, baking soda, cinnamon, and salt.

3.   In a separate medium bowl, whisk the egg with the egg white, buttermilk, and oil. Add the egg mixture to the dry ingredients and stir until just mixed. Gently fold in the bananas.

4.   Fill the muffin tins two-thirds full and sprinkle the tops evenly with the remaining 2 tablespoons of the brown sugar, pushing it through a strainer. Bake for 20 to 25 minutes, or until an inserted knife comes out clean.

5.   Remove from the oven and cool slightly on a wire rack. Turn out into a basket and serve warm or at room temperature.

*V*ARIATION:

❖   Blueberries can be substituted for the bananas.

Lemon Poppy Seed Muffins

Yield: 12 muffins

𝒮erve these low-fat muffins warm as part of a breakfast or brunch menu.

2 cups all-purpose flour

1½ teaspoons baking powder

1½ teaspoons baking soda

pinch of salt

½ cup sugar

3 tablespoons vegetable oil

2 eggs

¾ cup plain nonfat yogurt

2 tablespoons lemon juice

2 teaspoons freshly grated lemon rind

¼ cup poppy seeds

1.   Preheat the oven to 350°F. Lightly coat twelve 2½-inch muffin cups with non-stick cooking spray or line them with fluted paper or foil baking muffin cups.

2.   In a large bowl, mix the flour with the baking powder, baking soda, and salt, and stir to just combine.

3.   In a separate bowl, beat the sugar with the oil. Add the eggs and continue to beat until well mixed. Add the yogurt, lemon juice, and lemon rind and beat until just combined. Stir in the poppy seeds.

4.   Add the wet ingredients to the flour mixture and stir until just combined. Fill muffin tins two-thirds full and bake for 15 to 18 minutes, or until an inserted knife comes out clean.

5. Remove from the oven and cool slightly on a wire rack. Transfer the muffins from the tin to the rack and serve warm or at room temperature.

*V*ARIATION:

❖ Orange juice and orange rind can be substituted for the lemon.

*C*OOK NOTE:

❖ When preparing muffins, do not overmix the batter or your muffins will be tough and chewy.

*D*O-AHEAD PREP:

❖ The muffins can be prepared a day in advance, kept in an airtight container, and warmed just before serving. The muffins can also be frozen in a sealed container or plastic bag for 2 to 3 months

Spa Muffins

Yield: 12 muffins

This recipe is a variation of one created by Chef Michel Stroot, chef for The Golden Door spa and previously at the Cal-a-Vie spa, both in Southern California. Prepare these in large batches and freeze extras for a quick and healthful breakfast treat.

½ cup raisins

1½ cups whole wheat flour

1 cup shredded bran cereal (such as All-Bran)

⅓ cup sesame seeds

2 teaspoons ground cinnamon

1 teaspoon baking soda

1 teaspoon baking powder

½ teaspoon ground allspice

¼ teaspoon ground cloves

1½ cups finely shredded carrots

⅔ cup mashed ripe banana

½ cup fresh orange juice

¼ cup honey

2 tablespoons vegetable oil

1 tablespoon grated lemon rind

1. Preheat the oven to 350°F. Lightly coat twelve 2½-inch muffin cups with nonstick cooking spray or line them with fluted paper or foil baking muffin cups.

2. Place the raisins in a small bowl, cover them with boiling water, and let them stand until plump, about 15 minutes. Drain the raisins and pat dry.

3. Combine the flour with the bran cereal, sesame seeds, cinnamon, baking soda, baking powder, allspice, and cloves.

4. In a separate bowl, combine the raisins with the remaining ingredients and mix well. Fold the raisin-carrot mixture into the dry ingredients until just combined.

5. Spoon the batter into prepared muffin cups and bake until the muffins are golden brown and a toothpick inserted in the centers comes out clean, about 20 minutes.

6. Remove from the oven and cool slightly on a wire rack. Transfer the muffins to the rack, cool slightly, and serve warm or at room temperature.

*V*ARIATIONS:

❖ Currants or dried cranberries can be substituted for the raisins.

❖ The raisins can be soaked in hot apple or orange juice for added flavor.

*C*OOK NOTES:

❖ The freshest carrots come with crisp-looking greens attached, but these should be removed right after purchase to prevent drainage on the roots. Wrapped in plastic the carrots will keep for several weeks in the refrigerator.

❖ Although small, slender carrots have long been preferred, the large, thick California varieties now widely available are often sweeter.

*D*O-AHEAD PREP:

❖ The muffins can be prepared a day in advance, kept in an airtight container, and warmed just before serving. The muffins can also be frozen in a sealed container or plastic bag for 2 to 3 months.

DESSERTS

Light Orange Poppy Seed Pound Cake

Old-Fashioned Apple Cake

Chocolate Angel Food Cake

Traditional Pumpkin Pie

Mocha Pudding Cake

Orange Madeleines

Mocha Brownies

Summer Fruit Compote

Salade de Pèches

Poached Peaches with Raspberry Sauce

New Orleans Baked Bananas with Orange Sauce

Apple Crumble

Plum-Berry Cobbler

Betsy's Light Apple Bread Pudding

Light Rice Pudding

Summer Pudding

Strawberries with Orange-Amaretto Yogurt Cream

Poached Pears in Juice

Red, White, and Blue Bombe

Instant Strawberry-Peach Frozen Yogurt

Light Orange Poppy Seed Pound Cake

Yield: 1 large cake or about 16 servings

*Y*ou will need a nonstick 10-inch tube pan to make this incredible cake. It's a sort of angel food/pound cake combo made moist by nonfat sour cream, lightened by beaten whites, but with the texture of a rich pound cake. It is not a complicated recipe but does require a lot of bowls and dishes to prepare.

6 egg whites, at room temperature for 15 minutes before using

2 cups sugar

one 16-ounce carton nonfat sour cream

¼ cup frozen orange juice concentrate

⅓ cup poppy seeds

2 tablespoons grated orange rind

1 teaspoon pure vanilla extract

¼ cup vegetable oil

3 eggs

3 cups cake flour

1 teaspoon baking powder

¾ teaspoon baking soda

pinch of salt

*G*LAZE:

1½ cups confectioners' sugar

¼ cup fresh orange juice

1 tablespoon grated orange rind

*G*ARNISH: nonfat or low-fat vanilla or lemon frozen yogurt, or low-fat vanilla ice cream

1. Preheat the oven to 300°F. Generously coat a nonstick 10-inch tube pan with nonstick cooking spray.

2. In a large bowl, beat the egg whites on high with an electric mixer until just frothy. Gradually add ½ cup of the sugar, beating until soft peaks form.

3. In a small bowl, combine the sour cream with the orange juice concentrate, poppy seeds, orange rind, and vanilla; whisk until the mixture is smooth.

4. In a separate medium bowl, beat the remaining 1½ cups of the sugar with the oil until lightly combined. Add the whole eggs and beat until well mixed. Add the sour cream mixture and continue to beat until smooth.

5.   In a large bowl, combine the cake flour, baking powder, baking soda, and salt. Add to the sour cream mixture and continue beating until smooth. Fold in a small amount of the egg whites by hand and when combined add the remaining egg whites, folding until well incorporated.

6.   Pour the batter into the prepared pan and bake on the middle shelf of the oven for about 1 hour and 5 minutes or until the cake springs back to the touch. Remove from the oven, allow to cool in the pan for about 10 minutes, and then turn out onto a rack to cool thoroughly.

7.   While the cake is cooling, prepare the glaze by mixing the confectioners' sugar with the juice and rind and continue beating until smooth. When the cake is slightly cooled, prick holes lightly with a fork and pour the glaze over the cake.

8.   Allow the cake to cool slightly, slice, and serve it warm or at room temperature, topped with a dollop of nonfat or low-fat vanilla or lemon frozen yogurt, or low-fat vanilla ice cream.

*V*ARIATION:

❖   Lemon peel and frozen lemonade can be substituted for the orange flavoring.

*C*OOK NOTE:

❖   When buying poppy seeds, look for dark, shiny seeds. Dull seeds could be rancid. Store them in a tightly sealed bottle in a cool place. They may also be refrigerated for several weeks or frozen for several months.

❖   If you do not have cake flour, you can come close to the same results by subtracting 2 tablespoons of all-purpose flour for every cup of flour called for in the recipe. Replace the missing 2 tablespoons of flour with cornstarch to create a softer and more tender cake.

*D*O-AHEAD PREP:

❖   This cake is best served the day it is prepared but can be prepared a day in advance and covered tightly with plastic wrap to keep in the flavor. It can also be frozen for several weeks and then defrosted before serving.

Old-Fashioned Apple Cake

Yield: 1 layer cake or
about 16 servings

*T*his old-fashioned apple cake has all of the moistness of a rich, buttery cake but without lots of fat. Applesauce has been added to give the juicy texture. This cake is great for dinner but also makes a delicious breakfast treat.

2¼ cups all-purpose flour

1 cup sugar

1 teaspoon baking soda

1½ teaspoons ground cinnamon

¼ teaspoon ground nutmeg

pinch of ground mace

2 egg whites

2 whole eggs

½ cup low-fat buttermilk

½ cup applesauce

¼ cup vegetable oil

1 teaspoon pure vanilla extract

1½ cups peeled and coarsely chopped tart apples (2 medium
     Pippin or Granny Smith)

⅓ cup raisins

¼ cup brown sugar, firmly packed

3 tablespoons finely chopped walnuts (optional)

*A*CCOMPANIMENT: nonfat or low-fat vanilla frozen yogurt, or
     low-fat vanilla ice cream

1. Preheat the oven to 350°F. Lightly coat a 10-inch nonstick tube pan with non-stick cooking spray.

2. In a large mixing bowl, sift together the flour, sugar, baking soda, cinnamon, nutmeg, and mace.

3. In a separate bowl, beat the egg whites and eggs with the buttermilk, apple-sauce, oil, and vanilla until smooth.

4. Add the egg mixture to the dry ingredients and blend by hand until smooth. Add the apples and raisins and combine well.

5. Combine the brown sugar with the walnuts and sprinkle the mixture evenly over the top of the cake.

6. Pour the batter into the prepared pan and bake on the middle shelf of the oven for about 55 minutes or until an inserted knife comes out clean. Remove from the oven, allow to cool in the pan for about 10 minutes, and then turn out onto a rack to cool thoroughly.

7. Allow the cake to cool slightly, slice, and serve warm or at room temperature with a dollop of nonfat or low-fat vanilla frozen yogurt, or low-fat vanilla ice cream.

*V*ARIATIONS:

❖ If mace is unavailable, substitute ground allspice or ginger.

❖ The cake can be baked in a 10-inch bundt pan or even a 9-inch square baking pan.

❖ For an added zip, try stirring a little cinnamon into softened vanilla frozen yogurt.

*C*OOK NOTES:

❖ Mace is the bright red membrane that covers the nutmeg seed. The color of this spice changes to a tannish orange as it dries, and the skin becomes brittle. The flavor is more intense and pungent but less sweet than nutmeg.

❖ Do not store apples with carrots. Apples release a gas that gives carrots a bitter taste.

*D*O-AHEAD PREP:

❖ This cake is best served within a few days of baking, kept fresh covered in plastic wrap, and stored in the refrigerator. Remember to bring the cake to room temperature before serving or reheat just before you are about to eat it. It can also be frozen for several weeks and then defrosted before serving.

Chocolate Angel Food Cake

Serves: 12

*T*his recipe is adapted from one served at the Palm-Aire Resort and Spa in Pompano Beach, Florida. Angel food cakes do not call for greased pans since the beaten whites will rise better on an ungreased surface.

12 egg whites, at room temperature

½ teaspoon cream of tartar

1 cup plus ⅓ cup sugar

1 cup cake flour

¼ cup unsweetened cocoa

½ teaspoon almond extract

1 teaspoon pure vanilla extract

*G*ARNISH: nonfat or low-fat chocolate frozen yogurt or low-fat chocolate ice cream, fresh strawberries or raspberries, or raspberry sauce (see Cook Notes below), and sprigs of mint

1. Preheat the oven to 375°F.

2. In a very large bowl or in the bowl of a standing electric mixer, beat the egg whites until foamy. Add the cream of tartar and continue to beat until they form peaks, about 6 to 8 minutes. Very gradually add 1 cup of the sugar, beating until stiff peaks form.

3. In a medium bowl, sift the flour, cocoa, and remaining ⅓ cup of the sugar. Gently fold the cocoa mixture into the egg whites along with the almond and vanilla extracts. (Do not try to work out all the cocoa lumps or the egg whites will deflate.) Pour into a 10-inch nonstick angel food tube pan with removable bottom and bake about 35 to 40 minutes, or until an inserted knife comes out clean.

4. Remove the cake from the oven and allow it to cool; remove the cake from the pan by using a knife to loosen the cake, inverting a plate over the pan, and turning both over quickly, but carefully.

5. Serve the cake topped with nonfat or low-fat chocolate frozen yogurt or low-fat chocolate ice cream, fresh strawberries or raspberries, or raspberry sauce, and sprigs of mint.

*V*ARIATION:

❖ The almond extract can be omitted if desired.

COOK NOTES:

❖ It is important to sift the dry ingredients so that they fold easily into the whites. Do not overfold the dry ingredients with the egg whites or they will deflate.

❖ If you do not have cake flour, you can come close to the same results by subtracting 2 tablespoons of all-purpose flour for every cup of flour called for in the recipe. Replace the missing 2 tablespoons with cornstarch to create a softer and more tender cake.

❖ If you cannot find a nonstick angel food tube pan with removable bottom, use a regular tube pan, coat the bottom with nonstick cooking spray, and place a piece of parchment paper on the bottom of the pan.

❖ Select berries that are plump, fully colored, dry, and free of bruises and mold. Inspect the fruit through the slits of the container. Never buy fruit that is leaky, split, or soft, which is an indication of decay. Take a good whiff—the berries should have a strong sweet smell. Sort the berries immediately when you get them home from the market. Spread them out on a plate, cover it loosely with plastic wrap, and refrigerate. Do not wash the berries until just before serving and do not hull strawberries until after washing or they will absorb excess water.

❖ To prepare a raspberry sauce, puree the raspberries in a food processor or blender, strain to remove the seeds, and chill until ready to use.

DO-AHEAD PREP:

❖ The cake can be prepared a day in advance and kept fresh covered in plastic wrap. The cake can also be frozen in slices for future treats.

Traditional Pumpkin Pie

Yield: 9-inch pie, serves 10

*T*his quick and easy pumpkin pie has all the creaminess of a traditional pie, but substituting the new nonfat or low-fat sweetened condensed milk shaves off much of the fat.

*P*ASTRY:

1 cup all-purpose flour

1½ teaspoons sugar

¼ cup (½ stick) cold unsalted butter, diced

2 to 3 tablespoons ice water

*F*ILLING:

one 16-ounce can pumpkin (about 2 cups)

one 14-ounce can nonfat or low-fat sweetened condensed milk

3 egg whites

1 whole egg

1 teaspoon ground cinnamon

¼ teaspoon ground nutmeg

¼ teaspoon ground ginger

⅛ teaspoon ground allspice

pinch of ground cloves

pinch of salt

*G*ARNISH: nonfat or low-fat vanilla frozen yogurt, or low-fat vanilla ice cream

1. Place the flour and sugar in the bowl of a food processor and process for 10 seconds or until combined. Add the butter bits and continue to process the mixture for 20 to 30 seconds until just crumbly. While the machine is running, add 2 of the table-spoons of the ice water and process for an additional 20 to 30 seconds or until a ball of dough forms. If the dough does not hold together, add more water until the correct consistency is achieved—too much water and the dough becomes sticky, and too little water and the pastry may crack or tear. Wrap the dough in plastic and refrigerate for at least 30 minutes or freeze for 10 minutes.

2. On a lightly floured surface, flatten the ball of pastry to about ½ inch thick and roll into an 11-inch circle. Place the dough in a 9-inch pie pan and gently press into the pan, fluting the edges. The pie shell may be wrapped in plastic wrap and re-frigerated until ready to fill.

3. Preheat the oven to 400°F.

4. In a large mixing bowl, combine all the filling ingredients and whisk or beat until smooth. Pour into the prepared shell and bake for 15 minutes. Reduce the oven temperature to 350°F and continue to bake for an additional 30 to 35 minutes, or until an inserted knife comes out clean.

5. Remove the pie from the oven, allow to cool on a rack, and serve warm or at room temperature topped with nonfat or lowfat vanilla frozen yogurt, or low-fat vanilla ice cream.

*V*ARIATION:

❖ If pressed for time, a frozen, thawed pie shell can be substituted.

*C*OOK NOTE:

❖ Since spices deteriorate so quickly, put a small piece of masking tape on the bottom of newly purchased spice jars and note the date of purchase. After about a year, you might want to see if the flavor has lessened and it is time to purchase a new jar. For optimum flavor, store spices away from the heat in a cool area of the kitchen.

*D*O-AHEAD PREP:

❖ This pie can be prepared a day in advance, wrapped tightly in plastic wrap, and refrigerated overnight. Bring the pie to room temperature before serving. The pie can also be frozen successfully.

Mocha Pudding Cake

Serves: 8

*P*udding cakes are traditionally egg custards that contain a little flour and beaten egg whites that float to the top forming a spongy, cakelike top while the rest of the batter forms a pudding on the bottom. I've eliminated the eggs in this recipe but the texture is still cakey on top and gooey and custardy on the bottom. You can prepare this dish easily in one large pan or in individual dishes for a pretty presentation.

> 1 cup all-purpose flour
>
> ¾ cup granulated sugar
>
> 6 tablespoons unsweetened cocoa
>
> 2 teaspoons baking powder
>
> ¼ teaspoon salt
>
> ½ cup 1% low-fat milk
>
> 3 tablespoons nonfat or low-fat vanilla yogurt
>
> 2½ tablespoons canola oil
>
> 1 teaspoon pure vanilla extract
>
> ¾ cup brown sugar, firmly packed
>
> ¾ cup mild brewed coffee
>
> ¾ cup water
>
> *G*ARNISH: raspberries or strawberries and nonfat or low-fat vanilla frozen yogurt, or low-fat vanilla ice cream

1. Preheat the oven to 350°F. Lightly coat an 8-inch square pan or 6 to 8 small ramekins with nonstick cooking spray.

2. Sift the flour with the sugar, 3 tablespoons of the cocoa, the baking powder, and the salt into a mixing bowl. Whisk in the milk, yogurt, oil, and vanilla and pour into prepared pan or pans.

3. In a separate bowl, combine the brown sugar with the remaining 3 tablespoons of cocoa and sprinkle it over the top of the batter. Pour the coffee and water over the batter and bake for about 40 to 45 minutes or until the top springs back slightly when pressed.

4. Allow to cool slightly and serve warm topped with fresh berries and nonfat or low-fat vanilla frozen yogurt, or low-fat vanilla ice cream.

*V*ARIATION:

❖   If you are avoiding caffeine, use decaffeinated coffee.

*C*OOK NOTES:

❖   Cocoa is much lower in fat than baking chocolate, and it does not have the high saturated fat content. Cocoa will last for up to 2 years stored in an airtight container in a cool dark place.

❖   Store your bottle of pure vanilla extract in a dark, cool place since both heat and light hasten the deterioration of the vanilla flavor.

*D*O-AHEAD PREP:

❖   This pudding cake is best prepared an hour or two before serving.

Orange Madeleines

*M*adeleines are said to have been invented in the seventeenth century and brought into fashion at Versailles. The recipe for madeleines remained a secret for a very long time and was finally sold for a very large sum to the pastry maker of Commercy, France, who made this great delicacy one of the finest gastronomic specialties of their town.

Madeleines are baked in small individual molds. The molds bake a dozen at one time and are available at most cookware stores. If available buy the nonstick molds, which are easier to use.

    2 eggs, separated, at room temperature
    5 tablespoons sugar
    2 tablespoons fresh orange juice
    2 teaspoons freshly grated orange rind
    2 tablespoons unsalted butter, melted
    6 tablespoons cake flour

1. Preheat the oven to 350°F. Generously coat the madeleine pans (preferably nonstick) with nonstick cooking spray.

2. In a medium bowl, beat the egg whites until just foamy. Gradually add 2 tablespoons of the sugar and continue to beat the whites until stiff peaks form.

3. In a separate bowl, beat the yolks with the remaining 3 tablespoons sugar until light and lemony in color. Add the orange juice, rind, and butter and continue to beat until smooth. Gradually add the flour and continue to beat until just combined.

4. Gently fold a quarter of the whites into the yolks and then fold in the remaining amount, making sure not to deflate the whites.

5. Spoon 1 tablespoon of the batter into each madeleine form of the prepared pans and bake for 13 to 15 minutes, or until golden and the top springs back when touched.

6. Remove from the oven and allow to cool on a wire rack for 2 minutes. Lift out the madeleines with a spatula and cool, fluted side up on a wire rack. (You can also tap the pan against a hard surface and the madeleines will pop out.)

*V*ARIATION:

❖ Lemon juice and rind or half lemon and lime juice and rind can be substituted for the orange.

Cook Note:

❖ If you do not have cake flour, you can come close to the same results by subtracting 2 tablespoons of all-purpose flour for every cup of flour called for in the recipe. Replace the missing 2 tablespoons with cornstarch to create a softer and more tender cake.

Do-ahead prep:

❖ Madeleines taste their best the day they are baked, but they can be stored for several days in an airtight container or frozen for several months.

Mocha Brownies

Yield: 48 small squares

*T*hese brownies use pureed prunes as a substitute for the traditional butter and they still turn out moist and delicious.

    3 egg whites, at room temperature

    2 eggs, at room temperature

    2 cups sugar

    four 2½-ounce jars baby food pureed prunes

    2 teaspoons pure vanilla extract

    1 cup all-purpose flour

    1¼ cups unsweetened cocoa powder

    2 tablespoons instant coffee powder (not crystals if possible)

GARNISH: confectioners' sugar

1. Preheat the oven to 350°F. Lightly coat a 9-x-13-x-2-inch metal baking pan with nonstick cooking spray.

2. In the large bowl of an electric mixer, beat the egg whites and eggs with the sugar until pale and slightly thickened. Beat in the prunes and vanilla until smooth.

3. In a medium bowl, sift the flour with the cocoa and coffee and fold into the mixture until well combined. Spread the batter in the prepared pan and bake for 25 minutes, or until the brownies are set in the center. Remove from the oven and cool on a rack. Sprinkle lightly with confectioners' sugar.

4. When thoroughly cool, cut into 1-inch squares and serve.

*V*ARIATION:

❖ If you are avoiding caffeine, use decaffeinated coffee.

*C*OOK NOTES:

❖ Store eggs with the large end of the shell up (to keep the yolks centered in their shells) in a covered container in the refrigerator. Since egg shells are porous, eggs tend to absorb odors, so make sure to keep them away from strong-smelling foods such as onions and garlic.

❖ It is preferable to use the richer, darker Dutch cocoa, which has been treated with an alkali that helps to neutralize cocoa's natural acidity.

❖ These brownies can be prepared a day or two ahead and kept in an airtight container or they can be frozen successfully.

Summer Fruit Compote

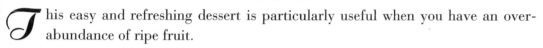

*T*his easy and refreshing dessert is particularly useful when you have an over-abundance of ripe fruit.

1 cup sugar

1 cup water

2 tablespoons honey

1 vanilla bean, split lengthwise

4 apricots, pitted and quartered

2 plums, pitted and quartered

2 nectarines, pitted and quartered

1 cantaloupe, cut into balls

1 pint raspberries

*G*arnish: nonfat or low-fat vanilla yogurt, or low-fat sour cream, and sprigs of mint

1. Bring the sugar, water, honey, and vanilla bean to a boil. Reduce heat, and simmer uncovered for 6 to 7 minutes, stirring occasionally, until the sugar has dissolved.

2. Add the apricots, plums, and nectarines, bring to a boil, reduce heat, and simmer for 6 to 7 minutes, or until tender. Add the cantaloupe and raspberries and cook for 2 to 3 minutes longer. Remove the vanilla bean, allow to dry, and rewrap it to be used again. Place the fruit in a covered container and refrigerate until ready to use.

3. Serve the compote chilled, garnished with a dollop of nonfat or low-fat vanilla yogurt, or low-fat sour cream, and sprigs of mint.

*V*ariations:

❖ Any variety of seasonal fruits can be substituted.

❖ If time permits, the apricots, plums, and nectarines can be peeled.

❖ Bury dried used vanilla beans in granulated or confectioners' sugar for added flavor.

𝒟O-AHEAD PREP:

❖ This dessert can be prepared several days in advance and kept in a covered container in the refrigerator.

Salade de Pèches

Serves: 4 to 6

*T*his recipe comes from the south of France where the peaches are so flavorful in the summer months. It is simple to prepare and the fresh taste is a perfect ending to any meal.

    4 to 6 ripe fresh peaches
    2 tablespoons fresh orange juice
    1 tablespoon lemon juice

𝒢ARNISH: nonfat or low-fat vanilla yogurt and mint sprigs

1. Peel the peaches by submerging them in boiling water for 1 minute, then in cold water, and use a paring knife to slip the skins off easily.

2. Halve the peaches lengthwise, discarding the pits, and slice them. Coat the peaches well with the orange and lemon juice to prevent browning, arrange attractively in a glass bowl, cover with plastic wrap, and chill for an hour, until ready to serve.

3. Serve the peaches chilled with a dollop of nonfat or low-fat vanilla yogurt and sprigs of fresh mint.

𝒱ARIATION:

❖ Any combination of fruits including the following will make wonderful and refreshing fruit salads in the summer: apricots, peaches, nectarines, oranges, all types of berries, grapes, pears, currants, apples, and bananas.

𝒞OOK NOTE:

❖ The peach originated in China where it was known 2,000 years before the birth of Christ, and was regarded as a symbol of immortality. The Chinese may have

been on to something judging from the reported effects of a peach on Madame Re-
camier, a French beauty of the nineteenth century. She was so ill that she refused all
food but her life was saved by a dish of peaches in syrup and cream, which restored
her appetite and her will to live.

$\mathcal{D}$o-ahead prep:

❖   It is advisable to prepare the peaches not more than 2 to 3 hours before serving or they might turn brown and lose their flavor.

Poached Peaches with Raspberry Sauce

Serves: 4

*T*his simple poached fruit dessert is made elegant by its presentation. The peaches (or any other seasonal fruit) are poached in a wine and sugar syrup. They are then placed atop an angel food cake or fat-free pound cake and finally drizzled with pureed raspberries. It's simple to create, easy to assemble, and impressive to present.

    4 ripe freestone peaches
    2 cups dry white wine
    1 cup sugar
    one 2-inch strip of orange peel
    one 10-ounce package frozen raspberries with sugar
        added, thawed
    8 thin slices angel food cake or fat-free pound cake
    ½ pint lemon sorbet or frozen nonfat or low-fat lemon yogurt

*G*ARNISH: sprigs of mint

1.　Peel the peaches by submerging them in boiling water for 1 minute, then in cold water, and use a paring knife to easily slip the skins off. Halve the peaches lengthwise and discard the pits.

2.　Put the wine, sugar, and orange peel in a saucepan that can hold the peaches in a single layer, bring the liquid to a boil, reduce the heat, and simmer, uncovered, for five minutes. Add the peach halves to the liquid and poach them for only 4 to 5 minutes, or until just tender. Remove the peaches with a slotted spoon, place on a plate, cover, and refrigerate until chilled, about 2 to 3 hours. Reserve the poaching liquid for another use.

3.　Puree the frozen berries in a food processor or blender, strain, and chill in a covered container until ready to use.

4.　To assemble the dessert: cut a few thin slices of the cake and arrange them slightly overlapping on 4 individual dessert plates. Top each of the cake layers with 2 peach halves and a scoop of lemon sorbet, and drizzle the raspberry puree on top. Serve immediately garnished with a sprig of mint.

*V*ARIATIONS:

❖　6 ripe fresh apricots or 4 ripe pears can be substituted for the peaches.

❖   Nonfat or low-fat vanilla frozen yogurt or low-fat vanilla ice cream can be substituted for the lemon sorbet.

𝒞OOK NOTE:

❖   When selecting peaches, look for firm, well-formed fruit, free from decay and bruising. A ripe peach should have a golden or creamy, yellow background color, and that wonderful "peach" smell. Peaches that are green have been picked too early, lack flavor, and will never properly ripen.

𝒟O-AHEAD PREP:

❖   The peaches can be poached 1 to 2 days in advance and kept in a covered container in the refrigerator. The dessert should not be assembled until just before serving.

New Orleans Baked Bananas
with Orange Sauce

Serves: 4

In the West Indies, this potassium-rich fruit is prepared in many different ways. This version, adapted from the Sonoma Mission Inn spa, is baked in foil with honey and butter, and scented with orange and vanilla. The aroma from the just-opened packet is heavenly.

1 tablespoon grated orange rind

1 tablespoon honey

1 tablespoon fresh orange juice

1 teaspoon pure vanilla extract

2 ripe bananas

1 teaspoon unsalted butter, cut into 4 pieces

GARNISH: julienned orange rind, 1 vanilla bean cut into 4 pieces, edible flowers (optional)

1. Preheat the oven to 350°F. Cut 4 pieces of foil, each 6 x 8 inches.

2. In a small bowl, mix the orange rind, honey, orange juice, and vanilla extract.

3. Peel the bananas, cut them in half lengthwise, and place each half on a foil rectangle. Spoon the sauce over the banana halves, top each half with a piece of butter, fold over the foil once, and crimp the edges to seal.

4. Place the packets on a baking sheet and bake for 5 to 8 minutes. If the bananas are really ripe, they will cook in about 5 minutes; if unripe, they may take a few minutes longer, but do not overcook or they will be mushy.

5. To serve, slash the banana halves in 5 places along the outside edge and curve into semicircles. Pour the juices over the fruit and garnish with the orange rind, vanilla bean, and edible flowers, if available.

COOK NOTES:

❖ Always wash bananas before eating. Bananas are grown in tropical countries and often packed under unsanitary conditions. Even though you peel the banana, your hand has touched the skin and then immediately touches the fruit that you are eating.

❖ To prevent discoloration of cut bananas, slice the bananas with a silver knife. Another method of preventing discoloration is to quickly coat cut bananas with citrus juice—orange, lemon, or lime.

❖   This dessert should be assembled just before baking.

Apple Crumble

*A*pple crumble is a combination of pie and Apple Brown Betty but can be pre-pared in only 15 minutes. It can be made in a 9-inch pie plate, in small ramekins, or in a flat oven-proof dish.

4 large tart apples

1 tablespoons orange juice

*S*TREUSEL TOPPING:

¼ cup all-purpose flour

¼ cup oatmeal or quick oats

⅓ cup dark brown sugar, firmly packed

½ teaspoon ground cinnamon

¼ teaspoon freshly grated nutmeg

2½ tablespoons unsalted butter, softened

*G*ARNISH: nonfat or low-fat vanilla frozen yogurt, or low-fat vanilla ice cream

1.   Preheat the oven to 375°F. Lightly coat a pie plate or individual dishes with nonstick cooking spray.

2.   Peel and slice the apples, place in the prepared dish, and immediately sprinkle with the orange juice.

3.   Prepare the streusel topping in a food processor, blender, or by hand by mixing flour, oats, brown sugar, cinnamon, nutmeg, and butter together until just crumbly but not overprocessed.

4.   Sprinkle the topping over the apples and bake for 40 to 45 minutes or until the top is golden and the apples are tender. Smaller dishes will only take 35 to 40 minutes.

5.   Serve the apple crumble warm, garnished with nonfat or low-fat vanilla frozen yogurt, or low-fat vanilla ice cream.

*V*ARIATIONS:

❖ Peaches, plums, or berries can be substituted for the apples.

❖ If you are in a hurry, substitute frozen peaches or berries, or a combination of both, thawed and drained.

*D*O-AHEAD PREP:

❖ The crumble can be baked a few hours earlier and reheated just before serving.

Plum-Berry Cobbler

Serves: 6 to 8

A cobbler is a deep-dish pie with no bottom crust and a top crust of streusel or biscuit dough. It is derived from the early American expression "to cobble up," meaning to put together quickly. By cutting down on the amount of butter in the topping, you can reduce the amount of fat in this lighter version.

3 cups peeled and sliced fresh ripe plums

1 pint fresh blueberries, washed and drained

1 tablespoon sugar

2 teaspoons lemon juice

1 teaspoon freshly grated lemon rind

½ teaspoon pure vanilla extract

½ cup (about 4 cookies) crushed macaroon cookies or crisp
    sugar cookies

⅓ cup all-purpose flour

¼ cup firmly packed brown sugar

½ teaspoon ground cinnamon

pinch ground nutmeg

2½ tablespoons unsalted butter

*G*ARNISH: nonfat or low-fat vanilla frozen yogurt, or low-fat
    vanilla ice cream, and orange slices

1. Preheat the oven to 350°F. Lightly coat a 10-inch round baking dish, or similar size oven-proof dish with nonstick cooking spray.

2. In a medium bowl, combine the plums and the blueberries with the sugar, lemon juice, lemon rind, and vanilla. Gently fold the ingredients together and pour into the prepared dish.

3.   In a food processor, combine the cookies, flour, brown sugar, cinnamon, and nutmeg, and process for a minute to combine. Add the butter and pulse until crumbly.

4.   Sprinkle the topping over the fruit and bake for 30 to 35 minutes, or until lightly browned.

5.   Serve the pudding warm with nonfat or low-fat vanilla frozen yogurt, or low-fat vanilla ice cream, and orange slices.

*V*ARIATIONS:

❖   The cobbler can be prepared in individual dishes.

❖   To prepare this comforting dessert in the winter months, substitute frozen sliced peaches and frozen blueberries for the plums and berries used in the summer months.

*C*OOK NOTES:

❖   To easily peel a plum, plunge it into boiling water for about one minute, then in cold water, and the peel will slip right off.

❖   Packaged frozen blueberries are less tasty than the ones you freeze yourself; while blueberries are in season, freeze some for the winter months. Simply spread the cleaned berries on a jelly-roll pan, allow them to freeze, and once frozen solid, place them in a resealable plastic storage bag for future use.

*D*O-AHEAD PREP:

❖   The cobbler can be baked a few hours earlier and reheated just before serving.

Betsy's Light Apple Bread Pudding

Serves: 6

*M*y friend Betsy Halpern serves this deliciously low-fat pudding for breakfast or as a dessert topped with vanilla frozen yogurt. For added fiber, substitute whole grain breads and if you are not a raisin fan, try substituting chopped dried apricots or cranberries as an alternative.

1 cup 1% low-fat milk

¼ cup pure maple syrup

½ teaspoon pure vanilla extract

¾ teaspoon ground cinnamon

¼ teaspoon ground nutmeg

4 egg whites, at room temperature for 15 minutes
before using

2 cups white bread, cubed (about 6 large slices with
crusts on)

2 cups peeled and chopped tart apples (about 2 large or 3
medium apples)

½ cup raisins, plumped in boiling water and then drained

*G*ARNISH: nonfat or low-fat vanilla frozen yogurt, or low-fat
vanilla ice cream

1. In a large bowl, lightly whisk the milk with the maple syrup, vanilla, cinnamon, and nutmeg.

2. In a separate bowl, beat the egg whites until very frothy but not quite stiff. Fold the egg whites into the milk mixture, add the bread cubes, gently stir to combine, and allow to soak for about 30 minutes, or until the bread is well saturated.

3. Preheat the oven to 350°F. Coat a 9-inch square baking pan with nonstick cooking spray.

4. Fold the apples and raisins into the mixture, pour into the prepared pan, and place in a large roasting pan. Add boiling water to the roasting pan to come 1 inch up the sides of the baking pan. Bake for about 50 to 60 minutes or until golden brown on top and an inserted knife comes out clean.

5. Serve warm for dessert topped with nonfat or low-fat vanilla frozen yogurt, or low-fat vanilla ice cream.

𝒱ARIATIONS:

❖ Prepare the pudding in small ramekins or custard dishes but bake only 40 to 50 minutes or until set in the center.

❖ Serve the apple bread pudding warm or cold for breakfast.

𝒟O-AHEAD PREP:

❖ The pudding can be cooked a day or two in advance. Store the cooked pudding covered in the refrigerator and reheat before serving.

Light Rice Pudding

Serves: 6 to 8

𝓘 can still remember drowning my sorrows in a vat of rice pudding from the local Horn & Hardart automat when I was a kid (OK, I'm over 30!). This version will ensure that you can assuage your depression, but not violate your low-fat regime. Served warm this is the optimum comfort food.

1¾ cups 1% low-fat milk

2 egg whites, at room temperature for 15 minutes before using

1 whole egg

½ cup sugar

1¼ cups cold cooked rice

½ cup golden raisins

1 teaspoon pure vanilla extract

ground cinnamon and ground nutmeg

𝒢ARNISH: raspberries or sliced strawberries

1. Preheat the oven to 325°F. Lightly coat 6 to 8 small custard cups, ramekins, or a large 1-quart baking dish with nonstick cooking spray.

2. Place the milk in a heavy-bottomed saucepan, cook over medium heat until steam rises and it is very hot, but *not* boiling. Remove the milk from the heat and place it in a large measuring cup.

3. Whisk the egg whites and egg together in a medium-sized bowl. Gradually whisk about one-fourth of the hot milk into the eggs. Add the remaining hot milk, whisking constantly. Stir in the sugar, rice, raisins, and vanilla until smooth.

4. Ladle the mixture into the prepared custard cups, ramekins, or a large

1-quart baking dish. Place the dishes in a shallow pan and sprinkle the tops lightly with ground cinnamon and nutmeg. Add water to a depth of 1 inch in the pan and bake for about 45 minutes, or until the pudding is set and an inserted knife comes out clean.

5. Remove the dishes from the pan, allow the pudding to cool slightly, and serve warm, or refrigerate and serve cold, garnished with raspberries or a few strawberry slices.

*V*ARIATION:

❖ Minced dried apricots or dried cranberries can be substituted for the raisins.

*C*OOK NOTE:

❖ The milk is added to the eggs slowly to prevent the eggs from curdling.

*D*O-AHEAD PREP:

❖ Although the pudding is at its best served warm, it can easily be prepared a day in advance and brought to room temperature before serving.

Summer Pudding

$\mathcal{S}$ummer pudding, which used to be known as hydropathic pudding, was an eighteenth-century invention expressly created for those who could not tolerate the rich pastry desserts so fashionable at the time. It is simply a fruit compote soaked in bread and uses no fat at all. Traditionally it is prepared with raspberries and red currants, but you can use any soft summer fruits that are available. Just top it with nonfat or low-fat vanilla yogurt or a little low-fat sour cream, and it is a perfect fresh finale to a summer dinner.

8 cups mixed summer fruits (raspberries, blueberries, strawberries, peeled peaches, plums, or apricots, singly or in
combination)

1½ cups water

1 cup sugar

1 tablespoon lemon juice

1 teaspoon grated lemon rind

12 very thin slices white bread (such as Pepperidge Farm),
crusts trimmed

$\mathcal{G}$ARNISH: nonfat or low-fat vanilla yogurt, or low-fat sour
cream, and fresh mint leaves

1. Lightly coat a round 4-cup dome-shaped metal bowl or similar shaped mold with nonstick cooking spray.

2. Wash the berries and peel any peaches or plums and set aside.

3. In a medium nonreactive saucepan, combine the water, sugar, lemon juice, and lemon rind, and bring to a boil. Boil for about 2 minutes or until the sugar has dissolved. Add the tougher fruits and bring to a boil, reduce heat to simmer, and stew until softened. Add the softer fruits like berries and continue to cook just until softened. Strain off the liquid and set aside.

4.   Cut a circle of bread for the bottom of the mold, and cut the remaining pieces in wedges. Dip the circle of bread in the fruit juices and lay the circle in the bottom of the bowl. Dip the remaining pieces in the liquid and place some of the wedges around the sides, allowing no gaps. Save any remaining pieces for the middle and top.

5.   Place half the cooked fruits in the bread-lined bowl, cover with a middle layer of soaked bread, and top with the remaining fruit. Place the remaining soaked bread wedges on top and place the pudding on a platter to catch any overflow. Cover the top of the mold with a small plate and press down with a weight or a couple of heavy cans. Cover with plastic and allow to chill overnight in the refrigerator.

6.   Run a knife around the edges to loosen the pudding, turn it out onto a large serving dish, spoon any remaining juices over and serve garnished with dollops of non-fat or low-fat vanilla yogurt, or low-fat sour cream, and fresh mint leaves.

*V*ARIATIONS:

❖   For extra flavor add a tablespoon of kirsch to the cooked fruits before placing in the mold.

❖   Mix the remaining fruit juice liquids with the yogurt for a creamy smooth topping.

❖   Top the finished pudding with Light English Creamy Topping (see page 51).

*C*OOK NOTES:

❖   When selecting berries at the market, look for see-through containers to reveal any bruised or decaying berries, which should be avoided. If the containers are cardboard, avoid ones with stained juice, which is an indication of bruising. Do not wash berries until just before using.

❖   Plums and peaches can be quickly ripened by placing them in a brown paper bag with an apple. The apple releases a natural ethylene gas that hastens the ripening process.

*D*O-AHEAD PREP:

❖   The pudding is best prepared a day in advance, covered with plastic wrap and refrigerated until ready to serve. It is best to bring the pudding to room temperature before serving.

Strawberries with Orange-Amaretto Yogurt Cream

Serves: 6

*W*hen fresh strawberries are in season there is no better way to serve them than with this light orange-flavored yogurt-based sauce.

3 pints strawberries, preferably with stems

*S*AUCE:

1 cup plain nonfat or low-fat yogurt

2 tablespoons sugar

1 tablespoon grated orange rind

1 tablespoon fresh orange juice

1 teaspoon Amaretto di Saronno liqueur

½ teaspoon almond extract

1. Wash and drain the berries but do not remove the caps or stems. Attractively arrange the berries on a large platter, leaving room for the sauce, and chill until ready to use.

2. Combine the sauce ingredients in a small bowl, stir well, and allow to chill until ready to use.

3. Serve the sauce surrounded by the berries.

*V*ARIATIONS:

❖ Substitute ¼ teaspoon ground ginger for the almond extract.

❖ Substitute low-fat sour cream for the yogurt.

*C*OOK NOTE:

❖ Select berries that are bright red and fully ripened, as they do not ripen after being picked.

*D*O-AHEAD PREP:

❖ Do not wash the berries until just before serving or they will begin to deteriorate. The almond yogurt cream can be prepared 1 to 2 days ahead and refrigerated in a covered container until ready to serve.

Poached Pears in Juice

Serves: 4

*T*hese light and luscious pears make an elegant end to a fall or winter dinner. Instead of being poached in sugar syrup, the whole pears are poached in juice.

3 cups pear nectar, pear juice, or apple juice

1 cinnamon stick

4 medium Bosc pears, peeled, cored, and halved

*G*ARNISH: nonfat or low-fat vanilla yogurt, or lightly sweetened low-fat sour cream, and sprigs of fresh mint

1. In a medium saucepan, bring the juice and the cinnamon stick to a boil, add the pear halves, reduce heat, cover, and simmer for 20 to 25 minutes, or until fork tender. Cool in the juice and then chill in a covered container.

2. Place each of the pear halves on a plate, garnish with the nonfat or low-fat vanilla yogurt, or low-fat sour cream, and mint, and serve chilled.

*V*ARIATION:

❖ The pears can be poached in the microwave.

*C*OOK NOTE:

❖ The Bosc pear is distinguished by its russet color, symmetrical body, long tapering neck, and slim stem. This winter pear is perfect for baking or poaching.

*D*O-AHEAD PREP:

❖ The pears can be cooked several days in advance and kept in a covered container in the refrigerator.

Red, White, and Blue Bombe

Serves: 10 to 12

*T*his is a very large dessert that is easy to prepare in advance, and by using frozen nonfat yogurt, it becomes a taste treat that is fat free as well. It is a perfect dessert to prepare in the summer months when berries are plentiful and inexpensive. If you prepare this when raspberries and blueberries are out of season, substitute strawberries, which will be much more affordable.

The secret to the success of a frozen dessert bombe is lining the mixing bowl with plastic wrap so the mold can be easily removed. It may seem a little difficult to master, but it is really quite easy.

1 quart (2 pints) nonfat or low-fat vanilla frozen yogurt, or low-fat vanilla ice cream, softened for 10 minutes

1 quart (2 pints) nonfat or low-fat strawberry or raspberry frozen yogurt or sorbet, softened for 10 minutes

2 pints blueberries

2 pints raspberries

*G*ARNISH: mint sprigs

1. Line a rounded 5- or 6-cup bowl (such as a metal mixing bowl) with plastic wrap, overlapping the sides. Layer the vanilla frozen yogurt on the bottom and up the sides of the bowl, pushing down with a slightly smaller bowl to make an even layer, and freeze until hard, about 1 hour.

2. Fill the cavity with the strawberry frozen yogurt, flatten the top, and cover tightly with plastic wrap. Freeze until hard, about 1 to 2 hours.

3. Remove the plastic wrap on the top of the bowl, place a platter on top of the bowl, and turn the bowl and platter over. The bombe will be perfectly placed in the center of the platter (if the bombe will not release easily, dip the bowl in hot water for 10 seconds).

4. Remove the remaining plastic wrap and, working quickly so that the dessert will not melt, surround the base of the platter with blueberries and decorate the rounded portion with the raspberries.

5. Serve immediately, cut in wedge-shaped pieces so that the colors will show through, and garnish with a sprig of mint.

*V*ARIATION:

❖ Any variety of frozen yogurt can be used. The key is to make this dessert spectacularly pretty. It is an awesome presentation!

*C*OOK NOTE:

❖ The peak month for blueberries is August. Select firm, plump blueberries with a dark blue color and a silvery bloom (this is the natural protective wax on the berry). While dark color is a sign of age, red traces around the stem of the blueberry signal immaturity.

*D*O-AHEAD PREP:

❖ The bombe can be kept tightly wrapped in the freezer for several weeks.

Instant Strawberry-Peach Frozen Yogurt

Serves: 4

*T*his is a very easy last-minute dessert. It is prepared just before serving and then must be eaten immediately. Use bags of frozen unsweetened fruit, but if you prefer you can use fresh peeled and sliced peaches and small, whole, cleaned, and hulled strawberries that have been frozen on cookie sheets and stored in resealable bags.

1 cup plain nonfat yogurt
2½ tablespoons honey
½ teaspoon pure vanilla extract
¾ cup frozen strawberries
¾ cup frozen sliced peaches

*G*ARNISH: strawberry halves

1.   Place the yogurt, honey, and vanilla in the bowl of a food processor and process until just smooth.

2.   While the machine is running, drop the frozen fruit down the feed tube in a steady stream until it has combined with the yogurt into a smooth mixture.

3.   Garnish with strawberry halves and serve immediately.

*V*ARIATION:

❖   Frozen unsweetened nectarines, raspberries, or other fruits can be substituted.

*C*OOK NOTE:

❖   Because honey is a supersaturated solution of fructose and glucose in water, it will eventually begin to crystallize, developing a murky look and a gritty texture. To bring it back, warm the glass jar in a pan of water over very low heat. Store honey in an airtight container to prevent it from absorbing moisture from the air and fermenting.

*D*O-AHEAD PREP:

❖   This dessert must be prepared just before serving.

BEVERAGES

Malibu Mary

Strawberry Lemonade

Fruited Herbal Iced Tea

Sparkling Cranberry Cooler

Christmas Glögg (Mulled Wine)

Hot Mulled Cider

Malibu Mary

Serves: 6

*T*his recipe comes from a friend, Dr. John Hertz, who likes to mix up a batch of this deliciously spicy Bloody Mary–like drink for a fantastic brunch beverage. This is a virgin Malibu Mary, but for the industrial strength version, add vodka to taste.

one 32-ounce jar Clamato juice

⅓ cup fresh orange juice

¼ cup fresh lemon juice

3 tablespoons fresh lime juice

3 tablespoons medium picante sauce, or to taste (I use the Pace brand; use your favorite variety)

2½ teaspoons white horseradish

2½ teaspoons celery salt

pepper to taste

*G*ARNISH: 10 to 12 sweet cherry peppers (I use the Mezzetta's brand available in California)

1. Combine all ingredients in a pitcher. Stir well, cover, and chill until ready to serve.

2. Pour over ice into tall glasses, add a sweet cherry pepper or two to each, and serve.

*V*ARIATIONS:

❖ If you can't find Clamato juice, substitute vegetable juice cocktail.

❖ For a spicier version use hot picante sauce.

❖ Vodka can be added to taste.

*C*OOK NOTE:

❖ Select oranges that are firm and heavy for their size and free of soft spots or wrinkles. Brown streaks on the skin of the orange have no bearing on the quality. Oranges do not ripen after harvest, and some green color on the skin does not necessarily mean the fruit is unripe. Oranges can be kept at room temperature for a few days but are best stored in the refrigerator where they will keep for weeks without significant nutrient loss. Oranges are excellent sources of vitamin C, potassium, and vitamin A.

DO-AHEAD PREP:

❖ The drink can be prepared 1 to 2 days in advance and stored in a covered container in the refrigerator.

Strawberry Lemonade

Serves: 4

*T*ired of chemical-laden fizzy diet drinks? Try this alternative cooling beverage from the chefs at The Four Seasons Hotel chain. This strawberry lemonade and variations are easy to prepare and provide a perfect light accompaniment to a summertime lunch or supper.

> 1 pint strawberries, washed, dried, and sliced
>
> 1 cup sugar
>
> 2 cups freshly squeezed lemon juice (about 10 to 12 ripe and
>   juicy lemons)
>
> 2½ cups cold water

1. Place the strawberries and sugar in a food processor or blender and puree until smooth.

2. Strain the mixture into a pitcher, add the lemon juice and cold water, stir well, and pour into ice-filled glasses or chill until ready to serve.

VARIATIONS:

❖ For raspberry lemonade use 2 pints raspberries, 1 cup sugar, 2 cups lemon juice, and 4 cups cold water.

❖ For pineapple lemonade use 1 peeled, cored, and sliced pineapple, ½ cup sugar, 2 cups lemon juice, and 2½ cups cold water.

❖ For peach lemonade use 6 very ripe peeled and sliced peaches, ¾ cup sugar, 2 cups lemon juice, and 3 cups cold water.

COOK NOTES:

❖ To get the most juice from a lemon, always squeeze them at room temperature and roll them on the counter with the palm of your hand before juicing. If they have been stored in the refrigerator, microwave them for 10 to 20 seconds or leave them in hot water for several minutes before juicing.

❖ Bottled lemon juice has an inferior taste. It is better to juice lots of lemons when available, freeze in ice cube trays, and pop into resealable storage bags until ready to use.

*D*O-AHEAD PREP:

❖ The lemonade can be prepared a day or two in advance and chilled until ready to serve.

Fruited Herbal Iced Tea

Serves: 12 to 16

*A*ny blend of herbal fruit teas can be used for this refreshing drink, especially the berry, orange, cranberry, and lemon flavors. Keep this deliciously healthful iced tea on hand at a party in place of diet soft drinks.

     2 quarts boiling water
     2 blackberry- or cranberry-flavored tea bags
     2 strawberry- or raspberry-flavored tea bags
     2 orange-flavored tea bags
     2 lemon-flavored tea bags
     1 peppermint tea bag
     3 cups fresh orange juice

*A*CCOMPANIMENTS: frozen unsweetened strawberries, peaches, and raspberries, and sprigs of fresh mint

1. Add the boiling water to a large pitcher, drop the tea bags in, and allow the tea to steep for 10 to 15 minutes. Remove the tea bags, squeeze, and discard. Allow the tea to cool to room temperature and then cover and refrigerate the tea for 3 to 4 hours or until well chilled.

2. Add the orange juice and stir well to blend. Pour the tea into chilled glasses and serve with the frozen fruit dropped in as ice cubes, garnished with sprigs of mint.

*V*ARIATION:

❖ Add the juice, 1 sliced navel orange, and 1 sliced lemon to the chilled tea and allow to steep for several hours or overnight. Do not leave the oranges in for more than 3 days or the skins will add a bitter taste to the tea.

COOK NOTES:

❖   After preparing the tea with boiling water, it is important to allow the mixture to cool to room temperature before chilling or the tea will become cloudy.

❖   To prevent iced tea from becoming foamy, add the water to the pitcher before you add the tea.

DO-AHEAD PREP:

❖   The iced tea can be prepared through Step 1 and chilled in a covered container until ready to serve.

Sparkling Cranberry Cooler

Serves: 8

*T*his wonderful fruity punchlike drink is delicious by itself or mixes beautifully with a little champagne.

2 cups fruit-sweetened cranberry juice (not cranberry cocktail)
2 cups unsweetened grapefruit juice
2 cups unsweetened pineapple juice
2 cups sparkling apple juice

*A*CCOMPANIMENT: champagne

1.   In a large pitcher, combine the cranberry, grapefruit, and pineapple juice, stir, and chill. Chill the sparkling apple juice while still in the bottle.

2.   When ready to serve, add the sparkling juice and/or champagne if desired, pop in the lemon ice cubes, and serve immediately.

*V*ARIATION:

❖   2 cups of orange juice can be substituted for the grapefruit juice or 1 cup can be poured in as a delicious addition.

*C*OOK NOTE:

❖   Add a few lemon twist ice cubes to the cooler. To prepare: place a small strip of lemon zest in the bottom of each square in an ice cube tray, fill the holes with water, and chill until frozen.

*D*O-AHEAD PREP:

❖   The cranberry cooler can be prepared through Step 1 and chilled in a covered container until ready to serve.

Christmas Glögg (Mulled Wine)

Serves: 12 to 16

This traditional Swedish-spiced mulled wine is always a big hit with the addition of American cranberry juice. Traditionally it is served spiked with aquavit or brandy, but here it is simply infused with fruits and spices. Prepare enough, but alert the guests that because the wine is warmed, it adds an extra punch to the punch!

2 cups cranberry juice

2 cups water

1 cup sugar

1 large lemon, very thinly sliced

6 allspice berries

4 whole cloves

2 cinnamon sticks

⅛ teaspoon ground ginger

pinch of nutmeg

2 bottles red wine (preferably red Bordeaux or
    California varietal)

l lemon, sliced

1 orange, sliced

½ cup raisins

GARNISH: cinnamon sticks

1. In a deep large nonreactive saucepan, combine the cranberry juice, water, sugar, ½ of a sliced lemon, allspice, cloves, cinnamon sticks, ginger, and nutmeg. Bring to a boil, stirring often, until the sugar is dissolved. Boil over medium heat for 15 minutes. Strain through a cheesecloth-lined strainer or very fine mesh strainer and set aside.

2. When ready to serve, heat the cranberry base and add the wine, remaining lemon slices, orange slices, and raisins. Heat until warm but do not allow the mixture to boil. Pour into a punch bowl and serve warm with a ladle and cinnamon stick stirrers.

VARIATIONS:

❖ For optimum flavor, use naturally sweetened cranberry juice.

❖ To avoid having to strain the glögg, tie up the whole spices in cheesecloth before adding to the liquid. After cooking the base through Step 1, squeeze and discard the cheesecloth.

*C*OOK NOTES:

❖ Use a heated tray to keep the punch warm throughout the party.

❖ Lemons freeze well, so you can store any unused portions in the freezer. If you use only small pieces of lemon or lime at a time, cut the fruit in quarters and store them in resealable plastic storage bags in the freezer.

*D*O-AHEAD PREP:

❖ The base can be prepared through Step 1, 3 to 4 days in advance and kept in a covered container in the refrigerator.

Hot Mulled Cider

Serves: 20 to 25

To mull a beverage is to slowly heat and infuse cider, wine, liqueur, or beer with spices, fruits, and flavorings. For holiday parties or cold winter dinners, try this comforting and warming hot mulled cider that is easy to prepare and economical to serve.

¼ cup mulling spices

1 orange, sliced horizontally

1 lemon, sliced horizontally

1 gallon freshly pressed apple cider

½ to 1 cup rum, or to taste

GARNISH: cinnamon sticks

1.   Combine the mulling spices and orange and lemon slices, place them in a cheesecloth bag, and tie the bag securely with kitchen twine.

2.   In a large nonreactive stockpot, place the bag of spices and the cider. Bring to a boil, reduce heat to a simmer, and mull for about 45 minutes to an hour.

3.   Remove the cheesecloth bag, squeeze the essence of the spices into the cider, and discard the bag.

4.   About 10 to 15 minutes before serving, add the rum, stir to combine, and allow the mixture to just heat through. Do not boil.

5.   Serve the mulled cider warm in cups with handles accompanied by cinnamon stick stirrers.

VARIATION:

❖   4 cinnamon sticks, 1½ teaspoons whole allspice, and 1½ teaspoons whole cloves can be substituted for the mulling spices.

COOK NOTES:

❖   Cinnamon is the bark of a tropical evergreen tree. The bark is left to dry and it rolls up into tight curls called cinnamon sticks. Select whole unblemished, smooth, unbroken cinnamon sticks.

❖   Apple cider is made by pressing the juice from apples. Before fermentation it is called *sweet cider. Hard cider* is the juice that has an alcoholic content after one or two cycles of fermentation. The drink called *cider* in European countries is always mildly alcoholic and frequently tastes much like beer.

❖ Hot mulled cider is often served in a *wassail* bowl. The word *wassail* comes from the Anglo-Saxon *weshal* or the Norse *ves heill* meaning "to be whole" or "good health," which was seen as an affirmation of friendship. The contents of the English wassail bowl were hot spiced ale and toasted apple. Known as "lambs wool," it had pieces of toast floating on it—hence the term *to toast*.

*D*O-AHEAD PREP:

❖ The mulled cider base can be prepared a day or two ahead through Step 2 and then refrigerated in a covered container until ready to heat with the rum.

$\mathcal{S}$UGGESTED MENUS FOR LIGHT AND EASY ENTERTAINING

❖ ❖ ❖ ❖ ❖ ❖ ❖

$\mathcal{H}$OLIDAY CELEBRATIONS:

New Year's Eve Midnight Supper

Thai Salad with Lemon Dressing (page 283)

Braised Lamb Curry (page 195)

White Rice*

Stir-Fried Spinach with Roasted Garlic (page 280)

Chocolate Angel Food Cake (page 344)

Valentine's Dinner for Lovers

Chilled Artichokes with Spicy Mustard Sauce
    (page 42)

Roast Rock Cornish Game Hens with Raspberry
    Flavor (page 128)

Vegetable Pasta (page 258)

Strawberries with Orange-Amaretto Yogurt
    Cream (page 367)

Fourth of July Picnic

Strawberry Lemonade (page 374)

Grilled Chinese Marinated Butterflied Leg of Lamb
    (page 192)

Spaghetti with Vegetables Chinoise (page 208)

Labor Day Picnic

Tomato Corn Soup (page 108)

Cold Barbecue Chicken*

New Potato and Green Bean Salad (page 299)

Summer Fruit Compote (page 353)

Mocha Brownies (page 352)

California Light Thanksgiving

Hot Mulled Cider (page 380)

Turkey Roasted on a Covered Charcoal Grill
    (page 130)

Light Sweet Potato Soufflé (page 276)

Brussels Sprouts with Chestnuts (page 262)

Cranberry Conserve with Cassis (page 54)

Traditional Pumpkin Pie (page 346)

Hanukkah Dinner

Sandy's Chicken Soup with Fine Noodles (page
    81)

Braised Veal Brisket (page 182)

Light and Crispy Potato-Zucchini Pancakes (pag
    274)

Stir-Fried Spinach with Roasted Garlic (page 28

Old-Fashioned Apple Cake (page 342)

I'm Dreaming of a Light Christmas

Christmas Glögg (Mulled Wine) (page 377)

Roast Butterflied Turkey Breast with Orange
Mustard Glaze and Raisin Bread Stuffing
(page 133)

Braised Onions with Sage (page 267)

Pumpkin-Cornmeal Spice Muffins (page 332)

Mixed Green Salad with Basic Light Vinaigrette
(pages 282, 286)

Kiwi Christmas Bread (page 328)

FESTIVE BREAKFASTS AND BRUNCHES:

Intimate Breakfasts in Bed

Berry-Filled Melon*

Cranberry-Orange Scones (page 326)

Café au Lait*

Breakfast Prepared the Night Before

Summer Fruit Compote (page 353)

Savory Strata (page 63)

Cinnamon-Flavored Coffee*

Power Breakfast

Malibu Mary (page 373)

Piquant Light Frittata (page 61)

Popovers (page 320)

Lemon Poppy Seed Muffins (page 335)

Cappuccino*

Continental Breakfast

Grapefruit/Cranberry Juice Mixed*

Basket of: Blueberry-Orange Muffins with
Crunchy Granola Topping (page 330)

Banana-Oatmeal Muffins (page 334)

Vanilla-Flavored Coffee*

Country French Picnic

Mushroom Pâté (page 28)

Cold Poached Lemon Chicken with Mustard-
Chive Sauce (page 120)

Crudités with Yogurt Cheese Caper Dip (page 35)

Salade de Pêches (page 354)

Baguette*

Orange Madeleines (page 350)

Book Group Luncheon

Sparkling Cranberry Cooler (page 377)

Chinese Chicken Salad (page 309)

Chilled Sesame Noodles with Vegetables (page
307)

Cut-up Fresh Fruit*

End-of-the-Summer Luncheon

Sweet Pea Guacamole (page 29)

Tex-Mex Salad with Grilled Chicken (page 312)

Summer Fruit Compote (page 353)

Luncheon in Winter

Celery Root and Carrot Soup (page 89)

Grilled Tuna Salad Niçoise or Shrimp Salad with
Watercress and Creamy Horseradish
Dressing (pages 315, 316)

Light Orange Poppy Seed Pound Cake (page 340)

Poached Pears in Juice (page 368)

MILESTONE MEALS:

Bridal Shower Tea Party

Fruited Herbal Iced Tea (page 375)

Smoked Salmon Tartare (page 39)

Thin Pumpernickel Bread*

Black Olive and Cheese Biscuits (page 322)

Cranberry-Orange Scones with Light English
 Creamy Topping (pages 326, 51)
Assorted Jams*
Orange Madeleines (page 350)

Guilt-Free Anniversary Cocktail Party

Malibu Mary (page 373)
Spinach Dip*
Crudités Platter*
Corn Blini with Salsa (page 43)
Spinach Meatballs (page 47)
Sun-Dried Tomato and Basil Chicken Pâté (page
 37)

Birthday Blowout

Spinach-Tomato Terrine (page 40)
Fish Cioppino on a Bed of Linguine (page 162)
Light Caesar Salad (page 284)
Presto Focaccia (page 325)
Light Orange Poppy Seed Pound Cake (page 340)

Open Housewarming Chili Party

Pico de Gallo (page 59)
Baked Tortilla Chips (page 48)
Eggplant Caviar Spread with Southwestern Flavor
 (page 33)
Outstanding Turkey Chili (page 137)
Mixed Green Salad with Basic Light Vinaigrette
 (pages 282, 286)
Southern Comfort Corn Sticks (page 321)
Apple Crumble (page 359)

First-Time Entertaining

Marinated Grilled Chicken Breast (page 112)
Radiatore with Mexican Salsa (page 219)
Light Caesar Salad (page 284)
Strawberries with Orange-Amaretto Yogurt
 Cream (page 367)

ℰLEGANT PARTIES:

A Midsummer Night's Supper

Chilled Trout Fillets with Creamy Dill Dressing
 (page 161)
Black Bean, Quinoa, and Corn Salad with Tomato
 (page 303)
Sourdough Bread*
Summer Pudding (page 365)

Sumptuous Italian Dinner Party

Spaghetti Squash Salad with Lemon-Basil Vinai-
 grette (page 301)
Grilled Osso Buco (page 186)
Presto Foccacia (page 325)
Fresh Fruit*

Elegantly Light Asian Dinner

Chinese Vegetable Egg Drop Soup
 (page 83)
Grilled Swordfish with Chinese Salsa
 (page 148)
Light Fried Rice (page 237)
Warm Chinese Green Bean Salad with Toasted
 Sesame Seeds (page 298)
Red, White, and Blue Bombe (page 369)

Guess Who's Coming to Dinner?

Potato Slices with Caviar (page 45)
Rack of Lamb with Pistachio-Mint Crumb Crust
 and Tangy Mint Sauce (page 190)
Polenta Squares (page 247)
Roasted Asparagus with Warm Vinaigrette (page
 288)
Poached Peaches with Raspberry Sauce (page
 356)
Biscotti*

Academy Award Buffet

Skewered Chicken with Papaya Salsa (page 46)

Yogurt Cheese Caper Dip (page 35)

Crudités Basket*

Vegetarian Lasagne (page 222)

Roasted Asparagus with Warm Vinaigrette (page 288)

Apple Crumble (page 359)

Looking Ahead Light: Elegant Dinner Prepared in Advance

Roasted Vegetable Spread (page 31)

Crackers*

Light Coq au Vin (page 124)

Fennel and Red Onion Salad (page 296)

Old-Fashioned Apple Cake (page 342)

Casual Feasts:

Hearty Winter Soup Supper

Seafood Minestrone (page 100)

Pesto Focaccia (page 325)

Fennel and Red Onion Salad (page 296)

New Orleans Baked Bananas with Orange Sauce (page 358)

Family Dinner That the Kids Will Love

Grilled Turkey Burger (page 135)

Hamburger Buns*

Oven-Roasted Cheese Fries (page 273)

Light Caesar Salad (page 284)

Mocha Brownies (page 352)

Impromptu Pasta Supper

Crunchy Radish and Cucumber Dip (page 36)

Farfalle with Caramelized Red Onion Sauce (page 209)

Mixed Green Salad with Creamy Dill Dressing (page 286)

Instant Strawberry-Peach Frozen Yogurt (page 371)

Pizza Party

Pizza with Caramelized Onion and Mushrooms (page 227)

Roasted Vegetables and Feta Cheese Pizza (page 228)

Light Caesar Salad (page 284)

Assorted Italian Ices*

Bistro Fare

Mixed Green Salad with Basic Light Vinaigrette Dressing (pages 282, 286)

Beef Burgundy with Porcini Mushrooms and Pearl Onions (page 179)

Baguette*

Poached Peaches with Raspberry Sauce (page 356)

Sunday Night Supper

Savory Shepherd's Pie (page 139)

Mixed Green Salad with Basic Light Vinaigrette Dressing (pages 282, 286)

Popovers (page 320)

Betsy's Light Apple Bread Pudding (page 362)

Down in the Dumps Comfort Food Feast

Meat Loaf with Porcini Mushrooms (page 177)

Crusty Light Baked Mashed Potatoes with Roasted Garlic (page 270)

Light Caesar Salad (page 284)

Light Rice Pudding (page 363)

Summer Evening Cookout

Grilled Pork Tenderloin with Hoisin Mustard Glaze
(page 197)
Grilled Green Beans with Peppers and Oregano
(page 261)
Corn Salad (page 292)
Summer Fruit Compote (page 353)

Pitch-in Party in the Kitchen

Spinach Meatballs (page 47)

Shrimp Risotto with Peas and Red Pepper (page
235)
Mixed Green Salad with Basic Light Vinaigrette
(pages 282, 286)
Mocha Pudding Cake (page 348)

Vegetarian Feast

Pea Soup with Roasted Garlic Flavor (page 92)
Spinach and Rice Pie with Vegetables (page 278)
Plum-Berry Cobbler (page 360)

---

* Starred dishes are suggestions for simply prepared additions to the menus; the recipes are not included in this book.

MAIL-ORDER SOURCE GUIDE

❖ ❖ ❖ ❖ ❖ ❖ ❖

EQUIPMENT AND GADGETS

Chef's Catalog
3215 Commercial Avenue
Northbrook, IL 60062-1900
800-388-3232
Huge selection of cookware and gadgets.

A Cook's Wares
211 37th Street
Beaver Falls, PA 15010-1263
412-846-9490
Good prices on name-brand cookware and knives as well as specialty foods.

Sur La Table
Catalogue Division
410 Terry Avenue North
Seattle, WA 98109-5229
800-243-0852
Great source for top-of-the-line kitchen equipment.

Williams-Sonoma
Mail Order Department
P.O. Box 7456
San Francisco, CA 94120-7456
800-521-2233
Huge selection of cookware and gadgets.

Zabar's
2245 Broadway
New York, NY 10024
212-787-2000
Great cookware, gadgets, and foods at reasonable prices.

FOODSTUFFS

Aidell's Sausage Co.
1625 Alvarado Street
San Leandro, CA 94577
800-546-5795
Good source for low-fat chicken and turkey sausages.

Balducci's Mail Order Department
4226 13th Street
Long Island City, NY 11101-4908
1-800-BALDUCCI (225-3822)
A cook's mail-order culinary paradise from condiments to caviar.

China Bowl Trading Co.
P.O. Box 454
Westport, CT 06881
203-222-0381
A wide variety of Asian groceries.

Clambake Celebrations
9 West Road
Orleans, MA 02653
800-423-4038
Many types of fresh shellfish delivered live.

Cotuit Oyster Co.
P.O. Box 563
Cotuit, MA 02635
508-428-6747
Oysters and clams available from October through April.

Dean & DeLuca
Mail Order Service
560 Broadway
New York, NY 10012
800-221-7714
Wide variety of international foodstuffs shipped to your doorstep.

Frieda's, Inc.
P.O. Box 58488
Los Angeles, CA 90058
800-241-1771
e-mail: Friedas@aol.com
Web site: http://www.friedas.com
Exotic produce, grains, dried fruits, and nuts from the people that helped to popularize the kiwi! The home page on the Internet will give you background and nutritional information plus recipes on how to use some of the exotic produce and ethnic foods.

The Herbfarm
32804 Issaquah-Fall City Road
Fall City, WA 98024
800-866-HERB
Hundreds of organically grown herb plants ready for shipping.

House of Spices
82–80 Broadway
Jackson Heights, NY 11373
718-476-1577
A bazaar of Indian and Pakistani foodstuffs.

Katagiri & Co.
224 E. 59th Street
New York, NY 10022
212-755-3566
Good source for Japanese ingredients and some Asian foodstuffs.

Penzeys, Ltd.
Post Office Box 1448
Waukesha, WI 53187
414-574-0277
Wide variety of quality herbs and spices.

Quinoa Corporation
P.O. Box 1039
Torrance, CA 90505
310-530-8666
Information on the grain quinoa available on request.

Todaro Brothers Mail Order
555 Second Avenue
New York, NY 10016
212-679-7766
Incredible source for Italian food products.

World Variety Produce, Inc.
P.O. Box 21127
Los Angeles 90021\800-588-0151
http://www.melissas.com
Quinoa, bulgur, dried mushrooms, dried fruits, and exotic produce.

INDEX

❖ ❖ ❖ ❖ ❖ ❖ ❖

METRIC EQUIVALENCIES

❖ ❖ ❖ ❖ ❖ ❖ ❖

LIQUID AND DRY MEASURE EQUIVALENCIES

Customary	Metric	Customary	Metric
¼ teaspoon	1.25 milliliters	1 ounce (by weight)	28 grams
½ teaspoon	2.5 milliliters	¼ pound (4 ounces)	114 grams
1 teaspoon	5 milliliters	1 pound (16 ounces)	454 grams
1 tablespoon	15 milliliters	2.2 pounds	1 kilogram
1 fluid ounce	30 milliliters		(1000 grams)
¼ cup	60 milliliters		
⅓ cup	80 milliliters		
½ cup	120 milliliters		
1 cup	240 milliliters		
1 pint (2 cups)	480 milliliters		
1 quart (4 cups)	960 milliliters (.96 liter)		
1 gallon (4 quarts)	3.84 liters		

OVEN-TEMPERATURE EQUIVALENCIES

Description	°Fahrenheit	°Celsius
Cool	200	90
Very slow	250	120
Slow	300–325	150–160
Moderately slow	325–350	160–180
Moderate	350–375	180–190
Moderately hot	375–400	190–200
Hot	400–450	200–230
Very hot	450–500	230–260